COLLEGE READINGS
IN POETRY

English and American

COLLEGE READINGS IN POETRY

IN POETRY

English and American

By

FRANCES KELLEY DEL PLAINE

and

ADAH GEORGINA GRANDY

Granger Poetry Library

GRANGER BOOK CO., INC.
Great Neck, NY

First Published 1933
Reprinted 1979

INTERNATIONAL STANDARD BOOK NUMBER
0-89609-111-2

library of congress catalog number
78-73485

PRINTED IN THE UNITED STATES OF AMERICA

PREFACE

The purpose in publishing this collection of poems is to put into the hands of college students a compact volume containing all of those poems and only those poems which are generally studied in freshman and sophomore English courses in college. This has been the basis of selection rather than any personal preference as to what should or should not be included. The poems, with very few exceptions, are printed entire. In general they are arranged in chronological order both as to authors and poems. The works of English and American authors have not been separated but have been grouped together in one chronological sequence since they represent, not two separate literatures, but rather two parts of one. The dates given at the close of the poems are those of first publication; and while care has been exercised, we realize that errors may have crept in, as this is not an easy matter to determine in all cases. The dates in parentheses, which are given for a few poems, are those of composition.

Our friends, both at Minnesota and elsewhere, have been generous in helping us with suggestions and criticism, and we wish to extend our thanks to them, especially to Mr. C. A. Moore and Mr. Joseph M. Thomas of the University of Minnesota.

THE EDITORS

MINNEAPOLIS, MINNESOTA
February, 1933

ACKNOWLEDGMENTS

The editors thank the following authors and publishers who have generously given permission to reprint the material indicated, which they control as holders of the copyright, or authorized publishers, or both:

Oxford University Press, New York: "The World Comes Not to an End" and "The Very Names of Things Belov'd Are Dear," from *The Collected Works of Robert Bridges*, 6 Vols.; and "The Wood Is Bare," from *The Shorter Poems of Robert Bridges*, Clarendon Press, 1931, by Robert Bridges.

Henry Holt and Company, New York: "To the Thawing Wind," from *A Boy's Will;* and "The Pasture" and "Mending Wall," from *North of Boston*, by Robert Frost; and "Chicago," "Lost," "The Harbor," "Under the Harvest Moon," and "Nocturne in a Deserted Brickyard," from *Chicago Poems*, by Carl Sandburg.

Edna St. Vincent Millay (Brandt and Brandt, Agents): "God's World" and "When the Year Grows Old," from *Renascence and Other Poems*, published by Harper & Brothers, copyright 1917, by Edna St. Vincent Millay; "Euclid Alone Has Looked on Beauty Bare," from *The Harp-Weaver and Other Poems*, published by Harper & Brothers, copyright 1920, 1921, 1922, 1923, by Edna St. Vincent Millay; Sonnets XIV and XVI from *Fatal Interview*, published by Harper & Brothers, copyright 1931, by Edna St. Vincent Millay.

Little, Brown & Company, Boston: "There Is No Frigate like a Book," "Not What We Did Shall Be the Test," and "As if the Sea Should Part," from *The Poems of Emily Dickinson*, Centenary Edition, edited by Martha Dickinson Bianchi and Alfred Leete Hampson. Reprinted by permission of Little, Brown & Company.

Houghton Mifflin Company, Boston: "Patterns," by Amy Lowell, used by permission of, and by arrangement with, Houghton Mifflin Company.

Dodd, Mead & Company, New York. "The Soldier" and "The Great Lover," by Rupert Brooke, copyright 1915, by Dodd, Mead & Company, Inc.

Doubleday, Doran & Company, Garden City: "Vigil Strange I Kept on the Field One Night," "Darest Thou Now, O Soul," "In Cabined Ships at Sea," "I Hear America Singing," and "When Lilacs Last in the Dooryard Bloomed," from *Leaves of Grass*, by Walt Whitman, reprinted by permission from Doubleday, Doran & Company, Inc., Publishers.

The Macmillan Company, New York: "Cargoes," "London Town," "Sea Fever," "The West Wind," and "On Growing Old," from *Collected Poems*, by John Masefield; "The Rose of the World," from *Minnie Maylow's Story and Other Tales and Scenes*, by John Masefield; and "Flammonde," "Cassandra," "The Gift of God," from *Collected Poems*, by Edwin Arlington Robinson; and "The Lake Isle of Innisfree," and "The Rose of the World," from *Early Poems and Stories*, by William Butler Yeats; and "Michael Robartes Remembers Forgotten Beauty," from *Later Poems*, by William Butler Yeats; and "She Hears the Storm," "In the Moonlight," and "The Man He Killed," from *Collected Poems*, by Thomas Hardy.

Harper & Brothers, New York: "The Youth of the Year," "The Life of Man," "The Garden of Proserpine," and "A Forsaken Garden," from *Collected Works*, by Algernon Swinburne.

Mr. A. E. Housman: Selections from *A Shropshire Lad*.

TABLE OF CONTENTS

BALLADS

SIXTEENTH CENTURY

SEVENTEENTH CENTURY

NINETEENTH CENTURY

TWENTIETH CENTURY

BALLADS

THOMAS RYMER

True Thomas lay oer yond grassy bank,
   And he beheld a ladie gay,
A ladie that was brisk and bold,
   Come riding oer the fernie brae.

Her skirt was of the grass-green silk,
   Her mantle of the velvet fine,
At ilka tett of her horse's mane
   Hung fifty silver bells and nine.

True Thomas he took off his hat,
   And bowed him low down till his knee: 10
"All hail, thou mighty Queen of Heaven!
   For your peer on earth I never did see."

"O no, O no, True Thomas," she says,
   "That name does not belong to me;
I am but the queen of fair Elfland,
    And I'm come here for to visit thee.

    .   .   .   .

"But ye maun go wi me now, Thomas,
   True Thomas, ye maun go wi me,
For ye maun serve me seven years,
   Thro weel or wae as may chance to be."   20

She turned about her milk-white steed,
   And took True Thomas up behind;
And aye wheneer her bridle rang,
   The steed flew swifter than the wind.

7. *ilka tett*, every lock.   17. *maun*, must.   20. *wae*, woe.

For forty days and forty nights
  He wade thro red blude to the knee,
And he saw neither sun nor moon,
  But heard the roaring of the sea.

O they rade on, and further on,
  Until they came to a garden green: 30
"Light down, light down, ye ladie free;
  Some of that fruit let me pull to thee."

"O no, O no, True Thomas," she says,
  "That fruit maun not be touched by thee,
For a' the plagues that are in hell
  Light on the fruit of this countrie.

"But I have a loaf here in my lap,
  Likewise a bottle of claret wine,
And now ere we go farther on,
  We 'll rest a while, and ye may dine."   40

When he had eaten and drunk his fill,
  "Lay down your head upon my knee,"
The lady sayd, "ere we climb yon hill,
  And I will show you fairlies three.

"O see not ye yon narrow road,
  So thick beset wi thorns and briers?
That is the path of righteousness,
  Tho after it but few enquires.

"And see not ye that braid, braid road,
  That lies across yon lillie leven?   50
That is the path of wickedness,
  Tho some call it the road to heaven.

44. *fairlies*, wonders.   50. *lillie leven*, lovely glade.

"And see not ye that bonny road
  Which winds about the fernie brae?
That is the road to fair Elfland,
  Where you and I this night maun gae.

"But Thomas, ye maun hold your tongue,
  Whatever you may hear or see,
For gin ae word you should chance to speak,
  You will neer get back to your ain countrie."   60

He has gotten a coat of the even cloth,
  And a pair of shoes of velvet green,
And till seven years were past and gone
  True Thomas on earth was never seen.

KEMP OWYNE

Her mother died when she was young,
  Which gave her cause to make great moan;
Her father married the warst woman
  That ever lived in Christendom.

She servéd her with foot and hand,
  In every thing that she could dee,
Till once, in an unlucky time,
  She threw her in ower Craigy's sea.

Says, "Lie you there, dove Isabel,
  And all my sorrows lie with thee;   10
Till Kemp Owyne come ower the sea,
  And borrow you with kisses three,
Let all the warld do what they will,
  Oh, borrowed shall you never be!"

11. *Kemp*, champion.   12. *borrow*, set free.

Her breath grew strang, her hair grew lang,
   And twisted thrice about the tree,
And all the people, far and near,
   Thought that a savage beast was she.

These news did come to Kemp Owyne,
   Where he lived, far beyond the sea;   20
He hasted him to Craigy's sea,
   And on the savage beast looked he.

Her breath was strang, her hair was lang,
   And twisted was about the tree,
And with a swing she came about:
   "Come to Craigy's sea, and kiss with me.

"Here is a royal belt," she cried,
   "That I have found in the green sea;
And while your body it is on,
   Drawn shall your blood never be;   30
But if you touch me, tail or fin,
   I vow my belt your death shall be."

He steppéd in, gave her a kiss;
   The royal belt he brought him wi.
Her breath was strang, her hair was lang,
   And twisted twice about the tree,
And with a swing she came about:
   "Come to Craigy's sea, and kiss with me.

"Here is a royal ring," she said,
   "That I have found in the green sea;   40
And while your finger it is on,
   Drawn shall your blood never be;
But if you touch me, tail or fin,
   I swear my ring your death shall be."

He steppéd in, gave her a kiss;
   The royal ring he brought him wi.

Her breath was strang, her hair was lang,
   And twisted ance about the tree,
And with a swing she came about:
   "Come to Craigy's sea, and kiss with me.   50

"Here is a royal brand," she said,
   "That I have found in the green sea;
And while your body it is on,
   Drawn shall your blood never be;
But if you touch me, tail or fin,
   I swear my brand your death shall be."

He steppéd in, gave her a kiss;
   The royal brand he brought him wi.
Her breath was sweet, her hair grew short,
   And twisted nane about the tree;   60
And smilingly she came about,
   As fair a woman as fair could be.

THE WIFE OF USHER'S WELL

There lived a wife at Usher's Well,
   And a wealthy wife was she;
She had three stout and stalwart sons,
   And sent them oer the sea.

They hadna been a week from her,
   A week but barely ane,
Whan word came to the carline wife
   That her three sons were gane.

They hadna been a week from her,
   A week but barely three,   10
Whan word came to the carline wife
   That her sons she 'd never see.

51. *brand*, sword.   7. *carline*, old woman.

"I wish the wind may never cease,
  Nor fashes in the flood,
Till my three sons come hame to me,
  In earthly flesh and blood."

It fell about the Martinmass,
  When nights are lang and mirk,
The carline wife's three sons came hame,
  And their hats were o the birk.   20

It neither grew in syke nor ditch,
  Nor yet in ony sheugh;
But at the gates o Paradise,
  That birk grew fair eneugh.

        .   .   .   .

"Blow up the fire, my maidens,
  Bring water from the well;
For a' my house shall feast this night,
  Since my three sons are well."

And she has made to them a bed,
  She's made it large and wide,   30
And she's taen her mantle her about,
  Sat down at the bed-side.

        .   .   .   .

Up then crew the red, red cock,
  And up and crew the gray;
The eldest to the youngest said,
  "'Tis time we were away."

The cock he hadna crawd but once,
  And clappd his wings at a',
When the youngest to the eldest said,
  "Brother, we must awa.   40

18. *mirk*, dark.   21. *syke*, trench.   22. *sheugh*, furrow.

"The cock doth craw, the day doth daw,
  The channerin worm doth chide;
Gin we be mist out o our place,
  A sair pain we maun bide.

"Fare ye weel, my mother dear!
  Fareweel to barn and byre!
And fare ye weel, the bonny lass
  That kindles my mother's fire!"

THE LAILY WORM AND THE MACHREL
OF THE SEA

"I was bat seven year alld
  Fan my mider she did dee,
My father marrëd the ae warst woman
  The wardle did ever see.

"For she has made me the lailly worm
  That lays att the fitt of the tree,
And o my sister Meassry
  The machrel of the sea.

"An every Saterday att noon
  The machrl comes to me,   10
An she takes my laylë head,
  An lays it on her knee,
An keames it we a silver kemm,
  An washes it in the sea.

"Seven knights ha I slain
  Sane I lay att the fitt of the tree;
An ye war na my ain father,
  The eight an ye sud be."

42. *channerin*, fretting.   8. *machrel*, mackerel.
  2. *fan*, when.   13. *keames*, combs.
  5. *lailly*, loathsome.   13. *kemm*, comb.

"Sing on your song, ye laily worm,
    That ye sung to me;"   20
"I never sung that song
    But fatt I wad sing to ye.

"I was but seven year aull
    Fan my mider she did dee,
My father marrëd the a warst woman
    The wardle did ever see.

"She changed me to the layely worm
    That layes att the fitt of the tree,
An my sister Messry
    To the makrell of the sea.   30

"And every Saterday att noon
    The machrell comes to me,
An she takes my layly head,
    An layes it on her knee,
An kames it weth a siller kame,
    An washes it in the sea.

"Seven knights ha I slain
    San I lay att the fitt of the tree;
An ye war na my ain father,
    The eight ye sud be."   40

He sent for his lady
    As fast as sen cod he:
"Far is my son,
    That ye sent fra me,
And my daughter,
    Lady Messry?"

"Yer son is att our king's court,
    Sarving for meatt an fee,
And yer daughter is att our quin's court,
    A mary suit an free."   50

22. *fatt*, what.   50. *mary*, maid-of-honor.
43. *far*, where.   50. *suit*, sweet.

"Ye lee, ye ill woman,
  Sa loud as I hear ye lea,
For my son is the layelly worm
  That lays at the fitt of the tree,
An my daughter Messry
  The machrell of the sea."

She has tain a silver wan
  An gine him stroks three,
And he started up the bravest knight
  Your eyes did ever see.   60

She has tane a small horn
  An loud an shill blue she,
An a' the fish came her tell but the proud machrell,
  An she stood by the sea:
"Ye shaped me ance an unshemly shape,
  An ye's never mare shape me."

He has sent to the wood
  For hathorn an fun,
An he has tane that gay lady,
  An ther he did her burne.   70

SWEET WILLIAM'S GHOST

There came a ghost to Margret's door,
  With many a grievous groan,
And ay he tirléd at the pin,
  But answer made she none.

"Is that my father Philip,
  Or is't my brother John?
Or is't my true-love Willy,
  From Scotland new come home?"

62. *blue*, blew.   68. *fun*, furze.   3. *tirléd at the pin*, rattle l the latch.

"'Tis not thy father Philip,
　　Nor yet thy brother John;   10
But 'tis thy true-love Willy,
　　From Scotland new come home.

"O sweet Margret, O dear Margret,
　　I pray thee speak to me;
Give me my faith and troth, Margret,
　　As I gave it to thee."

"Thy faith and troth thou's never get,
　　Nor yet will I thee lend,
Till that thou come within my bower,
　　And kiss my cheek and chin."   20

"If I should come within thy bower,
　　I am no earthly man;
And should I kiss thy rosy lips,
　　Thy days will not be lang.

"O sweet Margret, O dear Margret,
　　I pray thee speak to me;
Give me my faith and troth, Margret,
　　As I gave it to thee."

"Thy faith and troth thou's never get,
　　Nor yet will I thee lend,   30
Till you take me to yon kirk,
　　And wed me with a ring."

"My bones are buried in yon kirkyard,
　　Afar beyond the sea,
And it is but my spirit, Margret,
　　That's now speaking to thee."

18. *lend*, grant

She stretchd out her lilly-white hand,
   And, for to do her best,
"Hae, there's your faith and troth, Willy;
   God send your soul good rest."   40

Now she has kilted her robes of green
   A piece below her knee,
And a' the live-lang winter night
   The dead corp followed she.

"Is there any room at your head, Willy?
   Or any room at your feet?
Or any room at your side, Willy,
   Wherein that I may creep?"

"There's no room at my head, Margret,
   There's no room at my feet;   50
There's no room at my side, Margret,
   My coffin's made so meet."

Then up and crew the red, red cock,
   And up then crew the gray:
"'Tis time, 'tis time, my dear Margret,
   That you were going away."

No more the ghost to Margret said,
   But, with a grievous groan,
Evanishd in a cloud of mist,
   And left her all alone.   60

"O stay, my only true-love, stay,"
   The constant Margret cry'd;
Wan grew her cheeks, she closd her een,
   Stretchd her soft limbs, and dy'd.

52. *meet*, scant.

BONNY BARBARA ALLAN

It was in and about the Martinmas time,
  When the green leaves were a falling,
That Sir John Graeme, in the West Country,
  Fell in love with Barbara Allan.

He sent his men down through the town
  To the place where she was dwelling:
"O haste and come to my master dear,
  Gin ye be Barbara Allan."

O hooly, hooly rose she up,
  To the place where he was lying,   10
And when she drew the curtain by,
  "Young man, I think you're dying."

"O it's I'm sick, and very, very sick,
  And it's a' for Barbara Allan";
"O the better for me ye's never be,
  Tho your heart's blood were a spilling.

"O dinna ye mind, young man," said she,
  "When ye was in the tavern a drinking,
That ye made the healths gae round and round,
  And slighted Barbara Allan?"   20

He turned his face unto the wall,
  And death was with him dealing:
"Adieu, adieu, my dear friends all,
  And be kind to Barbara Allan."

And slowly, slowly raise she up,
  And slowly, slowly left him,
And sighing said she coud not stay,
  Since death of life had reft him.

9. *hooly*, softly.

She had not gane a mile but twa,
    When she heard the dead-bell ringing, 30
And every jow that the dead-bell geid,
    It cry'd, Woe to Barbara Allan!

"O mother, mother, make my bed!
    O make it saft and narrow!
Since my love died for me today,
    I'll die for him tomorrow."

EDWARD

"Why dois your brand sae drap wi bluid,
    Edward, Edward?
Why dois your brand sae drap wi bluid,
    And why sae sad gang yee O?"
"O I hae killed my hauke sae guid,
    Mither, mither,
O I hae killed my hauke sae guid,
    And I had nae mair bot hee O."

"Your haukis bluid was nevir sae reid,
    Edward, Edward, 10
Your haukis bluid was never sae reid,
    My deir son I tell thee O."
"O I hae killed my reid-roan steid,
    Mither, mither,
O I hae killed my reid-roan steid,
    That erst was sae fair and frie O."

"Your steid was auld, and ye hae gat mair,
    Edward, Edward,
Your steid was auld, and ye hae gat mair;
    Sum other dule ye drie O." 20

"O I hae killed my fadir deir,
    Mither, mither,
O I hae killed my fadir deir,
    Alas, and wae is mee O!"

"And whatten penance wul ye drie for that,
    Edward, Edward?
And whatten penance wul ye drie, for that?
    My deir son, now tell me O."
"Ile set my feit in yonder boat,
    Mither, mither,   30
Ile set my feit in yonder boat,
    And Ile fare ovir the sea O."

"And what wul ye doe wi your towirs and your ha,
    Edward, Edward?
And what wul ye doe wi your towirs and your ha,
    That were sae fair to see O?"
"Ile let thame stand tul they doun fa,
    Mither, mither,
Ile let thame stand tul they doun fa,
    For here nevir mair maun I bee O."   40

"And what wul ye leive to your bairns and your wife,
    Edward, Edward?
And what wul ye leive to your bairns and your wife,
    Whan ye gang ovir the sea O?"
"The warldis room, late them beg thrae life,
    Mither, mither,
The warldis room, late them beg thrae life,
    For thame nevir mair wul I see O."

"And what wul ye leive to your ain mither deir,
    Edward, Edward?   50
And what wul ye leive to your ain mither deir?
    My deir son, now tell me O."

45. *warldis*, world's.   45. *late*, let.

"The curse of hell frae me sall ye beir,
        Mither, mither,
The curse of hell frae me sall ye beir,
        Sic counseils ye gave to me O."

THE TWA SISTERS

There was twa sisters in a bowr,
        Edinburgh, Edinburgh,
There was twa sisters in a bowr,
        Stirling for ay;
There was twa sisters in a bowr,
There came a knight to be their wooer;
        Bonny Saint Johnston stands upon Tay.

He courted the eldest wi glove an ring,
But he lovd the youngest above a' thing.

He courted the eldest wi brotch an knife,   10
But he lovd the youngest as his life.

The eldest she was vexéd sair,
An much envied her sister fair.

Into her bowr she could not rest;
Wi grief an spite she almos brast.

Upon a morning fair an clear,
She cried upon her sister dear:

"O sister, come to yon sea stran,
An see our father's ships come to lan."

She's taen her by the milk-white han,   20
An led her down to yon sea stran.

2. Lines two, four, and seven are to be understood with each couplet as
a refrain.   10. *brotch*, brooch.

The youngest stood upon a stane;
The eldest came an threw her in.

She tooke her by the middle sma,
And dashed her bonny back to the jaw.

"O sister, sister, tak my han,
An Ise mack you heir to a' my lan.

"O sister, sister, tak my middle,
An yes get my goud and my gouden girdle.

"O sister, sister, save my life,   30
An I swear Ise never be nae man's wife."

"Foul fa the han that I should tacke;
It twind me an my wardles make.

"Your cherry cheeks an yallow hair
Gars me gae maiden for evermair."

Sometimes she sank, an sometimes she swam,
Till she came down yon bonny mill-dam.

O out it came the miller's son,
An saw the fair maid swimmin in.

"O father, father, draw your dam;   40
Here's either a mermaid or a swan."

The miller quickly drew the dam,
An there he found a drownd woman.

You couldna see her yallow hair
For gold and pearle that were so rare.

You coudna see her middle sma
For gouden girdle that was sae braw.

25. *jaw*, wave.   33. *wardles make*, world's mate.
33. *twind*, separated.

You coudna see her fingers white,
For gouden rings that were sae gryte.

An by there came a harper fine,   50
That harpéd to the king at dine.

When he did look that lady upon,
He sighd and made a heavy moan,

He's taen three locks o her yallow hair,
And wi them strung his harp sae fair.

The first tune he did play and sing,
Was, "Farewell to my father the king."

The nextin tune that he playd syne,
Was, "Farewell to my mother the queen."

The lasten tune that he playd then,   60
Was, "Wae to my sister, fair Ellen."

LORD RANDAL

"O where hae ye been, Lord Randal, my son?
O where hae ye been, my handsome young man?"
"I hae been to the wild wood; mother, make my bed soon,
For I'm weary wi hunting, and fain wald lie down."

"Where gat ye your dinner, Lord Randal, my son?
Where gat ye your dinner, my handsome young man?"
"I dined wi my true-love; mother, make my bed soon,
For I'm weary wi hunting, and fain wald lie down."

"What gat ye to your dinner, Lord Randal, my son?
What gat ye to your dinner, my handsome young man?" 10
"I gat eels boiled in broo; mother, make my bed soon,
For I'm weary wi hunting, and fain wald lie down."

"What became of your bloodhounds, Lord Randal, my
    son?
What became of your bloodhounds, my handsome young
    man?"
"O they swelld and they died; mother, make my bed soon,
For I'm weary wi hunting, and fain wald lie down."

"O I fear ye are poisond, Lord Randal, my son!
O I fear ye are poisond, my handsome young man!"
"O yes! I am poisond; mother, make my bed soon,
For I'm sick at the heart, and I fain wald lie down."   20

SIR PATRICK SPENS

The king sits in Dumferling toune,
    Drinking the blude-reid wine:
"O whar will I get guid sailor,
    To sail this schip of mine?"

Up and spak an eldern knicht,
    Sat at the kings richt kne:
"Sir Patrick Spens is the best sailor,
    That sails upon the se."

The king has written a braid letter,
    And signd it wi his hand,   10
And sent it to Sir Patrick Spens,
    Was walking on the sand.

The first line that Sir Patrick red,
    A loud lauch lauchéd he;
The next line that Sir Patrick red,
    The teir blinded his ee.

"O wha is this has don this deid,
    This il deid don to me,
To send me out this time o' the yeir,
    To sail upon the se!   20

"Mak hast, mak haste, my mirry men all,
  Our guid schip sails the morne."
"O say na sae, my master deir,
  For I feir a deadlie storme.

"Late, late yestreen I saw the new moone,
  Wi the auld moone in hir arme,
And I feir, I feir, my deir master,
  That we will cum to harme."

O our Scots nobles wer richt laith
  To weet their cork-heild schoone;   30
Bot lang owre a' the play wer playd,
  Thair hats they swam aboone.

O lang, lang may their ladies sit,
  Wi thair fans into their hand,
Or eir they se Sir Patrick Spens
  Cum sailing to the land.

O lang, lang may the ladies stand,
  Wi thair gold kems in their hair,
Waiting for thair ain deir lords,
  For they'll see thame na mair.   40

Haf owre, haf owre to Aberdour,
  It's fiftie fadom deip,
And thair lies guid Sir Patrick Spens,
  Wi the Scots lords at his feit.

YOUNG BEICHAN

In London city was Bicham born,
  He longd strange countries for to see,
But he was taen by a savage Moor,
  Who handld him right cruely.

For thro his shoulder he put a bore,
    An thro the bore has pitten a tree,
And he's gard him draw the carts o wine,
    Where horse and oxen had wont to be.

He's casten him in a dungeon deep,
    Where he could neither hear nor see;   10
He's shut him up in a prison strong,
    An he's handld him right cruely.

O this Moor he had but ae daughter,
    I wot her name was Shusy Pye;
She's doen her to the prison-house,
    And she's calld Young Bicham one word by.

"O hae ye ony lands or rents,
    Or citys in your ain country,
Could free you out of prison strong,
    An coud mantain a lady free?"   20

"O London city is my own,
    An other citys two or three,
Coud loose me out o prison strong,
    An coud mantain a lady free."

O she has bribed her father's men
    Wi meikle goud and white money,
She's gotten the key o the prison doors,
    An she has set Young Bicham free.

She's g'in him a loaf o good white bread,
    But an a flask o Spanish wine,   30
An she bad him mind on the ladie's love
    That sae kindly freed him out o pine.

"Go set your foot on good ship-board,
    An haste you back to your ain country,
An before that seven years has an end,
    Come back again, love, and marry me."

It was long or seven years had an end
   She longd fu sair her love to see;
She's set her foot on good ship-board,
   An turnd her back on her ain country. 40

She's saild up, so has she doun,
   Till she came to the other side;
She's landed at Young Bicham's gates,
   An I hope this day she sal be his bride.

"Is this Young Bicham's gates?" says she,
   "Or is that noble prince within?"
"He's up the stairs wi his bonny bride,
   An monny a lord and lady wi him."

"O has he taen a bonny bride,
   An has he clean forgotten me!" 50
An sighing said that gay lady,
   "I wish I were in my ain country!"

But she's pitten her han in her pocket,
   An gin the porter guineas three;
Says, "Take ye that, ye proud porter,
   An bid the bridegroom speak to me."

O whan the porter came up the stair,
   He's fa'n low down upon his knee:
"Won up, won up, ye proud porter,
   An what makes a' this courtesy?" 60

"O I've been porter at your gates
   This mair nor seven years an three,
But there is a lady at them now
   The like of whom I never did see."

"For on every finger she has a ring,
   An on the mid-finger she has three,
An there's as meikle goud aboon her brow
   As woud buy an earldome o lan to me."

Then up it started Young Bicham
  An sware so loud by Our Lady,   70
"It can be nane but Shusy Pye,
  That has come oer the sea to me."

O quickly ran he down the stair,
  O fifteen steps he has made but three;
He's tane his bonny love in his arms,
  An a wot he kissd her tenderly.

"O hae you tane a bonny bride?
  An hae you quite forsaken me?
An hae ye quite forgotten her
  That gae you life an liberty?"   80

She's lookit oer her left shoulder
  To hide the tears stood in her ee;
"Now fare thee well, Young Bicham," she says,
  "I'll strive to think nae mair on thee."

"Take back your daughter, madam," he says,
  "An a double dowry I'll gi her wi;
For I maun marry my first true love,
  That's done and suffered so much for me."

He's take his bonny love by the han,
  And led her to yon fountain stane;   90
He's changd her name frae Shusy Pye,
  An he's cald her his bonny love, Lady Jane.

HIND HORN

In Scotland there was a babie born,
  Lill lal, etc.
And his name it was called young Hind Horn.
  With a fal lal, etc.

He sent a letter to our king
That he was in love with his daughter Jean.

He 's gien to her a silver wand,
With seven living lavrocks sitting thereon.

She 's gien to him a diamond ring,
With seven bright diamonds set therein.   10

"When this ring grows pale and wan,
You may know by it my love is gane."

One day as he looked his ring upon,
He saw the diamonds pale and wan.

He left the sea and came to land,
And the first that he met was an old beggar man.

"What news, what news?" said young Hind Horn;
"No news, no news," said the old beggar man.

"No news," said the beggar, "no news at a',
But there is a wedding in the king's ha.   20

"But there is a wedding in the king's ha,
That has halden these forty days and twa."

"Will ye lend me your begging coat?
And I'll lend you my scarlet cloak.

"Will you lend me your beggar's rung?
And I'll gie you my steed to ride upon.

"Will you lend me your wig o hair,
To cover mine, because it is fair?"

The auld beggar man was bound for the mill,
But young Hind Horn for the king's hall.   30

25. *rung*, staff.

The auld beggar man was bound for to ride,
But young Hind Horn was bound for the bride.

When he came to the king's gate,
He sought a drink for Hind Horn's sake.

The bride came down with a glass of wine,
When he drank out the glass, and dropt in the ring.

"O got ye this by sea or land?
Or got ye it off a dead man's hand?"

"I got not it by sea, I got it by land,
And I got it, madam, out of your own hand." 40

"O I'll cast off my gowns of brown,
And beg wi you frae town to town.

"O I'll cast off my gowns of red,
And I'll beg wi you to win my bread."

"Ye needna cast off your gowns of brown,
For I'll make you lady o many a town.

"Ye needna cast off your gowns of red,
It's only a sham, the begging o my bread."

The bridegroom he had wedded the bride,
But young Hind Horn he took her to bed. 50

ROBIN HOOD'S DEATH

When Robin Hood and Little John,
Down a down, a down, a down,
Went oer yon bank of broom,
Said Robin Hood bold to Little John,
"We have shot for many a pound."
Hey down, a down, a down.

'But I am not able to shoot one shot more,
  My broad arrows will not flee;
But I have a cousin lives down below,
  Please God, she will bleed me."   10

Now Robin is to fair Kirkly gone,
  As fast as he can win;
But before he came there, as we do hear,
  He was taken very ill.

And when he came to fair Kirkly-hall,
  He knockd all at the ring,
But none was so ready as his cousin herself
  For to let bold Robin in.

"Will you please to sit down, cousin Robin," she said,
  "And drink some beer with me?"   20
"No, I will neither eat nor drink,
  Till I am blooded by thee."

"Well, I have a room, cousin Robin," she said,
  "Which you did never see,
And if you please to walk therein,
  You blooded by me shall be."

She took him by the lily-white hand,
  And led him to a private room,
And there she blooded bold Robin Hood,
  While one drop of blood would run down.   30

She blooded him in a vein of the arm,
  And locked him up in the room;
There did he bleed all the livelong day,
  Until the next day at noon.

He then bethought him of a casement there,
  Thinking for to get down;
But was so weak he could not leap,
  He could not get him down.

He then bethought him of his bugle-horn,
    Which hung low down to his knee;   40
He set his horn unto his mouth,
    And blew out weak blasts three.

Then Little John, when hearing him,
    As he sat under a tree,
"I fear my master is now near dead,
    He blows so wearily."

Then Little John to fair Kirkly is gone,
    As fast as he can dree;
But when he came to Kirkly-hall,
    He broke locks two or three;   50

Until he came bold Robin to see,
    Then he fell on his knee:
"A boon, a boon," cries Little John,
    "Master, I beg of thee."

"What is that boon," said Robin Hood,
    "Little John, thou begs of me?"
"It is to burn fair Kirkly-hall,
    And all their nunnery."

"Now nay, now nay," quoth Robin Hood,
    "That boon I'll not grant thee;   60
I never hurt woman in all my life,
    Nor men in woman's company.

"I never hurt fair maid in all my time,
    Nor at mine end shall it be;
But give me my bent bow in my hand,
    And a broad arrow I'll let flee;
And where this arrow is taken up,
    There shall my grave digged be.

"Lay me a green sod under my head,
　And another at my feet; 70
And lay my bent bow by my side,
　Which was my music sweet;
And make my grave of gravel and green,
　Which is most right and meet.

"Let me have length and breadth enough,
　With a green sod under my head;
That they may say, when I am dead,
　Here lies bold Robin Hood."

These words they readily granted him,
　Which did bold Robin please; 80
And there they buried bold Robin Hood,
　Within the fair Kirkleys.

SIXTEENTH CENTURY

EDMUND SPENSER (1552–1599)

AMORETTI

SONNET XVIII

The rolling wheele that runneth often round,
The hardest steele in tract of time doth teare:
  and drizling drops that often doe redound,
  the firmest flint doth in continuance weare.
Yet cannot I, with many a dropping teare,
  and long intreaty, soften her hard hart:
  that she will once vouchsafe my plaint to heare,
  or looke with pitty on my payneful smart.
But when I pleade, she bids me play my part,
  and when I weep, she sayes teares are but water: 10
  and when I sigh, she sayes I know the art,
  and when I waile she turnes hir selfe to laughter.
So doe I weepe, and wayle, and pleade in vaine,
  whiles she as steele and flint doth still remayne.

SONNET LXVIII

Most glorious Lord of lyfe, that on this day,
Didst make thy triumph over death and sin:
  and having harrowd hell, didst bring away
  captivity thence captive us to win:
This joyous day, deare Lord, with joy begin,
  and grant that we for whom thou diddest dye
  being with thy deare blood clene washt from sin,
  may live for ever in felicity.

33

And that thy love we weighing worthily,
  may likewise love thee for the same againe: 10
  and for thy sake that all lyke deare didst buy,
  with love may one another entertayne.
So let us love, deare love, lyke as we ought,
  love is the lesson which the Lord us taught.

                1595

EPITHALAMION

.   .   .   .

Open the temple gates unto my love,
Open them wide that she may enter in,
And all the postes adorne as doth behove,
And all the pillours deck with girlands trim,
For to recyve this Saynt with honour dew,
That commeth in to you.
With trembling steps and humble reverence,   210
She commeth in, before th' almighties vew,
Of her ye virgins learne obedience,
When so ye come into those holy places,
To humble your proud faces:
Bring her up to th' high altar, that she may
The sacred ceremonies there partake,
The which do endlesse matrimony make,
And let the roring Organs loudly play
The praises of the Lord in lively notes,
The whiles with hollow throates   220
The Choristers the joyous Antheme sing,
That al the woods may answere and their eccho ring.

Behold whiles she before the altar stands
Hearing the holy priest that to her speakes
And blesseth her with his two happy hands,
How the red roses flush up in her cheekes,
And the pure snow with goodly vermill stayne,
Like crimsin dyde in grayne,

That even th' Angels which continually,
About the sacred Altare doe remaine,   230
Forget their service and about her fly,
Ofte peeping in her face that seems more fayre,
The more they on it stare.
But her sad eyes still fastened on the ground,
Are governed with goodly modesty,
That suffers not one looke to glaunce awry,
Which may let in a little thought unsownd.
Why blush ye love to give to me your hand,
The pledge of all our band?
Sing ye sweet Angels, Alleluya sing,   240
That all the woods may answere and your eccho ring.

1595

.   .   .   .

THE FAERIE QUEENE

BOOK I

Canto I

34

A little lowly Hermitage it was,
Downe in a dale, hard by a forests side,
Far from resort of people, that did pas
In travell to and froe: a little wyde
There was an holy Chappell edifyde,
Wherein the Hermite dewly wont to say
His holy things each morne and eventyde:
Thereby a Christall streame did gently play,
Which from a sacred fountaine welled forth alway.

35

Arrived there, the little house they fill,   10
Ne looke for entertainement, where none was:
Rest is their feast, and all things at their will;

The noblest mind the best contentment has,
With faire discourse the evening so they pas:
For that old man of pleasing wordes had store,
And well could file his tongue as smooth as glas;
He told of Saintes and Popes, and evermore
He strowd an Ave-Mary after and before.

36

The drouping Night thus creepeth on them fast,
And the sad humour loading their eye liddes,   20
As messenger of *Morpheus* on them cast
Sweet slombring deaw, the which to sleepe them biddes.
Unto their lodgings then his guestes he riddes:
Where when all drownd in deadly sleepe he findes,
He to his study goes, and there amiddes
His Magick bookes and artes of sundry kindes,
He seekes out mighty charmes, to trouble sleepy mindes.

1596

CHRISTOPHER MARLOWE (1564-1593)

THE PASSIONATE SHEPHERD TO HIS LOVE

Come live with me and be my Love,
And we will all the pleasures prove
That hills and valleys, dales and fields,
Or woods or steepy mountain yields.

And we will sit upon the rocks,
And see the shepherds feed their flocks
By shallow rivers, to whose falls
Melodious birds sing madrigals.

And I will make thee beds of roses
And a thousand fragrant posies;   10
A cap of flowers, and a kirtle
Embroidered all with leaves of myrtle;

A gown made of the finest wool
Which from our pretty lambs we pull;
Fair-linéd slippers for the cold,
With buckles of the purest gold;

A belt of straw and ivy buds
With coral clasps and amber studs—
And if these pleasures may thee move,
Come live with me and be my Love.   20

The shepherd swains shall dance and sing
For thy delight each May morning—
If these delights thy mind may move,
Then live with me and be my Love.

1599

SIR WALTER RALEIGH (1552?–1618)

THE NYMPH'S REPLY TO THE SHEPHERD

If all the world and love were young,
And truth in every shepherd's tongue,
These pretty pleasures might me move,
To live with thee and be thy love.

But time drives flocks from field to fold,
When rivers rage, and rocks grow cold;
And Philomel becometh dumb;
The rest complains of cares to come.

The flowers do fade, and wanton fields
To wayward Winter reckoning yields;   10
A honey tongue, a heart of gall,
Is fancy's spring, but sorrow's fall.

Thy gowns, thy shoes, thy beds of roses,
Thy cap, thy kirtle, and thy posies,
Soon break, soon wither, soon forgotten,
In folly ripe, in reason rotten.

Thy belt of straw and ivy buds,
Thy coral clasps and amber studs,
All these in me no means can move,
To come to thee and be thy love.   20

But could youth last, and love still breed,
Had joys no date, nor age no need,
Then these delights my mind might move,
To live with thee and be thy love.

                                                1599

WILLIAM SHAKESPEARE (1564–1616)

SONGS FROM THE PLAYS

WHEN ICICLES HANG BY THE WALL

From LOVE'S LABOUR'S LOST

When icicles hang by the wall,
    And Dick the shepherd blows his nail,
And Tom bears logs into the hall,
    And milk comes frozen home in pail,
When blood is nipped and ways be foul,
Then nightly sings the staring owl,
Tu-whit, tu-who! a merry note,
While greasy Joan doth keel the pot.

When all aloud the wind doth blow,
    And coughing drowns the parson's saw,   10
And birds sit brooding in the snow,
    And Marian's nose looks red and raw,

When roasted crabs hiss in the bowl,
  Then nightly sings the staring owl,
  Tu-whit, tu-who! a merry note,
While greasy Joan doth keel the pot.

1598

SIGH NO MORE, LADIES, SIGH NO MORE

From MUCH ADO ABOUT NOTHING

Sigh no more, ladies, sigh no more,
  Men were deceivers ever,
One foot in sea and one on shore,
  To one thing constant never:
Then sigh not so, but let them go,
  And be you blithe and bonny,
Converting all your sounds of woe
  Into Hey nonny, nonny.

Sing no more ditties, sing no moe,
  Of dumps so dull and heavy;   10
The fraud of men was ever so,
  Since summer first was leafy:
Then sigh not so, but let them go,
  And be you blithe and bonny,
Converting all your sounds of woe
  Into Hey nonny, nonny!

1600

TELL ME, WHERE IS FANCY BRED

From THE MERCHANT OF VENICE

Tell me, where is fancy bred,
Or in the heart, or in the head?
How begot, how nourishéd?
      Reply, reply.

It is engendered in the eyes,
With gazing fed; and fancy dies
In the cradle where it lies.
Let us all ring fancy's knell;
I'll begin it—Ding-dong, bell.
        Ding, dong, bell.   10
                         1600

WHO IS SILVIA?

From TWO GENTLEMEN OF VERONA

Who is Silvia? what is she,
    That all our swains commend her?
Holy, fair, and wise is she;
    The heaven such grace did lend her
That she might admiréd be.

Is she kind as she is fair?
    For beauty lives with kindness.
Love doth to her eyes repair
    To help him of his blindness,
And, being helped, inhabits there.   10

Then to Silvia let us sing
    That Silvia is excelling;
She excels each mortal thing
    Upon the dull earth dwelling—
To her let us garlands bring.

                      1623

UNDER THE GREENWOOD TREE

From AS YOU LIKE IT

Under the greenwood tree
Who loves to lie with me,
And turn his merry note
Unto the sweet bird's throat,

Come hither! come hither! come hither!
    Here shall he see
    No enemy
But winter and rough weather.

    Who doth ambition shun
    And loves to live i' the sun,   10
    Seeking the food he eats
    And pleased with what he gets,
Come hither! come hither! come hither!
    Here shall he see
    No enemy
But winter and rough weather.

                1623

BLOW, BLOW, THOU WINTER WIND!

From AS YOU LIKE IT

Blow, blow, thou winter wind!
Thou art not so unkind
As man's ingratitude;
Thy tooth is not so keen,
Because thou art not seen,
    Although thy breath be rude.

Heigh ho! sing, heigh ho! unto the green holly;
Most friendship is feigning, most loving mere folly.
    Then, heigh ho, the holly!
    This life is most jolly.   10

    Freeze, freeze, thou bitter sky!
    That dost not bite so nigh
        As benefits forgot;

Though thou the waters warp,
Thy sting is not so sharp
   As friend remembered not.

Heigh ho! sing, heigh ho! etc.

1623

O MISTRESS MINE, WHERE ARE YOU ROAMING?

From TWELFTH NIGHT

O Mistress mine, where are you roaming?
Oh, stay and hear; your true love's coming,
   That can sing both high and low.
Trip no further, pretty sweeting,
Journeys end in lovers meeting,
   Every wise man's son doth know.

What is Love? 'tis not hereafter;
Present mirth hath present laughter;
   What's to come is still unsure.
In delay there lies no plenty;   10
Then come kiss me, sweet and twenty;
   Youth's a stuff will not endure.

1623

TAKE, O, TAKE THOSE LIPS AWAY

From MEASURE FOR MEASURE

Take, O, take those lips away
   That so sweetly were forsworn;
And those eyes, the break of day,
   Lights that do mislead the morn.
But my kisses bring again,
               Bring again;
Seals of love, but sealed in vain,
               Sealed in vain!

1623

HARK, HARK! THE LARK

From CYMBELINE

Hark, hark! the lark at heaven's gate sings
    And Phoebus 'gins arise,
His steeds to water at those springs
    On chaliced flowers that lies;
And winking Mary-buds begin
    To ope their golden eyes.
With every thing that pretty is,
    My lady sweet, arise!
      Arise, arise!

1623

FEAR NO MORE THE HEAT O' THE SUN

From CYMBELINE

Fear no more the heat o' the sun,
    Nor the furious winter's rages;
Thou thy worldly task hast done,
    Home art gone, and ta'en thy wages.
Golden lads and girls all must,
As chimney-sweepers, come to dust.

Fear no more the frown o' the great;
    Thou art past the tyrant's stroke;
Care no more to clothe and eat;
    To thee the reed is as the oak.   10
The scepter, learning, physic must
All follow this, and come to dust.

Fear no more the lightning-flash,
    Nor th' all-dreaded thunder-stone;
Fear not slander, censure rash;
    Thou hast finished joy and moan.

All lovers young, all lovers must
Consign to thee, and come to dust.

No exorciser harm thee!
   Nor no witchcraft charm thee!   20
Ghost unlaid forbear thee!
   Nothing ill come near thee!
Quiet consummation have;
And renownéd be thy grave!

1623

FULL FATHOM FIVE THY FATHER LIES

From THE TEMPEST

Full fathom five thy father lies.
   Of his bones are coral made;
Those are pearls that were his eyes;
   Nothing of him that doth fade
But doth suffer a sea change
Into something rich and strange.
Sea-nymphs hourly ring his knell:
                Ding-dong!
Hark! now I hear them—Ding-dong, bell!

1623

WHERE THE BEE SUCKS, THERE SUCK I

From THE TEMPEST

Where the bee sucks, there suck I;
In a cowslip's bell I lie;
There I couch when owls do cry.
On the bat's back I do fly
After summer merrily.
Merrily, merrily, shall I live now
Under the blossom that hangs on the bough.

1623

SONNETS

XVIII

Shall I compare thee to a summer's day?
Thou art more lovely and more temperate:
Rough winds do shake the darling buds of May,
And summer's lease hath all too short a date:
Sometime too hot the eye of heaven shines,
And often is his gold complexion dimm'd;
And every fair from fair sometime declines,
By change or nature's changing course untrimm'd;
But thy eternal summer shall not fade
Nor lose possession of that fair thou owest;   10
Nor shall Death brag thou wander'st in his shade,
When in eternal lines to time thou growest;
   So long as men can breathe or eyes can see,
   So long lives this and this gives life to thee.

XXIX

When, in disgrace with fortune and men's eyes,
I all alone beweep my outcast state
And trouble deaf heaven with my bootless cries
And look upon myself and curse my fate,
Wishing me like to one more rich in hope,
Featured like him, like him with friends possessed,
Desiring this man's art and that man's scope,
With what I most enjoy contented least;
Yet in these thoughts myself almost despising,
Haply I think on thee, and then my state,   10
Like to the lark at break of day arising
From sullen earth, sings hymns at heaven's gate;
   For thy sweet love remembered such wealth brings
   That then I scorn to change my state with kings.

XXX

When to the sessions of sweet silent thought
I summon up remembrance of things past,
I sigh the lack of many a thing I sought,

And with old woes new wail my dear time's waste.
Then can I drown an eye, unused to flow,
For precious friends hid in death's dateless night,
And weep afresh love's long since canceled woe,
And moan the expense of many a vanished sight—
Then can I grieve at grievances foregone,
And heavily from woe to woe tell o'er   10
The sad account of fore-bemoanéd moan,
Which I new pay as if not paid before.
    But if the while I think on thee, dear friend,
    All losses are restored and sorrows end.

XXXIII

Full many a glorious morning have I seen
Flatter the mountain-tops with sovereign eye,
Kissing with golden face the meadows green,
Gilding pale streams with heavenly alchemy;
Anon permit the basest clouds to ride
With ugly rack on his celestial face,
And from the forlorn world his visage hide,
Stealing unseen to west with this disgrace.
Even so my sun one early morn did shine
With all-triumphant splendor on my brow;   10
But out, alack! he was but one hour mine;
The region cloud hath masked him from me now.
    Yet him for this my love no whit disdaineth;
    Suns of the world may stain when heaven's sun staineth.

XXXV

No more be griev'd at that which thou hast done:
Roses have thorns, and silver fountains mud;
Clouds and eclipses stain both moon and sun,
And loathsome canker lives in sweetest bud.
All men make faults, and even I in this,
Authorizing thy trespass with compare,
Myself corrupting, salving thy amiss,
Excusing thy sins more than thy sins are;

For to thy sensual fault I bring in sense—
Thy adverse party is thy advocate—   10
And 'gainst myself a lawful plea commence:
Such civil war is in my love and hate
    That I an accessary needs must be
    To that sweet thief which sourly robs from me.

LXXI

No longer mourn for me when I am dead
Than you shall hear the surly, sullen bell
Give warning to the world that I am fled
From this vile world, with vilest worms to dwell.
Nay, if you read this line, remember not
The hand that writ it; for I love you so
That I in your sweet thoughts would be forgot
If thinking on me then should make you woe.
Oh, if, I say, you look upon this verse
When I perhaps compounded am with clay,   10
Do not so much as my poor name rehearse,
But let your love even with my life decay,
    Lest the wise world should look into your moan
    And mock you with me after I am gone.

LXXIII

That time of year thou mayst in me behold
When yellow leaves, or none, or few, do hang
Upon those boughs which shake against the cold,
Bare ruined choirs, where late the sweet birds sang.
In me thou see'st the twilight of such day
As after sunset fadeth in the west,
Which by and by black night doth take away,
Death's second self, that seals up all in rest.
In me thou see'st the glowing of such fire
That on the ashes of his youth doth lie,   10
As the deathbed whereon it must expire,
Consumed with that which it was nourished by.

This thou perceivest, which makes thy love more strong,
To love that well which thou must leave ere long.

CIV

To me, fair friend, you never can be old,
For as you were when first your eye I ey'd,
Such seems your beauty still. Three winters cold
Have from the forests shook three summers' pride,
Three beauteous springs to yellow autumn turn'd
In process of the seasons have I seen.
Three April perfumes in three hot Junes burn'd,
Since first I saw you fresh, which yet are green.
Ah! yet doth beauty, like a dial-hand,
Steal from his figure and no pace perceived;   10
So your sweet hue, which methinks still doth stand,
Hath motion and mine eye may be deceived:
    For fear of which, hear this, thou age unbred;
    Ere you were born was beauty's summer dead.

CVI

When in the chronicle of wasted time
I see descriptions of the fairest wights,
And beauty making beautiful old rime
In praise of ladies dead and lovely knights,
Then, in the blazon of sweet beauty's best,
Of hand, of foot, of lip, of eye, of brow,
I see their antique pen would have expressed
Even such a beauty as you master now.
So all their praises are but prophecies
Of this our time, all you prefiguring;   10
And, for they looked but with divining eyes,
They had not skill enough your worth to sing;
    For we, which now behold these present days,
    Have eyes to wonder, but lack tongues to praise.

CIX

Oh, never say that I was false of heart,
Though absence seemed my flame to qualify.

As easy might I from myself depart
As from my soul, which in thy breast doth lie.
That is my home of love; if I have ranged,
Like him that travels I return again,
Just to the time, not with the time exchanged,
So that myself bring water for my stain.
Never believe, though in my nature reigned
All frailties that besiege all kinds of blood,　　　10
That it could so preposterously be stained,
To leave for nothing all thy sum of good;
　For nothing this wide universe I call,
　Sáve thou, my rose; in it thou art my all.

CXVI

Let me not to the marriage of true minds
Admit impediments. Love is not love
Which alters when it alteration finds,
Or bends with the remover to remove.
Oh, no! it is an ever-fixéd mark
That looks on tempests and is never shaken;
It is the star to every wandering bark,
Whose worth's unknown, although his height be taken,
Love's not Time's fool, though rosy lips and cheeks
Within his bending sickle's compass come;　　　10
Love alters not with his brief hours and weeks,
But bears it out even to the edge of doom.
　If this be error and upon me proved,
　I never writ, nor no man ever loved.

CXLIV

Two loves I have of comfort and despair,
Which like two spirits do suggest me still:
The better angel is a man right fair,
The worser spirit a woman color'd ill.
To win me soon to hell, my female evil
Tempteth my better angel from my side,
And would corrupt my saint to be a devil,

Wooing his purity with her foul pride.
And whether that my angel be turn'd fiend
Suspect I may, yet not directly tell;   10
But being both from me, both to each friend,
I guess one angel in another's hell;
   Yet this shall I ne'er know, but live in doubt,
   Till my bad angel fire my good one out.

1609

SEVENTEENTH CENTURY

BEN JONSON (1573?–1637)

TO CELIA

Drink to me only with thine eyes,
    And I will pledge with mine;
Or leave a kiss but in the cup
    And I'll not look for wine.
The thirst that from the soul doth rise
    Doth ask a drink divine;
But might I of Jove's nectar sup,
    I would not change for thine.

I sent thee late a rosy wreath,
    Not so much honoring thee   10
As giving it a hope that there
    It could not withered be;
But thou thereon didst only breathe,
    And sent'st it back to me;
Since when it grows, and smells, I swear,
    Not of itself but thee!

                          1616

TO THE MEMORY OF MY BELOVED, MASTER WILLIAM SHAKESPEARE

To draw no envy, Shakespeare, on thy name,
Am I thus ample to thy book and fame;
While I confess thy writings to be such
As neither man, nor muse, can praise too much.
'Tis true, and all men's suffrage. But these ways
Were not the paths I meant unto thy praise;

For silliest ignorance on these may light,
Which, when it sounds at best, but echoes right;
Or blind affection, which doth ne'er advance
The truth, but gropes, and urgeth all by chance;   10
Or crafty malice might pretend this praise,
And think to ruin, where it seemed to raise.
These are, as some infamous bawd or whore
Should praise a matron. What could hurt her more?
But thou art proof against them, and, indeed,
Above the ill fortune of them, or the need.
I therefore will begin. Soul of the age!
The applause, delight, the wonder of our stage!
My Shakespeare, rise! I will not lodge thee by
Chaucer, or Spenser, or bid Beaumont lie   20
A little further, to make thee a room;
Thou art a monument without a tomb,
And art alive still while thy book doth live
And we have wits to read and praise to give.
That I not mix thee so, my brain excuses,
I mean with great, but disproportioned Muses;
For if I thought my judgment were of years,
I should commit thee surely with thy peers,
And tell how far thou didst our Lyly outshine,
Or sporting Kyd, or Marlowe's mighty line.   30
And though thou hadst small Latin and less Greek,
From thence to honor thee, I would not seek
For names; but call forth thundering Aeschylus,
Euripides, and Sophocles to us;
Pacuvius, Accius, him of Cordova dead,
To life again, to hear thy buskin tread,
And shake a stage; or, when thy socks were on,
Leave thee alone for the comparison
Of all that insolent Greece or haughty Rome
Sent forth, or since did from their ashes come.   40
Triumph, my Britain, thou hast one to show
To whom all scenes of Europe homage owe.

He was not of an age, but for all time!
And all the Muses still were in their prime,
When, like Apollo, he came forth to warm
Our ears, or like a Mercury to charm!
Nature herself was proud of his designs
And joyed to wear the dressing of his lines!
Which were so richly spun, and woven so fit,
As, since, she will vouchsafe no other wit.   50
The merry Greek, tart Aristophanes,
Neat Terence, witty Plautus, now not please,
But antiquated and deserted lie,
As they were not of Nature's family.
Yet must I not give Nature all; thy art,
My gentle Shakespeare, must enjoy a part.
For though the poet's matter nature be,
His art doth give the fashion; and, that he
Who casts to write a living line, must sweat
(Such as thine are) and strike the second heat   60
Upon the Muses' anvil; turn the same
(And himself with it) that he thinks to frame,
Or, for the laurel, he may gain a scorn;
For a good poet's made, as well as born.
And such wert thou! Look how the father's face
Lives in his issue; even so the race
Of Shakespeare's mind and manners brightly shines
In his well turnéd, and true filéd lines;
In each of which he seems to shake a lance,
As brandished at the eyes of ignorance.   70
Sweet Swan of Avon! what a sight it were
To see thee in our waters yet appear,
And make those flights upon the banks of Thames,
That so did take Eliza, and our James!
But stay, I see thee in the hemisphere
Advanced, and made a constellation there!
Shine forth, thou Star of poets, and with rage
Or influence, chide or cheer the drooping stage,

Which, since thy flight from hence, hath mourned like
    night,
And despairs day, but for thy volume's light.

1623

JOHN DONNE (1573–1631)

THE EXTASIE

Where, like a pillow on a bed,
    A Pregnant banke swel'd up, to rest
The violets reclining head,
    Sat we two, one anothers best.
Our hands were firmely cimented
    With a fast balme, which thence did spring,
Our eye-beames twisted, and did thred
    Our eyes, upon one double string;
So to'entergraft our hands, as yet
    Was all the meanes to make us one,   10
And pictures in our eyes to get
    Was all our propagation.
As 'twixt two equall Armies, Fate
    Suspends uncertaine victorie,
Our soules (which to advance their state,
    Were gone out,) hung 'twixt her, and mee.
And whil'st our soules negotiate there,
    Wee like sepulchrall statues lay;
All day, the same our postures were,
    And wee said nothing, all the day.   20
If any, so by love refin'd,
    That he soules language understood,
And by good love were growen all minde,
    Within convenient distance stood,
He (though he knew not which soule spake,
    Because both meant, both spake the same)

Might thence a new concoction take,
    And part farre purer then he came.
This Extasie doth unperplex
    (We said) and tell us what we love,   30
Wee see by this, it was not sexe,
    Wee see, we saw not what did move:
But as all severall soules containe
    Mixture of things, they know not what,
Love, these mixt soules, doth mixe againe,
    And makes both one, each this and that.
A single violet transplant,
    The strength, the colour, and the size,
(All which before was poore, and scant,)
    Redoubles still, and multiplies.   40
When love, and one another so
    Interinanimates two soules,
That abler soule, which thence doth flow,
    Defects of lonelinesse controules.
Wee then, who are this new soule, know,
Of what we are compos'd, and made,
For, th' Atomies of which we grow,
    Are soules, whom no change can invade.
But O alas, so long, so farre
    Our bodies why doe wee forbeare?   50
They are ours, though they are not wee, Wee are
    The intelligences, they the spheare.
We owe them thankes, because they thus,
    Did us, to us, at first convay,
Yeelded their forces, sense, to us,
    Nor are dlrosse to us, but allay.
On man heavens influence workes not so,
    But that it first imprints the ayre,
Soe soule into the soule may flow,
    Though it to body first repaire.   60
As our blood labours to beget
    Spirits, as like soules as it can,

Because such fingers need to knit
    That subtile knot, which makes us man:
So must pure lovers soules descend
    T'affections, and to faculties,
Which sense may reach and apprehend,
    Else a great Prince in prison lies.
To'our bodies turne wee then, that so
    Weake men on love reveal'd may looke;   70
Loves mysteries in soules doe grow,
    But yet the body is his booke.
And if some lover, such as wee,
    Have heard this dialogue of one,
Let him still marke us, he shall see
    Small change, when we'are to bodies gone.

        1633

THE FUNERALL

Who ever comes to shroud me, do not harme
    Nor question much
That subtile wreath of haire, which crowns my arme;
The mystery, the signe you must not touch,
    For 'tis my outward Soule,
Viceroy to that, which then to heaven being gone,
    Will leave this to controule,
And keepe these limbes, her Provinces, from dissolution.

For if the sinewie thread my braine lets fall
    Through every part,   10
Can tye those parts, and make mee one of all;
These haires which upward grew, and strength and art
    Have from a better braine,
Can better do'it; Except she meant that I
    By this should know my pain,
As prisoners then are manacled, when they'are condemn'd
    to die.

What ere shee meant by'it, bury it with me,
    For since I am
Loves martyr, it might breed idolatrie,
If into others hands these Reliques came;   20
    As 'twas humility
To afford to it all that a Soule can doe,
    So, 'tis some bravery,
That since you would save none of mee, I bury some of
    you.

        1633

DIVINE POEMS
IX

If poisonous mineralls, and if that tree,
Whose fruit threw death on else immortall us,
If lecherous goats, if serpents envious
Cannot be damn'd; Alas; why should I bee?
Why should intent or reason, borne in mee,
Make sinnes, else equall, in mee more heinous?
And mercy being easie, and glorious
To God; in his sterne wrath, why threatens hee?
But who am I, that dare dispute with thee
O God? Oh! of thine only worthy blood,   10
And my teares, make a heavenly Lethean flood,
And drowne in it my sinnes blacke memorie;
That thou remember them, some claime as debt,
I thinke it mercy, if thou wilt forget.

        1633

A HYMNE TO GOD THE FATHER
I

Wilt thou forgive that sinne where I begunne,
    Which was my sin, though it were done before?
Wilt thou forgive that sinne; through which I runne,
    And do run still: though still I do deplore?
      When thou hast done, thou hast not done,
          For, I have more.

II

Wilt thou forgive that sinne which I have wonne
  Others to sinne? and, made my sinne their doore?
Wilt thou forgive that sinne which I did shunne
  A yeare, or two: but wallowed in, a score?   10
    When thou hast done, thou hast not done,
      For I have more.

III

I have a sinne of feare, that when I have spunne
  My last thred, I shall perish on the shore;
But sweare by thy selfe, that at my death thy sonne
  Shall shine as he shines now, and heretofore;
    And, having done that, Thou haste done,
      I feare no more.

1633

THOMAS CAREW (1598?–1639?)

SONG

Ask me no more where Jove bestows,
When June is past, the fading rose;
For in your beauty's orient deep
These flowers, as in their causes, sleep.

Ask me no more whither do stray
The golden atoms of the day;
For in pure love heaven did prepare
Those powders to enrich your hair.

Ask me no more whither doth haste
The nightingale when May is past;   10
For in your sweet, dividing throat
She winters and keeps warm her note.

Ask me no more where those stars 'light
That downwards fall in dead of night;
For in your eyes they sit, and there
Fixéd become as in their sphere.

Ask me no more if east or west
The phoenix builds her spicy nest;
For unto you at last she flies,
And in your fragrant bosom dies.

1640

ROBERT HERRICK (1591-1674)

CORINNA'S GOING A-MAYING

Get up, get up for shame! The blooming morn
Upon her wings presents the god unshorn.
  See how Aurora throws her fair,
  Fresh-quilted colors through the air.
  Get up, sweet slug-a-bed, and see
  The dew bespangling herb and tree!
Each flower has wept and bowed toward the east
Above an hour since, yet you not drest;
  Nay! not so much as out of bed?
  When all the birds have matins said   10
And sung their thankful hymns, 'tis sin,
  Nay, profanation, to keep in,
Whereas a thousand virgins on this day
Spring sooner than the lark, to fetch in May.

Rise and put on your foliage, and be seen
To come forth, like the springtime, fresh and green,
  And sweet as Flora. Take no care
  For jewels for your gown or hair.
  Fear not; the leaves will strew
  Gems in abundance upon you.   20

Besides, the childhood of the day has kept
Against you come, some orient pearls unwept.
   Come, and receive them while the light
   Hangs on the dew-locks of the night;
   And Titan on the eastern hill
   Retires himself, or else stands still
Till you come forth! Wash, dress, be brief in praying;
Few beads are best when once we go a-Maying.

Come, my Corinna, come; and coming, mark
How each field turns a street, each street a park,   30
   Made green and trimmed with trees! see how
   Devotion gives each house a bough
   Or branch! each porch, each door, ere this,
   An ark, a tabernacle is,
Made up of whitethorn neatly interwove,
As if here were those cooler shades of love.
   Can such delights be in the street
   And open fields, and we not see't?
   Come, we'll abroad; and let's obey
   The proclamation made for May,   40
And sin no more, as we have done, by staying;
But, my Corinna, come, let's go a-Maying.

There's not a budding boy or girl this day
But is got up and gone to bring in May.
   A deal of youth ere this is come
   Back, and with whitethorn laden home.
   Some have dispatched their cakes and cream,
   Before that we have left to dream;
And some have wept and wooed, and plighted troth,
And chose their priest, ere we can cast off sloth.   5c
   Many a green-gown has been given,
   Many a kiss, both odd and even;
   Many a glance, too, has been sent
   From out the eye, love's firmament;

Many a jest told of the keys betraying
.This night, and locks picked; yet we're not a-Maying!

Come, let us go, while we are in our prime,
And take the harmless folly of the time!
   We shall grow old apace, and die
   Before we know our liberty.   60
   Our life is short, and our days run
   As fast away as does the sun.
And, as a vapor or a drop of rain,
Once lost, can ne'er be found again,
   So when or you or I are made
   A fable, song, or fleeting shade,
   All love, all liking, all delight
   Lies drowned with us in endless night.
Then, while time serves, and we are but decaying,
Come, my Corinna, come, let's go a-Maying.

                         1648

TO ANTHEA, WHO MAY COMMAND
HIM ANYTHING

Bid me to live, and I will live
   Thy protestant to be;
Or bid me love, and I will give
   A loving heart to thee.

A heart as soft, a heart as kind,
   A heart as sound and free
As in the whole world thou canst find,
   That heart I'll give to thee.

Bid that heart stay, and it will stay
   To honor thy decree;   10
Or bid it languish quite away,
   And 't shall do so for thee.

Bid me to weep, and I will weep
  While I have eyes to see;
And, having none, yet will I keep
  A heart to weep for thee.

Bid me despair, and I'll despair
  Under that cypress-tree;
Or bid me die, and I will dare
  E'en death to die for thee.   20

Thou art my life, my love, my heart,
  The very eyes of me;
And hast command of every part
  To live and die for thee.

          1648

TO DAFFODILS

Fair daffodils, we weep to see
  You haste away so soon;
As yet the early-rising sun
  Has not attained his noon.
      Stay, stay
    Until the hasting day
      Has run
    But to the evensong;
And, having prayed together, we
  Will go with you along.   10

We have short time to stay, as you,
  We have as short a spring;
As quick a growth to meet decay,
  As you, or anything.
      We die
    As your hours do, and dry
      Away
    Like to the summer's rain;

Or as the pearls of morning's dew,
Ne'er to be found again.

1648

TO THE VIRGINS, TO MAKE
MUCH OF TIME

Gather ye rosebuds while ye may,
Old Time is still a-flying,
And this same flower that smiles today
Tomorrow will be dying.

The glorious lamp of heaven, the sun,
The higher he's a-getting,
The sooner will his race be run,
And nearer he's to setting.

That age is best which is the first,
When youth and blood are warmer;   10
But being spent, the worse, and worst
Times still succeed the former.

Then be not coy, but use your time,
And while ye may, go marry;
For having lost but once your prime,
You may forever tarry.

1648

UPON JULIA'S CLOTHES

Whenas in silks my Julia goes,
Then, then, methinks, how sweetly flows
The liquefaction of her clothes.

Next, when I cast mine eyes, and see
That brave vibration, each way free,
O, how that glittering taketh me!

1648

EDMUND WALLER (1606–1687)

GO, LOVELY ROSE

Go, lovely Rose—
Tell her that wastes her time and me
    That now she knows,
When I resemble her to thee,
How sweet and fair she seems to be.

Tell her that's young,
And shuns to have her graces spied,
    That hadst thou sprung
In deserts where no men abide,
Thou must have uncommended died.   10

Small is the worth
Of beauty from the light retired;
    Bid her come forth,
Suffer herself to be desired,
And not blush so to be admired.

Then die—that she
The common fate of all things rare
    May read in thee;
How small a part of time they share
That are so wondrous sweet and fair!

1640

ON A GIRDLE

That which her slender waist confined,
Shall now my joyful temples bind;
No monarch but would give his crown,
His arms might do what this has done.

It was my heaven's extremest sphere,
The pale which held that lovely deer.
My joy, my grief, my hope, my love,
Did all within this circle move!

A narrow compass! and yet there
Dwelt all that's good, and all that's fair;   10
Give me but what this ribband bound,
Take all the rest the sun goes round.

1645

SIR JOHN SUCKLING (1609–1642)

WHY SO PALE AND WAN, FOND LOVER?

From AGLAURA

Why so pale and wan, fond lover?
    Prithee, why so pale?
Will, when looking well can't move her,
    Looking ill prevail?
    Prithee, why so pale?

Why so dull and mute, young sinner?
    Prithee, why so mute?
Will, when speaking well can't win her,
    Saying nothing do 't?
    Prithee, why so mute?   10

Quit, quit for shame! This will not move;
    This cannot take her.
If of herself she will not love,
    Nothing can make her.
    The devil take her!

1638

A POEM WITH THE ANSWER

Out upon it, I have loved
    Three whole days together!
And am like to love three more,
    If it prove fair weather.

Time shall moult away his wings
    Ere he shall discover
In the whole wide world again
    Such a constant lover.

But the spite on't is, no praise
    Is due at all to me;   10
Love with me had made no stays,
    Had it any been but she.

Had it any been but she,
    And that very face,
There had been at least ere this
    A dozen dozen in her place.

1646

RICHARD LOVELACE (1618–1658)

TO LUCASTA, GOING TO THE WARS

Tell me not, Sweet, I am unkind,
    That from the nunnery
Of thy chaste breast and quiet mind
    To war and arms I fly.

True, a new mistress now I chase,
    The first foe in the field;
And with a stronger faith embrace
    A sword, a horse, a shield.

Yet this inconstancy is such
   As thou too shalt adore;   10
I could not love thee, Dear, so much,
   Loved I not honour more.

1649

TO ALTHEA, FROM PRISON

When Love with unconfinéd wings
   Hovers within my gates,
And my divine Althea brings
   To whisper at the grates;
When I lie tangled in her hair
   And fettered to her eye,
The birds that wanton in the air
   Know no such liberty.

When flowing cups run swiftly round
   With no allaying Thames,   10
Our careless heads with roses bound,
   Our hearts with loyal flames;
When thirsty grief in wine we steep,
   When healths and drafts go free—
Fishes that tipple in the deep
   Know no such liberty.

When, like committed linnets, I
   With shriller throat shall sing
The sweetness, mercy, majesty,
   And glories of my King;   20
When I shall voice aloud how good
   He is, how great should be,
Enlargéd winds, that curl the flood,
   Know no such liberty.

Stone walls do not a prison make,
    Nor iron bars a cage;
Minds innocent and quiet take
    That for an hermitage;
If I have freedom in my love
    And in my soul am free,   30
Angels alone, that soar above,
    Enjoy such liberty.

1640

JOHN MILTON (1608–1674)

LYCIDAS

In this Monody the Author bewails a learned Friend, unfortunately drowned in his passage from Chester on the Irish Seas, 1637; and by occasion, foretells the ruin of our corrupted Clergy, then in their height.

Yet once more, O ye laurels, and once more,
Ye myrtles brown, with ivy never sear,
I come to pluck your berries harsh and crude,
And with forced fingers rude
Shatter your leaves before the mellowing year.
Bitter constraint and sad occasion dear
Compels me to disturb your season due;
For Lycidas is dead, dead ere his prime,
Young Lycidas, and hath not left his peer.
Who would not sing for Lycidas? He knew   10
Himself to sing, and build the lofty rime.
He must not float upon his watery bier
Unwept, and welter to the parching wind,
Without the meed of some melodious tear.
   Begin, then, Sisters of the sacred well,
That from beneath the seat of Jove doth spring;
Begin, and somewhat loudly sweep the string.
Hence with denial vain and coy excuse;

So may some gentle muse
With lucky words favor my destined urn,   20
And as he passes, turn
And bid fair peace be to my sable shroud!
   For we were nursed upon the selfsame hill,
Fed the same flock, by fountain, shade, and rill;
Together both, ere the high lawns appeared
Under the opening eyelids of the Morn,
We drove afield, and both together heard
What time the gray-fly winds her sultry horn,
Battening our flocks with the fresh dews of night,
Oft till the star that rose at evening, bright,   30
Toward heaven's descent had sloped his westering
   wheel.
Meanwhile the rural ditties were not mute,
Tempered to the oaten flute;
Rough Satyrs danced, and Fauns with cloven heel
From the glad sound would not be absent long;
And old Damoetas loved to hear our song.
   But, oh! the heavy change, now thou art gone,
Now thou art gone, and never must return!
Thee, Shepherd, thee the woods and desert caves,
With wild thyme and the gadding vine o'ergrown,   40
And all their echoes, mourn.
The willows, and the hazel copses green,
Shall now no more be seen
Fanning their joyous leaves to thy soft lays.
As killing as the canker to the rose,
Or taint-worm to the weanling herds that graze,
Or frost to flowers, that their gay wardrobe wear,
When first the white-thorn blows—
Such, Lycidas, thy loss to shepherd's ear.
   Where were ye, Nymphs, when the remorseless deep   50
Closed o'er the head of your loved Lycidas?
For neither were ye playing on the steep
Where your old bards, the famous Druids, lie,

Nor on the shaggy top of Mona high,
Nor yet where Deva spreads her wizard stream.
Aye me! I fondly dream
"Had ye been there"—for what could that have done?
What could the Muse herself that Orpheus bore,
The Muse herself, for her enchanting son,
Whom universal nature did lament,   60
When, by the rout that made the hideous roar,
His gory visage down the stream was sent,
Down the swift Hebrus to the Lesbian shore?
    Alas! what boots it with uncessant care
To tend the homely, slighted shepherd's trade,
And strictly meditate the thankless Muse?
Were it not better done as others use,
To sport with Amaryllis in the shade,
Or with the tangles of Neaera's hair?
Fame is the spur that the clear spirit doth raise   70
(That last infirmity of noble mind)
To scorn delights, and live laborious days;
But, the fair guerdon when we hope to find,
And think to burst out into sudden blaze,
Comes the blind Fury with the abhorréd shears,
And slits the thin-spun life. "But not the praise,"
Phoebus replied, and touched my trembling ears;
"Fame is no plant that grows on mortal soil,
Nor in the glistering foil
Set off to the world, nor in broad rumor lies,   80
But lives and spreads aloft by those pure eyes
And perfect witness of all-judging Jove;
As he pronounces lastly on each deed,
Of so much fame in heaven expect thy meed."
    O fountain Arethuse, and thou honored flood,
Smooth-sliding Mincius, crowned with vocal reeds,
That strain I heard was of a higher mood.
But now my oat proceeds,
And listens to the Herald of the Sea

That came in Neptune's plea.   90
He asked the waves, and asked the felon winds,
What hard mishap hath doomed this gentle swain!
And questioned every gust of rugged wings
That blows from off each beakéd promontory.
They knew not of his story;
And sage Hippotades their answer brings,
That not a blast was from his dungeon strayed;
The air was calm, and on the level brine
Sleek Panope with all her sisters played.
It was that fatal and perfidious bark,   100
Built in the eclipse, and rigged with curses dark,
That sunk so low that sacred head of thine.
   Next, Camus, reverend sire, went footing slow,
His mantle hairy, and his bonnet sedge,
Inwrought with figures dim, and on the edge
Like to that sanguine flower inscribed with woe.
"Ah! who hath reft," quoth he, "my dearest pledge?"
Last came, and last did go,
The Pilot of the Galilean Lake;
Two massy keys he bore of metals twain   110
(The golden opes, the iron shuts amain).
He shook his mitered locks, and stern bespake:
"How well could I have spared for thee, young swain,
Enow of such as, for their bellies' sake,
Creep, and intrude, and climb into the fold!
Of other care they little reckoning make
Than how to scramble at the shearers' feast,
And shove away the worthy bidden guest.
Blind mouths! that scarce themselves know how to
   hold
A sheep-hook, or have learned aught else the least   120
That to the faithful herdman's art belongs!
What recks it them?   What need they?   They are
   sped;

103. *Camus*, presiding genius of the River Cam.

And, when they list, their lean and flashy songs
Grate on their scrannel pipes of wretched straw;
The hungry sheep look up, and are not fed,
But, swoln with wind and the rank mist they draw,
Rot inwardly, and foul contagion spread;
Besides what the grim wolf with privy paw
Daily devours apace, and nothing said.
But that two-handed engine at the door   130
Stands ready to smite once, and smite no more."
    Return, Alpheus, the dread voice is past
That shrunk thy streams; return, Sicilian Muse,
And call the vales, and bid them hither cast
Their bells and flowerets of a thousand hues.
Ye valleys low, where the mild whispers use
Of shades, and wanton winds, and gushing brooks,
On whose fresh lap the swart star sparely looks,
Throw hither all your quaint enameled eyes,
That on the green turf suck the honeyed showers,   140
And purple all the ground with vernal flowers.
Bring the rathe primrose that forsaken dies,
The tufted crow-toe, and pale jessamine,
The white pink, and the pansy freaked with jet,
The glowing violet,
The musk-rose, and the well-attired woodbine,
With cowslips wan that hang the pensive head,
And every flower that sad embroidery wears;
Bid amaranthus all his beauty shed,
And daffadillies fill their cups with tears,   150
To strew the laureate hearse where Lycid lies.
For so, to interpose a little ease,
Let our frail thoughts dally with false surmise.
Aye me! Whilst thee the shores and sounding seas
Wash far away, where'er thy bones are hurled,
Whether beyond the stormy Hebrides,
Where thou perhaps under the whelming tide
Visit'st the bottom of the monstrous world;

Or whether thou, to our moist vows denied,
Sleep'st by the fable of Bellerus old, 160
Where the great Vision of the guarded mount
Looks toward Namancos and Bayona's hold.
Look homeward, Angel, now, and melt with ruth;
And, O ye dolphins, waft the hapless youth.
   Weep no more, woeful shepherds, weep no more,
For Lycidas, your sorrow, is not dead,
Sunk though he be beneath the watery floor;
So sinks the day-star in the ocean bed,
And yet anon repairs his drooping head,
And tricks his beams, and with new-spangled ore 170
Flames in the forehead of the morning sky.
So Lycidas sunk low, but mounted high,
Through the dear might of Him that walked the waves,
Where, other groves and other streams along,
With nectar pure his oozy locks he laves,
And hears the unexpressive nuptial song,
In the blest kingdoms meek of joy and love.
There entertain him all the Saints above,
In solemn troops, and sweet societies,
That sing, and singing in their glory move, 180
And wipe the tears forever from his eyes.
Now, Lycidas, the shepherds weep no more;
Henceforth thou art the Genius of the shore,
In thy large recompense, and shalt be good
To all that wander in that perilous flood.
   Thus sang the uncouth swain to the oaks and rills,
While the still morn went out with sandals gray;
He touched the tender stops of various quills,
With eager thought warbling his Doric lay.
And now the sun had stretched out all the hills, 190
And now was dropped into the western bay.
At last he rose, and twitched his mantle blue;
Tomorrow to fresh woods and pastures new.

1638

ON HIS HAVING ARRIVED AT THE AGE OF TWENTY-THREE

How soon hath Time, the subtle thief of youth,
Stolen on his wing my three and twentieth year!
My hasting days fly on with full career,
But my late spring no bud or blossom shew'th.
Perhaps my semblance might deceive the truth
That I to manhood am arrived so near;
And inward ripeness doth much less appear,
That some more timely-happy spirits endu'th.
Yet be it less or more, or soon or slow,
It shall be still in strictest measure even   10
To that same lot, however mean or high,
Toward which Time leads me, and the will of Heaven;
All is, if I have grace to use it so,
As ever in my great Task-Master's eye.

1645

ON THE LATE MASSACRE IN PIEDMONT

Avenge, O Lord, thy slaughtered saints, whose bones
Lie scattered on the Alpine mountains cold;
Even them who kept thy truth so pure of old,
When all our fathers worshiped stocks and stones,
Forget not; in thy book record their groans
Who were thy sheep, and in their ancient fold
Slain by the bloody Piemontese, that rolled
Mother with infant down the rocks. Their moans
The vales redoubled to the hills, and they
To heaven. Their martyred blood and ashes sow   10
O'er all the Italian fields, where still doth sway
The triple tyrant; that from these may grow
A hundredfold, who, having learnt thy way,
Early may fly the Babylonian woe.

1673

ON HIS BLINDNESS

When I consider how my light is spent
Ere half my days, in this dark world and wide,
And that one talent which is death to hide
Lodged with me useless, though my soul more bent
To serve therewith my Maker, and present
My true account, lest he returning chide;
"Doth God exact day-labor, light denied?"
I fondly ask. But Patience, to prevent
That murmur, soon replies, "God doth not need
Either man's work or his own gifts. Who best   10
Bear his mild yoke, they serve him best. His state
Is kingly; thousands at his bidding speed,
And post o'er land and ocean without rest;
They also serve who only stand and wait."

                                           1673

TO CYRIACK SKINNER

Cyriack, this three years' day these eyes, though clear
To outward view, of blemish or of spot,
Bereft of light, their seeing have forgot;
Nor to their idle orbs doth sight appear
Of sun or moon or star throughout the year,
Or man or woman. Yet I argue not
Against Heaven's hand or will, nor bate a jot
Of heart or hope, but still bear up and steer
Right onward. What supports me, dost thou ask?
The conscience, friend, to have lost them overplied   10
In liberty's defense, my noble task,
Of which all Europe talks from side to side.
This thought might lead me through the world's vain mask
Content, though blind, had I no better guide.

                                           1673

ON HIS DECEASED WIFE

Methought I saw my late espoused saint
Brought to me like Alcestis from the grave,
Whom Jove's great son to her glad husband gave,
Rescued from death by force though pale and faint.
Mine as whom washed from spot of child-bed taint,
Purification in the old law did save,
And such, as yet once more I trust to have
Full sight of her in heaven without restraint,
Came vested all in white, pure as her mind.
Her face was veiled, yet to my fancied sight,   10
Love, sweetness, goodness, in her person shined
So clear, as in no face with more delight.
But O, as to embrace me she inclined,
I waked, she fled, and day brought back my night.

                                                    1673

TO THE LORD GENERAL CROMWELL, MAY, 1652

ON THE PROPOSALS* OF CERTAIN MINISTERS AT THE COMMITTEE FOR PROPAGATION OF THE GOSPEL

Cromwell, our chief of men, who through a cloud
Not of war only, but detractions rude,
Guided by faith and matchless fortitude,
To peace and truth thy glorious way hast plowed,
And on the neck of crownéd Fortune proud
Hast reared God's trophies, and his work pursued,
While Darwen stream, with blood of Scots imbrued,
And Dunbar field resounds thy praises loud,
And Worcester's laureate wreath. Yet much remains
To conquer still; peace hath her victories   10
No less renowned than war; new foes arise,

* *Proposals*, especially that the Government support the Puritan ministers.

Threatening to bind our souls with secular chains.
Help us to save free conscience from the paw
Of hireling wolves, whose gospel is their maw.

1694

JOHN DRYDEN (1631–1700)

A SONG FOR ST. CECILIA'S DAY, NOVEMBER 22, 1687

From harmony, from heavenly harmony
    This universal frame began;
  When Nature underneath a heap
    Of jarring atoms lay,
  And could not heave her head,
The tuneful voice was heard from high,
    Arise, ye more than dead.

Then cold and hot and moist and dry
    In order to their stations leap,
    And Music's power obey.   10
From harmony, from heavenly harmony
    This universal frame began;
    From harmony to harmony
Through all the compass of the notes it ran,
The diapason closing full in Man.

What passion cannot Music raise and quell?
    When Jubal struck the chorded shell,
  His listening brethren stood around,
    And, wondering, on their faces fell
  To worship that celestial sound.   20
Less than a god they thought there could not dwell
  Within the hollow of that shell,
  That spoke so sweetly, and so well.
What passion cannot Music raise and quell?

The trumpet's loud clangor
   Excites us to arms
With shrill notes of anger
   And mortal alarms.
The double, double, double beat
   Of the thundering drum   30
   Cries, hark! the foes come;
Charge, charge, 'tis too late to retreat!
   The soft complaining flute
   In dying notes discovers
   The woes of hopeless lovers,
Whose dirge is whispered by the warbling lute.

   Sharp violins proclaim
Their jealous pangs and desperation,
Fury, frantic indignation,
Depth of pains and height of passion,   40
   For the fair, disdainful dame.

But, oh! what art can teach,
What human voice can reach
   The sacred organ's praise?
   Notes inspiring holy love,
Notes that wing their heavenly ways
   To mend the choirs above.

Orpheus could lead the savage race,
And trees unrooted left their place,
   Sequacious of the lyre;   50
But bright Cecilia raised the wonder higher;
When to her organ vocal breath was given,
An angel heard, and straight appeared,
   Mistaking earth for heaven.

GRAND CHORUS

As from the power of sacred lays
   The spheres began to move,

And sung the great Creator's praise
  To all the blest above;
So when the last and dreadful hour
This crumbling pageant shall devour,   60
The trumpet shall be heard on high,
The dead shall live, the living die,
And Music shall untune the sky.

                    1687

EPIGRAM ON MILTON

Three poets, in three distant ages born,
Greece, Italy, and England did adorn.
The first in loftiness of thought surpassed,
The next in majesty, in both the last.
The force of Nature could no further go—
To make a third she joined the other two.

                    1688

ALEXANDER'S FEAST; OR, THE POWER OF MUSIC

A SONG IN HONOUR OF ST. CECILIA'S DAY: 1697

I

'Twas at the royal feast for Persia won
  By Philip's warlike son:
 Aloft in awful state
 The godlike hero sate
  On his imperial throne.
 His valiant peers were placed around;
 Their brows with roses and with myrtles bound:
 (So should desert in arms be crowned.)
The lovely Thais, by his side,
Sate like a blooming Eastern bride,   10

In flower of youth and beauty's pride.
 Happy, happy, happy pair!
  None but the brave,
  None but the brave,
 None but the brave deserves the fair.

CHORUS

Happy, happy, happy pair!
 None but the brave,
 None but the brave,
None but the brave deserves the fair.

2

Timotheus placed on high   20
 Amid the tuneful quire,
With flying fingers touched the lyre:
 The trembling notes ascend the sky,
 And heavenly joys inspire.
 The song began from Jove,
 Who left his blissful seats above,
 (Such is the power of mighty love.)
 A dragon's fiery form belied the god:
 Sublime on radiant spires he rode,
 When he to fair Olympia pressed: 30
 And while he sought her snowy breast,
 Then round her slender waist he curled,
And stamped an image of himself, a sovereign of the world.
 The listening crowd admire the lofty sound,
 A present deity, they shout around;
 A present deity, the vaulted roofs rebound:
  With ravished ears
  The monarch hears,
  Assumes the god,
  Affects to nod,   40
 And seems to shake the spheres.

20. *Timotheus*, musician to Alexander.

CHORUS

With ravished ears
The monarch hears,
Assumes the god,
Affects to nod,
And seems to shake the spheres.

3

The praise of Bacchus then the sweet musician sung,
 Of Bacchus ever fair, and ever young.
  The jolly god in triumph comes;
  Sound the trumpets, beat the drums;   50
   Flushed with a purple grace
   He shows his honest face:
Now give the hautboys breath; he comes, he comes.
  Bacchus ever fair and young,
   Drinking joys did first ordain;
  Bacchus' blessings are a treasure,
  Drinking is the soldier's pleasure;
   Rich the treasure,
   Sweet the pleasure,
  Sweet is pleasure after pain.   60

CHORUS

Bacchus' blessings are a treasure,
Drinking is the soldier's pleasure;
 Rich the treasure,
 Sweet the pleasure,
Sweet is pleasure after pain.

4

Soothed with the sound the king grew vain;
 Fought all his battles o'er again;
And thrice he routed all his foes, and thrice he slew the
  slain.
 The master saw the madness rise,

His glowing cheeks, his ardent eyes;   70
And while he heaven and earth defied,
Changed his hand, and checked his pride.
   He chose a mournful Muse,
    Soft pity to infuse;
He sung Darius great and good,
   By too severe a fate,
Fallen, fallen, fallen, fallen,
   Fallen from his high estate,
And weltering in his blood;
Deserted at his utmost need   80
By those his former bounty fed;
On the bare earth exposed he lies,
With not a friend to close his eyes.

With downcast looks the joyless victor sate,
   Revolving in his altered soul
     The various turns of chance below;
   And, now and then, a sigh he stole,
    And tears began to flow.

CHORUS

Revolving in his altered soul
   The various turns of chance below;   90
And, now and then, a sigh he stole,
   And tears began to flow.

5

The mighty master smiled to see
That love was in the next degree;
'Twas but a kindred-sound to move,
For pity melts the mind to love.
   Softly sweet, in Lydian measures,
   Soon he soothed his soul to pleasures,
War, he sung, is toil and trouble;
Honour but an empty bubble;   100

> Never ending, still beginning,
> Fighting still, and still destroying:
>   If the world be worth thy winning,
> Think, O think it worth enjoying:
>   Lovely Thais sits beside thee,
>   Take the good the gods provide thee.

The many rend the skies with loud applause;
So Love was crowned, but Music won the cause.
  The prince, unable to conceal his pain,
    Gazed on the fair   110
    Who caused his care,
  And sighed and looked, sighed and looked,
  Sighed and looked, and sighed again;
At length, with love and wine at once oppressed,
The vanquished victor sunk upon her breast.

CHORUS

  The prince, unable to conceal his pain,
    Gazed on the fair
    Who caused his care,
  And sighed and looked, sighed and looked,
  Sighed and looked, and sighed again;   120
At length, with love and wine at once oppressed,
The vanquished victor sunk upon her breast.

6

Now strike the golden lyre again;
A louder yet, and yet a louder strain.
Break his bands of sleep asunder,
And rouse him, like a rattling peal of thunder.
    Hark, hark, the horrid sound
      Has raised up his head;
      As awaked from the dead,
    And amazed, he stares around.   130

Revenge, revenge, Timotheus cries,
   See the Furies arise;
   See the snakes that they rear,
   How they hiss in their hair,
And the sparkles that flash from their eyes!
   Behold a ghastly band,
   Each a torch in his hand!
Those are Grecian ghosts, that in battle were slain,
      And unburied remain
      Inglorious on the plain: 140
      Give the vengeance due
      To the valiant crew.
Behold how they toss their torches on high,
   How they point to the Persian abodes,
And glittering temples of their hostile gods.
The princes applaud with a furious joy;
And the king seized a flambeau with zeal to destroy;
   Thais led the way,
   To light him to his prey,
And, like another Helen, fired another Troy.   150

CHORUS

And the king seized a flambeau with zeal to destroy;
   Thais led the way,
   To light him to his prey,
And, like another Helen, fired another Troy.

7

   Thus long ago,
  Ere heaving bellows learned to blow,
   While organs yet were mute,
   Timotheus, to his breathing flute
    And sounding lyre,
Could swell the soul to rage, or kindle soft desire.   160
  At last divine Cecilia came,
  Inventress of the vocal frame;

The sweet enthusiast, from her sacred store,
    Enlarged the former narrow bounds,
    And added length to solemn sounds,
With Nature's mother-wit, and arts unknown before.
    Let old Timotheus yield the prize,
        Or both divide the crown:
    He raised a mortal to the skies;
        She drew an angel down.   170

GRAND CHORUS

At last divine Cecilia came,
Inventress of the vocal frame;
The sweet enthusiast, from her sacred store,
    Enlarged the former narrow bounds,
    And added length to solemn sounds,
With Nature's mother-wit, and arts unknown before.
    Let old Timotheus yield the prize,
        Or both divide the crown:
    He raised a mortal to the skies;
        She drew an angel down.

1697

EIGHTEENTH CENTURY

ALEXANDER POPE (1688–1744)

THE RAPE OF THE LOCK
AN HEROI–COMICAL POEM
Canto I

What dire offense from am'rous causes springs,
What mighty contests rise from trivial things,
I sing. This verse to Caryl, Muse! is due:
This, ev'n Belinda may vouchsafe to view:
Slight is the subject, but not so the praise,
If she inspire, and he approve my lays.

  Say what strange motive, Goddess! could compel
A well-bred lord t' assault a gentle belle?
O say what stranger cause, yet unexplor'd,
Could make a gentle belle reject a lord?   10
In tasks so bold, can little men engage,
And in soft bosoms dwells such mighty rage?

  Sol thro' white curtains shot a tim'rous ray,
And op'd those eyes that must eclipse the day;
Now lap-dogs give themselves the rousing shake,
And sleepless lovers just at twelve awake;
Thrice rung the bell, the slipper knock'd the ground,
And the press'd watch return'd a silver sound.
Belinda still her downy pillow prest,
Her guardian Sylph prolong'd the balmy rest: 20
'Twas he had summon'd to her silent bed
The morning dream that hover'd o'er her head;
A youth more glitt'ring than a Birth-night Beau,
(That ev'n in slumber caused her cheek to glow)
Seem'd to her ear his winning lips to lay,
And thus in whispers said, or seem'd to say:
  "Fairest of mortals, thou distinguish'd care

Of thousand bright Inhabitants of Air!
If e'er one vision touch'd thy infant thought,
Of all the nurse and all the priest have taught—   30
Of airy elves by moonlight shadows seen,
The silver token, and the circled green,
Or virgins visited by Angel-pow'rs,
With golden crowns and wreaths of heav'nly flow'rs—
Hear and believe! thy own importance know,
Nor bound thy narrow views to things below.
Some secret truths, from learned pride conceal'd,
To maids alone and children are reveal'd.
What tho' no credit doubting Wits may give?
The fair and innocent shall still believe.   40
Know, then, unnumber'd Spirits round thee fly,
The light militia of the lower sky:
These, tho' unseen, are ever on the wing,
Hang o'er the Box, and hover round the Ring.
Think what an equipage thou hast in air,
And view with scorn two pages and a chair.
As now your own, our beings were of old,
And once inclos'd in woman's beauteous mould;
Thence, by a soft transition, we repair
From earthly vehicles to these of air.   50
Think not, when woman's transient breath is fled,
That all her vanities at once are dead;
Succeeding vanities she still regards,
And tho' she plays no more, o'erlooks the cards.
Her joy in gilded chariots, when alive,
And love of Ombre, after death survive.
For when the Fair in all their pride expire,
To their first elements their souls retire.
The sprites of fiery termagants in flame
Mount up, and take a salamander's name.   60
Soft yielding minds to water glide away
And sip, with nymphs, their elemental tea.
The graver prude sinks downward to a Gnome,

In search of mischief still on earth to roam.
The light coquettes in Sylphs aloft repair,
And sport and flutter in the fields of air.
   "Know further yet: whoever fair and chaste
Rejects mankind, is by some Sylph embrac'd;
For spirits, freed from mortal laws, with ease
Assume what sexes and what shapes they please.   70
What guards the purity of melting maids,
In courtly balls and midnight masquerades,
Safe from the treach'rous friend, the daring spark,
The glance by day, the whisper in the dark,
When kind occasion prompts their warm desires,
When music softens, and when dancing fires?
'Tis but their Sylph, the wise celestials know,
Tho' honour is the word with men below.
Some nymphs there are too conscious of their face,
For life predestin'd to the Gnome's embrace.   80
These swell their prospects and exalt their pride,
When offers are disdain'd, and love deny'd;
Then gay ideas crowd the vacant brain,
While peers, and dukes, and all their sweeping train,
And garters, stars, and coronets appear,
And in soft sounds, 'Your Grace' salutes their ear.
'Tis these that early taint the female soul,
Instruct the eyes of young coquettes to roll,
Teach infant-cheeks a hidden blush to know,
And little hearts to flutter at a Beau.   90
   "Oft, when the world imagine women stray,
The Sylphs thro' mystic mazes guide their way;
Thro' all the giddy circle they pursue,
And old impertinence expel by new.
What tender maid but must a victim fall
To one man's treat, but for another's ball?
When Florio speaks what virgin could withstand,
If gentle Damon did not squeeze her hand?
With varying vanities, from ev'ry part,

They shift the moving toyshop of their heart;   100
Where wigs with wigs, with sword-knots sword-knots
    strive,
Beaus banish beaus, and coaches coaches drive.
This erring mortals levity may call;
Oh blind to truth! the Sylphs contrive it all.
   "Of these am I, who thy protection claim,
A watchful sprite, and Ariel is my name.
Late, as I rang'd the crystal wilds of air,
In the clear mirror of thy ruling star
I saw, alas! some dread event impend,
Ere to the main this morning sun descend,   110
But heav'n reveals not what, or how, or where.
Warn'd by the Sylph, oh pious maid, beware!
This to disclose is all thy guardian can:
Beware of all, but most beware of Man!"
   He said; when Shock, who thought she slept too long,
Leap'd up, and wak'd his mistress with his tongue,
'Twas then, Belinda! if report say true,
Thy eyes first open'd on a billet-doux;
Wounds, charms, and ardours were no sooner read,
But all the vision vanish'd from thy head.   120
   And now, unveil'd, the toilet stands display'd,
Each silver vase in mystic order laid.
First, rob'd in white, the nymph intent adores,
With head uncover'd, the cosmetic pow'rs.
A heav'nly image in the glass appears;
To that she bends, to that her eyes she rears.
Th' inferior priestess, at her altar's side,
Trembling begins the sacred rites of Pride.
Unnumber'd treasures ope at once, and here
The various off'rings of the world appear;   130
From each she nicely culls with curious toil,
And decks the goddess with the glitt'ring spoil.
This casket India's glowing gems unlocks,
And all Arabia breathes from yonder box;

The tortoise here and elephant unite,
Transform'd to combs, the speckled and the white.
Here files of pins extend their shining rows,
Puffs, powders, patches, Bibles, billet-doux.
Now awful beauty puts on all its arms;
The Fair each moment rises in her charms,   140
Repairs her smiles, awakens ev'ry grace,
And calls forth all the wonders of her face;
Sees by degrees a purer blush arise,
And keener lightnings quicken in her eyes.
The busy Sylphs surround their darling care,
These set the head, and those divide the hair,
Some fold the sleeve, whilst others plait the gown;
And Betty's prais'd for labours not her own.

·   ·   ·   ·   ·   ·   ·

Canto III

Close by those meads, for ever crown'd with flow'rs
Where Thames with pride surveys his rising tow'rs,
There stands a structure of majestic frame,
Which from the neighb'ring Hampton takes its name.
Here Britain's statesmen oft the fall foredoom
Of foreign tyrants, and of nymphs at home;
Here thou, great ANNA! whom three realms obey,
Dost sometimes counsel take—and sometimes tea.

Hither the heroes and the nymphs resort,
To taste awhile the pleasures of a court.   10
In various talk th' instructive hours they past,
Who gave the ball, or paid the visit last;
One speaks the glory of the British Queen,
And one describes a charming Indian screen;
A third interprets motions, looks, and eyes;
At ev'ry word a reputation dies.
Snuff, or the fan, supply each pause of chat,
With singing, laughing, ogling, *and all that.*

Meanwhile, declining from the noon of day,

The sun obliquely shoots his burning ray;   20
The hungry judges soon the sentence sign,
And wretches hang that jury-men may dine;
The merchant from th' Exchange returns in peace,
And the long labours of the toilet cease.
Belinda now, whom thirst of fame invites,
Burns to encounter two advent'rous knights,
At Ombre singly to decide their doom;
And swells her breast with conquests yet to come.
Straight the three bands prepare in arms to join,
Each band the number of the sacred nine.   30
Soon as she spreads her hand, th' aërial guard
Descend, and sit on each important card:
First Ariel perch'd upon a Matadore,
Then each according to the rank they bore;
For Sylphs, yet mindful of their ancient race,
Are, as when women, wondrous fond of place.
    Behold four Kings in majesty rever'd,
With hoary whiskers and a forky beard;
And four fair Queens, whose hands sustain a flow'r,
Th' expressive emblem of their softer pow'r;   40
Four Knaves in garbs succinct, a trusty band,
Caps on their heads, and halberds in their hand;
And particolor'd troops, a shining train,
Drawn forth to combat on the velvet plain.
    The skillful nymph reviews her force with care;
Let Spades be trumps! she said; and trumps they were.
    Now move to war her sable Matadores,
In show like leaders of the swarthy Moors.
Spadillio first, unconquerable lord!
Led off two captive trumps, and swept the board.   50
As many more Manillio forced to yield,
And march'd a victor from the verdant field.
Him Basto follow'd, but his fate more hard
Gain'd but one trump and one plebeian card.
With his broad sabre next, a chief in years,

The hoary Majesty of Spades appears,
Puts forth one manly leg, to sight reveal'd;
The rest his many-color'd robe conceal'd.
The rebel Knave, who dares his prince engage,
Proves the just victim of his royal rage.   60
Ev'n mighty Pam, that Kings and Queens o'erthrew
And mow'd down armies in the fights of Loo,
Sad chance of war! now destitute of aid,
Falls undistinguish'd by the victor Spade!
    Thus far both armies to Belinda yield;
Now to the Baron fate inclines the field.
His warlike amazon her host invades,
Th' imperial consort of the crown of Spades.
The Club's black tyrant first her victim dy'd,
Spite of his haughty mien, and barb'rous pride: 70
What boots the regal circle on his head,
His giant limbs, in state unwieldy spread,
That long behind he trails his pompous robe,
And of all monarchs only grasps the globe?
    The Baron now his Diamonds pours apace;
Th' embroider'd King who shows but half his face,
And his refulgent Queen, with pow'rs combin'd,
Of broken troops an easy conquest find.
Clubs, Diamonds, Hearts, in wild disorder seen,
With throngs promiscuous strow the level green.   80
Thus when dispers'd a routed army runs
Of Asia's troops, and Afric's sable sons,
With like confusion different nations fly,
Of various habit, and of various dye;
The pierc'd battalions disunited fall,
In heaps on heaps; one fate o'erwhelms them all.
    The Knave of Diamonds tries his wily arts,
And wins (oh shameful chance!) the Queen of Hearts.
At this the blood the virgin's cheek forsook,
A livid paleness spreads o'er all her look;   90
She sees, and trembles at th' approaching ill,

Just in the jaws of ruin, and Codille.
And now (as oft in some distemper'd state)
On one nice trick depends the gen'ral fate;
An Ace of Hearts steps forth; The King unseen
Lurk'd in her hand, and mourn'd his captive Queen:
He springs to vengeance with an eager pace,
And falls like thunder on the prostrate Ace.
The nymph exulting fills with shouts the sky;
The walls, the woods, and long canals reply.   100

   Oh thoughtless mortals! ever blind to fate,
Too soon dejected, and too soon elate,
Sudden these honours shall be snatch'd away,
And curs'd for ever this victorious day.

   For lo! the board with cups and spoons is crown'd,
The berries crackle, and the mill turns round;
On shining altars of Japan they raise
The silver lamp; the fiery spirits blaze:
From silver spouts the grateful liquors glide,
While China's earth receives the smoking tide.   110
At once they gratify their scent and taste,
And frequent cups prolong the rich repast.
Straight hover round the Fair her airy band;
Some, as she sipp'd, the fuming liquor fann'd,
Some o'er her lap their careful plumes display'd,
Trembling, and conscious of the rich brocade.
Coffee (which makes the politician wise,
And see thro' all things with his half-shut eyes)
Sent up in vapors to the Baron's brain
New stratagems, the radiant Lock to gain.   120
Ah cease, rash youth! desist ere 'tis too late,
Fear the just gods, and think of Scylla's fate!
Chang'd to a bird, and sent to flit in air,
She dearly pays for Nisus' injur'd hair!

   But when to mischief mortals bend their will,
How soon they find fit instruments of ill!
Just then Clarissa drew with tempting grace

A two-edg'd weapon from her shining case;
So ladies in romance assist their knight,
Present the spear, and arm him for the fight.　　　130
He takes the gift with rev'rence, and extends
The little engine on his fingers' ends;
This just behind Belinda's neck he spread,
As o'er the fragrant steams she bends her head.
Swift to the Lock a thousand sprites repair;
A thousand wings by turns blow back the hair;
And thrice they twitch'd the diamond in her ear;
Thrice she look'd back, and thrice the foe drew near.
Just in that instant, anxious Ariel sought
The close recesses of the virgin's thought;　　　140
As on the nosegay in her breast reclin'd,
He watch'd th' ideas rising in her mind,
Sudden he view'd, in spite of all her art,
An earthly lover lurking at her heart.
Amaz'd, confus'd, he found his pow'r expir'd,
Resign'd to fate, and with a sigh retir'd.
The Peer now spreads the glitt'ring forfex wide,
T' inclose the Lock; now joins it, to divide.
Ev'n then, before the fatal engine clos'd,
A wretched Sylph too fondly interpos'd;　　　150
Fate urg'd the shears, and cut the Sylph in twain
(But airy substance soon unites again):
The meeting points the sacred hair dissever
From the fair head, for ever, and for ever!
　　Then flash'd the living lightning from her eyes,
And screams of horror rend th' affrighted skies.
Not louder shrieks to pitying heav'n are cast,
When husbands, or when lapdogs breathe their last;
Or when rich China vessels fall'n from high,
In glittering dust and painted fragments lie!　　　160
　　"Let wreaths of triumph now my temples twine,"
The victor cried; "the glorious prize is mine!
While fish in streams, or birds delight in air,

Or in a coach and six the British Fair,
As long as Atalantis shall be read,
Or the small pillow grace a lady's bed;
While visits shall be paid on solemn days,
When num'rous waxlights in bright order blaze;
While nymphs take treats, or assignations give,
So long my honour, name, and praise shall live! "   170
What Time would spare, from Steel receives its date,
And monuments, like men, submit to fate!
Steel could the labor of the gods destroy,
And strike to dust th' imperial tow'rs of Troy;
And hew triumphal arches to the ground.
What wonder then, fair nymph! thy hair should feel
The conqu'ring force of unresisted steel?

.   .   .   .

Canto V *

She said: the pitying audience melt in tears;
But Fate and Jove had stopp'd the Baron's ears.
In vain Thalestris with reproach assails;
For who can move when fair Belinda fails?
Not half so fix'd the Trojan could remain,
While Anna begg'd and Dido rag'd in vain.
Then grave Clarissa graceful wav'd her fan;
Silence ensu'd, and thus the nymph began:
   "Say, why are beauties prais'd and honour'd most,
The wise man's passion, and the vain man's toast?   10
Why deck'd with all that land and sea afford,
Why angels call'd, and angel-like ador'd?
Why round our coaches crowd the white-glov'd beaux?
Why bows the side-box from its inmost rows?
How vain are all these glories, all our pains,
Unless good sense preserve what beauty gains,

* Canto IV ends with Belinda's lament.

That men may say, when we the front-box grace,
'Behold the first in virtue as in face!'
Oh! if to dance all night, and dress all day,
Charm'd the small-pox, or chas'd old age away;   20
Who would not scorn what housewife's cares produce,
Or who would learn one earthly thing of use?
To patch, nay ogle, might become a saint;
Nor could it sure be such a sin to paint.
But since, alas! frail beauty must decay;
Curl'd or uncurl'd, since locks will turn to gray;
Since painted, or not painted, all shall fade,
And she who scorns a man, must die a maid;
What then remains but well our pow'r to use,
And keep good-humour still whate'er we lose?   30
And trust me, dear! good-humour can prevail,
When airs, and flights, and screams, and scolding fail.
Beauties in vain their pretty eyes may roll;
Charms strike the sight, but merit wins the soul."
    So spoke the dame, but no applause ensu'd;
Belinda frowned, Thalestris call'd her prude.
"To arms, to arms!" the fierce virago cries,
And swift as lightning to the combat flies.
All side in parties, and begin th' attack;
Fans clap, silks rustle, and tough whalebones crack;   40
Heroes' and heroines' shouts confus'dly rise,
And bass, and treble voices strike the skies.
No common weapons in the hands are found;
Like gods they fight, nor dread a mortal wound.
    So when bold Homer makes the gods engage,
And heav'nly breasts with human passions rage;
'Gainst Pallas, Mars; Latona, Hermes arms;
And all Olympus rings with loud alarms;
Jove's thunder roars, heav'n trembles all around;
Blue Neptune storms, the bellowing deeps resound;   50
Earth shakes her nodding tow'rs, the ground gives way,
And the pale ghosts start at the flash of day!

Triumphant Umbriel, on a sconce's height,
Clapp'd his glad wings, and sate to view the fight.
Propp'd on their bodkin spears, the sprites survey
The growing combat, or assist the fray.

    While thro' the press enrag'd Thalestris flies,
And scatters death around from both her eyes,
A beau and witling perish'd in the throng;
One died in metaphor, and one in song.   60
"O cruel nymph! a living death I bear."
Cried Dapperwit, and sunk beside his chair.
A mournful glance Sir Fopling upward cast;
"Those eyes are made so killing"—was his last.
Thus on Maeander's flow'ry margin lies
Th' expiring swan, and as he sings he dies.

    When bold Sir Plume had drawn Clarissa down,
Chloe stepp'd in, and kill'd him with a frown;
She smil'd to see the doughty hero slain,
But, at her smile, the beau reviv'd again.   70

    Now Jove suspends his golden scales in air,
Weighs the men's wits against the lady's hair;
The doubtful beam long nods from side to side;
At length the wits mount up, the hairs subside.

    See, fierce Belinda on the Baron flies,
With more than usual lightning in her eyes;
Nor fear'd the chief th' unequal fight to try,
Who sought no more than on his foe to die.
But this bold lord, with manly strength endu'd,
She with one finger and a thumb subdu'd: 80
Just where the breath of life his nostrils drew,
A charge of snuff the wily virgin threw;
The Gnomes direct, to ev'ry atom just,
The pungent grains of titillating dust.
Sudden with starting tears each eye o'erflows,
And the high dome re-echoes to his nose.

    "Now meet thy fate," incens'd Belinda cry'd,
And drew a deadly bodkin from her side.

(The same, his ancient personage to deck,
Her great-great-grandsire wore about his neck,   90
In three seal-rings; which after, melted down,
Form'd a vast buckle for his widow's gown;
Her infant grandame's whistle next it grew,
The bells she jingled, and the whistle blew;
Then in a bodkin grac'd her mother's hairs,
Which long she wore, and now Belinda wears.)
    "Boast not my fall," he cried, "insulting foe!
Thou by some other shalt be laid as low.
Nor think, to die dejects my lofty mind:
All that I dread is leaving you behind!   100
Rather than so, ah let me still survive,
And burn in Cupid's flames—but burn alive."
    "Restore the Lock!" she cries; and all around
"Restore the Lock!" the vaulted roofs rebound.
Not fierce Othello in so loud a strain
Roar'd for the handkerchief that caus'd his pain.
But see how oft ambitious aims are cross'd,
And chiefs contend till all the prize is lost!
The Lock, obtain'd with guilt, and kept with pain,
In ev'ry place is sought, but sought in vain.   110
With such a prize no mortal must be blest,
So heav'n decrees! with heav'n who can contest?
    Some thought it mounted to the lunar sphere,
Since all things lost on earth are treasur'd there.
There heroes' wits are kept in pond'rous vases,
And beaux in snuff-boxes and tweezer-cases.
There broken vows and death-bed alms are found,
And lovers' hearts with ends of riband bound,
The courtier's promises, and sick man's pray'rs,
The smiles of harlots, and the tears of heirs,   120
Cages for gnats, and chains to yoke a flea,
Dried butterflies, and tomes of casuistry.
    But trust the Muse—she saw it upward rise,
Tho' mark'd by none but quick poetic eyes;

(So Rome's great founder to the heav'ns withdrew,
To Proculus alone confess'd in view)
A sudden star, it shot thro' liquid air,
And drew behind a radiant trail of hair.
Not Berenice's locks first rose so bright,
The heav'ns bespangling with dishevel'd light.   130
The Sylphs behold it kindling as it flies,
And pleas'd pursue its progress thro' the skies.
   This the beau monde shall from the Mall survey,
And hail with music its propitious ray.
This the blest lover shall for Venus take,
And send up vows from Rosamonda's lake;
This Partridge soon shall view in cloudless skies,
When next he looks thro' Galileo's eyes;
And hence th' egregious wizard shall foredoom
The fate of Louis, and the fall of Rome.   140
   Then cease, bright nymph! to mourn thy ravish'd hair
Which adds new glory to the shining sphere!
Not all the tresses that fair head can boast,
Shall draw such envy as the Lock you lost:
For after all the murders of your eye,
When, after millions slain, yourself shall die:
When those fair suns shall set, as set they must,
And all those tresses shall be laid in dust,
This Lock the Muse shall consecrate to fame,
And 'midst the stars inscribe Belinda's name.

1712, 1714

UNIVERSAL PRAYER

Father of all! in ev'ry age,
   In ev'ry clime adored,
By saint, by savage, and by sage,
   Jehovah, Jove, or Lord!

Thou Great First Cause, least understood,
   Who all my sense confined
To know but this, that thou art good,
   And that myself am blind;

Yet gave me, in this dark estate,
   To see the good from ill;   10
And binding nature fast in fate,
   Left free the human will.

What conscience dictates to be done,
   Or warns me not to do;
This teach me more than hell to shun,
   That more than heaven pursue.

What blessings thy free bounty gives
   Let me not cast away;
For God is paid when man receives;
   T' enjoy is to obey.   20

Yet not to earth's contracted span
   Thy goodness let me bound,
Or think thee Lord alone of man,
   When thousand worlds are round.

Let not this weak, unknowing hand
   Presume thy bolts to throw,
And deal damnation round the land
   On which I judge thy foe.

If I am right, thy grace impart,
   Still in the right to stay;   30
If I am wrong, O teach my heart
   To find that better way.

Save me alike from foolish pride
   Or impious discontent,
At aught thy wisdom has denied,
   Or aught thy goodness lent.

Teach me to feel another's woe,
    To hide the fault I see;
That mercy I to others show,
    That mercy show to me.   40

Mean though I am, not wholly so,
    Since quickened by thy breath,
O lead me, whereso'er I go,
    Through this day's life or death!

This day be bread and peace my lot;
    All else beneath the sun
Thou know'st if best bestowed or not,
    And let thy will be done.

To Thee, whose temple is all space,
    Whose altar earth, sea, skies,   50
One chorus let all being raise,
    All nature's incense rise!

                      1738

THOMAS GRAY (1716–1771)

ELEGY WRITTEN IN A COUNTRY CHURCHYARD

The curfew tolls the knell of parting day,
    The lowing herd wind slowly o'er the lea,
The plowman homeward plods his weary way,
    And leaves the world to darkness and to me.

Now fades the glimmering landscape on the sight,
    And all the air a solemn stillness holds
Save where the beetle wheels his droning flight,
    And drowsy tinklings lull the distant folds;

Save that from yonder ivy-mantled tower
　　The moping owl does to the moon complain　　10
Of such, as wandering near her secret bower,
　　Molest her ancient solitary reign.

Beneath those rugged elms, that yew-tree's shade,
　　Where heaves the turf in many a mould'ring heap,
Each in his narrow cell forever laid,
　　The rude forefathers of the hamlet sleep.

The breezy call of incense-breathing morn,
　　The swallow twittering from the straw-built shed,
The cock's shrill clarion, or the echoing horn,
　　No more shall rouse them from their lowly bed.　　20

For them no more the blazing hearth shall burn,
　　Or busy housewife ply her evening care;
No children run to lisp their sire's return,
　　Or climb his knees the envied kiss to share.

Oft did the harvest to their sickle yield;
　　Their furrow oft the stubborn glebe has broke;
How jocund did they drive their team afield!
　　How bowed the woods beneath their sturdy stroke!

Let not ambition mock their useful toil,
　　Their homely joys, and destiny obscure;　　30
Nor grandeur hear with a disdainful smile,
　　The short and simple annals of the poor.

The boast of heraldry, the pomp of power,
　　And all that beauty, all that wealth e'er gave,
Awaits alike th' inevitable hour.
　　The paths of glory lead but to the grave.

26. *glebe*, soil.

Nor you, ye proud, impute to these the fault,
  If memory o'er their tomb no trophies raise,
Where through the long drawn aisle and fretted vault
  The pealing anthem swells the note of praise.   40

Can storied urn or animated bust
  Back to its mansion call the fleeting breath?
Can honour's voice provoke the silent dust,
  Or flattery soothe the dull, cold ear of death?

Perhaps in this neglected spot is laid
  Some heart once pregnant with celestial fire;
Hands that the rod of empire might have swayed,
  Or waked to ecstasy the living lyre.

But knowledge to their eyes her ample page
  Rich with the spoils of time did ne'er unroll;   50
Chill penury repressed their noble rage,
  And froze the genial current of the soul.

Full many a gem of purest ray serene
  The dark, unfathomed caves of ocean bear;
Full many a flower is born to blush unseen,
  And waste its sweetness on the desert air.

Some village Hampden, that with dauntless breast
  The little tyrant of his fields withstood;
Some mute, inglorious Milton here may rest;
  Some Cromwell guiltless of his country's blood.   60

The applause of listening senates to command,
  The threats of pain and ruin to despise,
To scatter plenty o'er a smiling land,
  And read their history in a nation's eyes,

41. *storied*, carved with an epitaph or relief.
51. *rage*, poetical genius.

Their lot forbade; nor circumscribed alone
   Their growing virtues, but their crimes confined;
Forbade to wade through slaughter to a throne,
   And shut the gates of mercy on mankind,

The struggling pangs of conscious truth to hide,
   To quench the blushes of ingenuous shame,   70
Or heap the shrine of luxury and pride
   With incense kindled at the muse's flame.

Far from the madding crowd's ignoble strife,
   Their sober wishes never learned to stray;
Along the cool, sequestered vale of life
   They kept the noiseless tenor of their way.

Yet ev'n these bones from insult to protect,
   Some frail memorial still erected nigh,
With uncouth rimes and shapeless sculpture decked,
   Implores the passing tribute of a sigh.   80

Their name, their years, spelt by th' unlettered muse,
   The place of fame and elegy supply;
And many a holy text around she strews,
   That teach the rustic moralist to die.

For who to dumb forgetfulness a prey,
   This pleasing anxious being e'er resigned,
Left the warm precincts of the cheerful day,
   Nor cast one longing, lingering look behind?

On some fond breast the parting soul relies,
   Some pious drops the closing eye requires;   90
Ev'n from the tomb the voice of nature cries,
   Ev'n in our ashes live their wonted fires.

For thee, who mindful of th' unhonoured dead
   Dost in these lines their artless tale relate,
If chance, by lonely contemplation led,
   Some kindred spirit shall inquire thy fate,

Haply some hoary-headed swain may say:
　"Oft have we seen him at the peep of dawn
Brushing with hasty steps the dews away
　To meet the sun upon the upland lawn.   100

"There at the foot of yonder nodding beech
　That wreathes its old fantastic roots so high
His listless length at noontide would he stretch,
　And pore upon the brook that babbles by.

"Hard by yon wood, now smiling as in scorn,
　Muttering his wayward fancies he would rove,
Now drooping, woeful wan, like one forlorn,
　Or crazed with care, or crossed in hopeless love.

"One morn I missed him on.the customed hill,
　Along the heath and near his favourite tree;   110
Another came; nor yet beside the rill,
　Nor up the lawn, nor at the wood was he;

"The next with dirges due in sad array
　Slow through the church-way path we saw him borne.
Approach and read (for thou can'st read) the lay,
　Graved on the stone beneath yon aged thorn."

THE EPITAPH

Here rests his head upon the lap of earth,
　A youth to fortune and to fame unknown.
Fair science frowned not on his humble birth,
　And melancholy marked him for her own.   120

Large was his bounty, and his soul sincere,
　Heaven did a recompense as largely send.
He gave to misery, all he had, a tear,
　He gained from Heaven ('twas all he wished) a friend.

No farther seek his merits to disclose,
  Or draw his frailties from their dread abode.
(There they alike in trembling hope repose),
  The bosom of his Father and his God.

1751

THE FATAL SISTERS

AN ODE FROM THE NORSE TONGUE

Now the storm begins to lower
(Haste, the loom of hell prepare);
Iron-sleet of arrowy shower
Hurtles in the darkened air.

Glitt'ring lances are the loom,
Where the dusky warp we strain,
Weaving many a soldier's doom,
Orkney's woe, and Randver's bane.

See the grisly texture grow
('Tis of human entrails made),   10
And the weights, that play below,
Each a gasping warrior's head.

Shafts for shuttles, dipped in gore,
Shoot the trembling cords along.
Sword, that once a monarch bore,
Keep the tissue close and strong.

Mista black, terrific maid,
Sangrida, and Hilda see,
Join the wayward work to aid;
'Tis the woof of victory.   20

Ere the ruddy sun be set,
Pikes must shiver, javelins sing,
Blade with clattering buckler meet,
Hauberk crash, and helmet ring.

(Weave the crimson web of war.)
Let us go, and let us fly,
Where our friends the conflict share,
Where they triumph, where they die.

As the paths of fate we tread,
Wading through th' ensanguined field,   30
Gondula, and Geira, spread
O'er the youthful king your shield.

We the reins to slaughter give,
Ours to kill, and ours to spare;
Spite of danger he shall live.
(Weave the crimson web of war.)

They, whom once the desert-beach
Pent within its bleak domain,
Soon their ample sway shall stretch
O'er the plenty of the plain.   40

Low the dauntless earl is laid,
Gored with many a gaping wound.
Fate demands a nobler head;
Soon a king shall bite the ground.

Long his loss shall Eirin weep;
Ne'er again his likeness see.
Long her strains in sorrow steep,
Strains of immortality!

Horror covers all the heath;
Clouds of carnage blot the sun.   50
Sisters, weave the web of death;
Sisters, cease, the work is done.

Hail the task, and hail the hands!
Songs of joy and triumph sing!
Joy to the victorious bands;
Triumph to the younger king.

Mortal, thou that hear'st the tale,
Learn the tenor of our song.
Scotland, through each winding vale
Far and wide the notes prolong.   60

Sisters hence with spurs of speed;
Each her thundering falchion wield;
Each bestride her sable steed.
Hurry, hurry to the field.

1768

WILLIAM COLLINS (1721–1759)

ODE

WRITTEN IN THE BEGINNING OF THE YEAR 1746

How sleep the brave who sink to rest
By all their country's wishes blest!
When Spring, with dewy fingers cold,
Returns to deck their hallowed mould,
She there shall dress a sweeter sod
Than Fancy's feet have ever trod.

By fairy hands their knell is rung;
By forms unseen their dirge is sung.
There Honour comes, a pilgrim gray,
To bless the turf that wraps their clay;   10
And Freedom shall awhile repair,
To dwell a weeping hermit there!

1746

ODE TO EVENING

If aught of oaten stop, or pastoral song,
May hope, chaste Eve, to soothe thy modest ear,
    Like thy own solemn springs,
    Thy springs and dying gales;

O nymph reserved—while now the bright-haired sun
Sits in yon western tent, whose cloudy skirts,
    With brede ethereal wove,
    O'erhang his wavy bed;

Now air is hushed, save where the weak-eyed bat
With short shrill shriek flits by on leathern wing,   10
    Or where the beetle winds
    His small but sullen horn,

As oft he rises, 'midst the twilight path
Against the pilgrim borne in heedless hum—
    Now teach me, maid composed,
    To breathe some softened strain,

Whose numbers, stealing through thy darkening vale,
May not unseemly with its stillness suit,
    As, musing slow, I hail
    Thy genial loved return!   20

For when thy folding-star arising shows
His paly circlet, at his warning lamp
    The fragrant Hours, and elves
    Who slept in buds the day,

And many a nymph who wreathes her brows with sedge,
And sheds the freshening dew, and, lovelier still,
    The pensive Pleasures sweet,
    Prepare thy shadowy car.

Then lead, calm votaress, where some sheety lake
Cheers the lone heath, or some time-hallowed pile,   30
    Or upland fallows grey
    Reflect its last cool gleam.

But when chill blustering winds, or driving rain,
Prevent my willing feet, be mine the hut
    That from the mountain's side
    Views wilds and swelling floods,

And hamlets brown, and dim-discovered spires,
And hears their simple bell, and marks o'er all
    Thy dewy fingers draw
    The gradual dusky veil.   40

While Spring shall pour his show'rs, as oft he wont,
And bathe thy breathing tresses, meekest Eve!
    While Summer loves to sport
    Beneath thy lingering light;

While sallow Autumn fills thy lap with leaves,
Or Winter, yelling through the troublous air,
    Affrights thy shrinking train,
    And rudely rends thy robes;

So long, regardful of thy quiet rule,
Shall Fancy, Friendship, Science, rose-lipped Health, 50
    Thy gentlest influence own,
    And hymn thy favorite name!

                 1746

THE PASSIONS

AN ODE FOR MUSIC

When Music, heavenly maid, was young,
While yet in early Greece she sung,
The Passions oft, to hear her shell,
Thronged around her magic cell,
Exulting, trembling, raging, fainting,
Possessed beyond the Muse's painting;
By turns they felt the glowing mind
Disturbed, delighted, raised, refined;
Till once, 'tis said, when all were fired,
Filled with fury, rapt, inspired,   10
From the supporting myrtles round
They snatched her instruments of sound;
And as they oft had heard apart

Sweet lessons of her forceful art,
Each, for madness rules the hour,
Would prove his own expressive power.

First Fear his hand, its skill to try,
    Amid the chords bewildered laid,
And back recoiled, he knew not why,
    Ev'n at the sound himself had made.   20

Next Anger rushed; his eyes, on fire,
    In lightnings owned his secret stings;
In one rude clash he struck the lyre,
    And swept with hurried hand the strings.

With woeful measures wan Despair
    Low sullen sounds his grief beguiled;
A solemn, strange, and mingled air;
    'Twas sad by fits, by starts 'twas wild.

But thou, O Hope, with eyes so fair,
    What was thy delightful measure?   30
Still it whispered promised pleasure,
    And bade the lovely scenes at distance hail!
Still would her touch the strain prolong,
    And from the rocks, the woods, the vale,
She called on Echo still through all the song;
    And where her sweetest theme she chose,
A soft responsive voice was heard at ev'ry close,
And Hope enchanted smiled, and waved her golden hair.

And longer had she sung—but with a frown
    Revenge impatient rose;   40
He threw his blood-stained sword in thunder down
    And with a with'ring look
    The war-denouncing trumpet took,
And blew a blast so loud and dread,

Were ne'er prophetic sounds so full of woe.
   And ever and anon he beat
   The doubling drum with furious heat;
And though sometimes, each dreary pause between,
     Dejected Pity, at his side,
     Her soul-subduing voice applied,   50
   Yet still he kept his wild unaltered mien,
While each strained ball of sight seemed bursting from his
     head.

Thy numbers, Jealousy, to nought were fixed,
   Sad proof of thy distressful state;
Of diff'ring themes the veering song was mixed,
   And now it courted Love, now raving called on Hate.

With eyes upraised, as one inspired,
Pale Melancholy sate retired,
And from her wild sequestered seat,
In notes by distance made more sweet,   60
Poured through the mellow horn her pensive soul;
   And, dashing soft from rocks around,
   Bubbling runnels joined the sound;
Through glades and glooms the mingled measure stole;
   Or o'er some haunted stream with fond delay
     Round an holy calm diffusing,
     Love of peace and lonely musing,
   In hollow murmurs died away.

But oh, how altered was its sprightlier tone,
When Cheerfulness, a nymph of healthiest hue,   70
   Her bow across her shoulder flung,
   Her buskins gemmed with morning dew,
Blew an inspiring air, that dale and thicket rung,
   The hunter's call to faun and dryad known!
   The oak-crowned sisters, and their chaste-eyed queen,
   Satyrs, and silvan boys, were seen,

Peeping from forth their alleys green;
Brown Exercise rejoiced to hear,
   And Sport leaped up, and seized his beechen spear.

Last came Joy's ecstatic trial. 80
He, with viny crown advancing,
   First to the lively pipe his hand addrest;
But soon he saw the brisk awak'ning viol,
   Whose sweet entrancing voice.he loved the best.
      They would have thought, who heard the strain,
      They saw in Tempe's vale her native maids
      Amidst the vestal sounding shades,
To some unwearied minstrel dancing,
While, as his flying fingers kissed the strings,
   Love framed with Mirth a gay fantastic round; 90
   Loose were her tresses seen, her zone unbound,
   And he, amidst his frolic play,
   As if he would the charming air repay,
Shook thousand odors from his dewy wings.
O Music, sphere-descended maid,
Friend of Pleasure, Wisdom's aid,
Why, goddess, why, to us denied,
Lay'st thou thy ancient lyre aside?
As in that loved Athenian bow'r
You learned an all-commanding pow'r 100
Thy mimic soul, O nymph endeared,
Can well recall what then it heard.
Where is thy native simple heart,
Devote to Virtue, Fancy, Art?
Arise as in that elder time,
Warm, energic, chaste, sublime!
Thy wonders, in that godlike age,
Fill thy recording sister's page.—
   'Tis said, and I believe the tale,
Thy humblest reed could more prevail, 110
Had more of strength, diviner rage,

Than all which charms this laggard age,
Ev'n all at once together found,
Cecilia's mingled world of sound.
Oh, bid our vain endeavors cease,
Revive the just designs of Greece,
Return in all thy simple state,
Confirm the tales her sons relate!

1746

WILLIAM COWPER (1731–1800)

WALKING WITH GOD

GENESIS V, 24

From THE OLNEY HYMNS

Oh! for a closer walk with God,
A calm and heavenly frame;
A light to shine upon the road
That leads me to the Lamb!

Where is the blessedness I knew
When first I saw the Lord?
Where is the soul-refreshing view
Of Jesus and his word?

What peaceful hours I once enjoyed!
How sweet their memory still!   10
But they have left an aching void
The world can never fill.

Return, O holy Dove, return,
Sweet messenger of rest!
I hate the sins that made thee mourn
And drove thee from my breast.

The dearest idol I have known,
Whate'er that idol be,
Help me to tear it from thy throne,
And worship only thee.   20

So shall my walk be close with God,
Calm and serene my frame;
So purer light shall mark the road
That leads me to the Lamb.

1779

LIGHT SHINING OUT OF DARKNESS

From THE OLNEY HYMNS

God moves in a mysterious way
    His wonders to perform;
He plants his footsteps in the sea,
    And rides upon the storm.

Deep in unfathomable mines,
    With never-failing skill,
He treasures up his bright designs,
    And works his sovereign will.

Ye fearful saints, fresh courage take;
    The clouds ye so much dread   10
Are big with mercy, and shall break
    In blessings on your head.

Judge not the Lord by feeble sense,
    But trust him for his grace;
Behind a frowning providence
    He hides a smiling face.

His purposes will ripen fast,
    Unfolding every hour;
The bud may have a bitter taste,
    But sweet will be the flower.   20

Blind unbelief is sure to err,
. And scan his work in vain;
God is his own interpreter,
And he will make it plain.

1779

THE DIVERTING HISTORY OF JOHN GILPIN

SHOWING HOW HE WENT FARTHER THAN HE INTENDED, AND CAME HOME SAFE AGAIN

John Gilpin was a citizen
Of credit and renown;
A trainband captain eke was he
Of famous London town.

John Gilpin's spouse said to her dear,
"Though wedded we have been
These twice ten tedious years, yet we
No holiday have seen.

"Tomorrow is our wedding day,
And we will then repair   10
Unto the Bell at Edmonton
All in a chaise and pair.

"My sister, and my sister's child,
Myself, and children three,
Will fill the chaise; so you must ride
On horseback after we."

He soon replied, "I do admire
Of womankind but one,
And you are she, my dearest dear;
Therefore it shall be done.   20

"I am a linendraper bold,
    As all the world doth know,
And my good friend the calender
    Will lend his horse to go."

Quoth Mrs. Gilpin, "That's well said;
    And for that wine is dear,
We will be furnished with our own,
    Which is both bright and clear."

John Gilpin kissed his loving wife;
    O'erjoyed was he to find,   30
That, though on pleasure she was bent,
    She had a frugal mind.

The morning came, the chaise was brought,
    But yet was not allowed
To drive up to the door, lest all
    Should say that she was proud.

So three doors off the chaise was stayed,
    Where they did all get in;
Six precious souls, and all agog
    To dash through thick and thin.   40

Smack went the whip, round went the wheels,
    Were never folks so glad;
The stones did rattle underneath,
    As if Cheapside were mad.

John Gilpin at his horse's side
    Seized fast the flowing mane,
And up he got, in haste to ride,
    But soon came down again;

For saddletree scarce reached had he
    His journey to begin,   50
When, turning round his head, he saw
    Three customers come in.

So down he came; for loss of time,
　　Although it grieved him sore,
Yet loss of pence, full well he knew,
　　Would trouble him much more.

'Twas long before the customers
　　Were suited to their mind,
When Betty screaming came downstairs,
　　"The wine is left behind!"　　　　　　　60

"Good lack!" quoth he—"yet bring it me,
　　My leathern belt likewise,
In which I bear my trusty sword
　　When I do exercise."

Now Mistress Gilpin (careful soul!)
　　Had two stone bottles found,
To hold the liquor that she loved,
　　And keep it safe and sound.

Each bottle had a curling ear,
　　Through which the belt he drew,　　　　70
And hung a bottle on each side,
　　To make his balance true.

Then over all, that he might be
　　Equipped from top to toe,
His long red cloak, well brushed and neat,
　　He manfully did throw.

Now see him mounted once again
　　Upon his nimble steed,
Full slowly pacing o'er the stones,
　　With caution and good heed.　　　　　　80

But finding soon a smoother road
　　Beneath his well-shod feet,
The snorting beast began to trot,
　　Which galled him in his seat.

So, "Fair and softly," John he cried,
   But John he cried in vain;
That trot became a gallop soon,
   In spite of curb and rein.

So stooping down, as needs he must
   Who cannot sit upright,   90
He grasped the mane with both his hands,
   And eke with all his might.

His horse, who never in that sort
   Had handled been before,
What thing upon his back had got
   Did wonder more and more.

Away went Gilpin, neck or nought;
   Away went hat and wig;
He little dreamt, when he set out,
   Of running such a rig.   100

The wind did blow, the cloak did fly,
   Like streamer long and gay,
Till, loop and button failing both,
   At last it flew away.

Then might all people well discern
   The bottles he had slung;
A bottle swinging at each side,
   As hath been said or sung.

The dogs did bark, the children screamed,
   Up flew the windows all;   110
And every soul cried out, "Well done!"
   As loud as he could bawl.

Away went Gilpin—who but he?
   His fame soon spread around—
"He carries weight! he rides a race!
   'Tis for a thousand pound!"

And still as fast as he drew near,
  'Twas wonderful to view
How in a trice the turnpike men
  Their gates wide open threw.   120

And now, as he went bowing down,
  His reeking head full low,
The bottles twain behind his back
  Were shattered at a blow.

Down ran the wine into the road,
  Most piteous to be seen,
Which made his horse's flanks to smoke
  As they had basted been.

But still he seemed to carry weight,
  With leathern girdle braced;   130
For all might see the bottle necks
  Still dangling at his waist.

Thus all through merry Islington
  These gambols did he play,
Until he came unto the Wash
  Of Edmonton so gay;

And there he threw the Wash about
  On both sides of the way,
Just like unto a trundling mop,
  Or a wild goose at play.   140

At Edmonton his loving wife
  From the balcony spied
Her tender husband, wondering much
  To see how he did ride.

"Stop, stop, John Gilpin!—Here's the house,"
  They all at once did cry;
"The dinner waits, and we are tired."
  Said Gilpin—"So am I!"

But yet his horse was not a whit
   Inclined to tarry there;   150
For why?—his owner had a house
   Full ten miles off, at Ware.

So like an arrow swift he flew,
   Shot by an archer strong;
So did he fly—which brings me to
   The middle of my song.

Away went Gilpin out of breath,
   And sore against his will,
Till at his friend the calender's
   His horse at last stood still.   160

The calender, amazed to see
   His neighbor in such trim,
Laid down his pipe, flew to the gate,
   And thus accosted him:

"What news? what news? your tidings tell;
   Tell me you must and shall—
Say why bareheaded you are come,
   Or why you come at all?"

Now Gilpin had a pleasant wit,
   And loved a timely joke;   170
And thus unto the calender
   In merry guise he spoke:

"I came because your horse would come;
   And, if I well forbode,
My hat and wig will soon be here—
   They are upon the road."

The calender, right glad to find
   His friend in merry pin,
Returned him not a single word,
   But to the house went in;   180

Whence straight he came with hat and wig—
   A wig that flowed behind,
A hat not much the worse for wear,
   Each comely in its kind.

He held them up, and in his turn
   Thus showed his ready wit:
"My head is twice as big as yours,
   They therefore needs must fit.

"But let me scrape the dirt away
   That hangs upon your face;   190
And stop and eat, for well you may
   Be in a hungry case."

Said John, "It is my wedding day,
   And all the world would stare,
If wife should dine at Edmonton,
   And I should dine at Ware."

So turning to his horse, he said,
   "I am in haste to dine;
'Twas for your pleasure you came here,
   You shall go back for mine."   200

Ah luckless speech, and bootless boast!
   For which he paid full dear;
For, while he spake, a braying ass
   Did sing most loud and clear;

Whereat his horse did snort, as he
    Had heard a lion roar,
And galloped off with all his might,
    As he had done before.

Away went Gilpin, and away
    Went Gilpin's hat and wig;   210
He lost them sooner than at first,
    For why?—they were too big.

Now Mistress Gilpin, when she saw
    Her husband posting down
Into the country far away,
    She pulled out half-a-crown;

And thus unto the youth she said,
    That drove them to the Bell,
"This shall be yours, when you bring back
    My husband safe and well."   220

The youth did ride, and soon did meet
    John coming back amain;
Whom in a trice he tried to stop,
    By catching at his rein.

But not performing what he meant,
    And gladly would have done,
The frighted steed he frighted more,
    And made him faster run.

Away went Gilpin, and away
    Went postboy at his heels,   230
The postboy's horse right glad to miss
    The lumbering of the wheels.

Six gentlemen upon the road,
    Thus seeing Gilpin fly,
With postboy scampering in the rear,
    They raised the hue and cry:

"Stop thief! stop thief! a highwayman!"
  Not one of them was mute;
And all and each that passed that way
  Did join in the pursuit.   240

And now the turnpike gates again
  Flew open in short space,
The toll-men thinking as before,
  That Gilpin rode a race.

And so he did, and won it too,
  For he got first to town,
Nor stopped till where he had got up
  He did again get down.

Now let us sing, "Long live the king,
  And Gilpin, long live he";   250
And when he next doth ride abroad,
  May I be there to see!

                                                  1782

WILLIAM BLAKE (1757–1827)

NEVER SEEK TO TELL THY LOVE

Never seek to tell thy love,
  Love that never told can be;
For the gentle wind doth move
  Silently, invisibly.

I told my love, I told my love,
  I told her all my heart;
Trembling, cold, in ghastly fears,
  Ah! she did depart!

Soon after she was gone from me,
   A traveler came by,   10
Silently, invisibly;
   He took her with a sigh.

1863

I SAW A CHAPEL ALL OF GOLD

I saw a Chapel all of gold
That none did dare to enter in,
And many weeping stood without,
Weeping, mourning, worshiping.

I saw a Serpent rise between
The white pillars of the door,
And he forced and forced and forced,
Down the golden hinges tore,

And along the pavement sweet,
Set with pearls and rubies bright,   10
All his shining length he drew,
Till upon the altar white

Vomiting his poison out
On the Bread and on the Wine.
So I turned into a sty,
And laid me down among the swine.

1863

TO THE EVENING STAR

Thou fair-haired angel of the evening,
Now, whilst the sun rests on the mountains, light
Thy bright torch of love; thy radiant crown
Put on, and smile upon our evening bed!

Smile on our loves, and while thou drawest the
Blue curtains of the sky, scatter thy silver dew
On every flower that shuts its sweet eyes
In timely sleep. Let thy west wind sleep on
The lake; speak silence with thy glimmering eyes,
And wash the dusk with silver. Soon, full soon,   10
Dost thou withdraw; then the wolf rages wide,
And the lion glares through the dun forest.
The fleeces of our flocks are covered with
Thy sacred dew; protect them with thine influence.

1783

THE LAMB

Little Lamb, who made thee?
Dost thou know who made thee?
Gave thee life and bid thee feed
By the stream and o'er the mead;
Gave thee clothing of delight,
Softest clothing, woolly, bright;
Gave thee such a tender voice,
Making all the vales rejoice?
Little Lamb, who made thee?
Dost thou know who made thee?   10

Little Lamb, I'll tell thee;
Little Lamb, I'll tell thee:
He is callèd by thy name,
For he calls himself a Lamb.
He is meek, and he is mild;
He became a little child.
I a child, and thou a lamb,
We are callèd by his name.
Little Lamb, God bless thee!
Little Lamb, God bless thee!

1789

THE TIGER

Tiger! tiger! burning bright
In the forests of the night,
What immortal hand or eye
Could frame thy fearful symmetry?

In what distant deeps or skies
Burned the fire of thine eyes?
On what wings dare he aspire?
What the hand dare seize the fire?

And what shoulder, and what art,
Could twist the sinews of thy heart?   10
And when thy heart began to beat,
What dread hand? and what dread feet?

What the hammer? what the chain?
In what furnace was thy brain?
What the anvil? what dread grasp
Dare its deadly terrors clasp?

When the stars threw down their spears,
And watered heaven with their tears,
Did he smile his work to see?
Did he who made the Lamb make thee?   20

Tiger! tiger! burning bright
In the forests of the night,
What immortal hand or eye
Dare frame thy fearful symmetry?

1794

A POISON TREE

I was angry with my friend;
I told my wrath, my wrath did end.
I was angry with my foe;
I told it not, my wrath did grow.

And I watered it in fears
Night and morning with my tears,
And I sunnéd it with smiles
And with soft deceitful wiles.

And it grew both day and night,
Till it bore an apple bright,   10
And my foe beheld it shine,
And he knew that it was mine—

And into my garden stole
When the night had veiled the pole;
In the morning, glad, I see
My foe outstretched beneath the tree.

1794

AH, SUNFLOWER

Ah, Sunflower! weary of time,
Who countest the steps of the sun,
Seeking after that sweet golden clime
Where the traveler's journey is done—

Where the youth pined away with desire,
And the pale virgin, shrouded in snow,
Arise from their graves, and aspire
Where my sunflower wishes to go!

1794

ROBERT BURNS (1759-1796)

ADDRESS TO THE UNCO GUID, OR THE RIGIDLY RIGHTEOUS

My son, these maxims make a rule,
   And lump them aye thegither:
The rigid righteous is a fool,
   The rigid wise anither;
The cleanest corn that e'er was dight,
   May hae some pyles o' caff in;
So ne'er a fellow-creature slight
   For random fits o' daffin.

O ye wha are sae guid yoursel,
   Sae pious and sae holy,
Ye've nought to do but mark and tell
   Your neibor's fauts and folly!
Whase life is like a weel-gaun mill,
   Supplied wi' store o' water;
The heapéd happer's ebbing still,
   And still the clap plays clatter.

Hear me, ye venerable core,
   As counsel for poor mortals,   10
That frequent pass douce Wisdom's door,
   For glaikit Folly's portals;
I, for their thoughtless careless sakes,
   Would here propone defenses—
Their donsie tricks, their black mistakes,
   Their failings and mischances.

Ye see your state wi' theirs compared,
   And shudder at the niffer;
But cast a moment's fair regard—
   What maks the mighty differ?   20
Discount what scant occasion gave,
   That purity ye pride in,
And (what's aft mair than a' the lave)
   Your better art o' hidin'.

Think, when your castigated pulse
  Gies now and then a wallop,
What ragings must his veins convulse,
  That still eternal gallop!
Wi' wind and tide fair i' your tail,
  Right on ye scud your seaway;   30
But in the teeth o' baith to sail,
  It makes an unco leeway.

See Social life and Glee sit down,
  All joyous and unthinking,
Till, quite transmogrified, they 're grown
  Debauchery and Drinking.
O would they stay to calculate .
  Th' eternal consequences;
Or your more dreaded hell to state,
  Damnation of expenses!   40

Ye high, exalted, virtuous Dames,
  Tied up in godly laces,
Before ye gie poor Frailty names,
  Suppose a change o' cases;
A dear loved lad, convenience snug,
  A treacherous inclination—
But, let me whisper i' your lug,
  Ye 're aiblins nae temptation.

Then gently scan your brother man,
  Still gentler sister woman;   50
Though they may gang a kennin wrang,
  To step aside is human.
One point must still be greatly dark,
  The moving why they do it;
And just as lamely can ye mark
  How far perhaps they rue it.

Who made the heart, 'tis He alone
  Decidedly can try us;

He knows each chord, its various tone,
  Each spring, its various bias.   60
Then at the balance let's be mute,
  We never can adjust it;
What's done we partly may compute,
  But know not what's resisted.

1787

OF A' THE AIRTS THE WIND CAN BLAW

Of a' the airts the wind can blaw,
  I dearly like the west,
For there the bonnie lassie lives,
  The lassie I lo'e best.
There wild woods grow, and rivers row,
  And monie a hill between;
But day and night my fancy's flight
  Is ever wi' my Jean.

I see her in the dewy flowers,
  I see her sweet and fair.   10
I hear her in the tunefu' birds,
  I hear her charm the air.
There's not a bonnie flower that springs
  By fountain, shaw, or green;
There's not a bonnie bird that sings,
  But minds me o' my Jean.

1790

OH, WILLIE BREWED A PECK O' MAUT

Oh, Willie brewed a peck o' maut,
  And Rob and Allan cam to see;
Three blyther hearts, that lee-lang night,
  Ye wad na found in Christendie.

TO MARY IN HEAVEN

Chorus

We are na fou, we're nae that fou,
  But just a drappie in our e'e;
The cock may craw, the day may daw,
  And aye we'll taste the barley bree!

Here are we met, three merry boys,
  Three merry boys, I trow, are we;   10
And mony a night we've merry been,
  And mony mae we hope to be!

It is the moon, I ken her horn,
  That's blinkin in the lift sae hie;
She shines sae bright to wyle us hame,
  But, by my sooth, she'll wait a wee!

Wha first shall rise to gang awa,
  A cuckold, coward loun is he!
Wha first beside his chair shall fa',
  He is the king amang us three!

1790

TO MARY IN HEAVEN

Thou ling'ring star, with less'ning ray,
  That lov'st to greet the early morn,
Again thou usher'st in the day
  My Mary from my soul was torn.
O Mary! dear departed shade!
  Where is thy place of blissful rest?
See'st thou thy lover lowly laid?
  Hear'st thou the groans that rend his breast?

That sacred hour can I forget,
  Can I forget the hallowed grove,   10
Where by the winding Ayr we met
  To live one day of parting love?

Eternity will not efface
  Those records dear of transports past,
Thy image at our last embrace—
    Ah! little thought we 'twas our last!

Ayr, gurgling, kissed his pebbled shore,
  O'erhung with wild woods, thick'ning green;
The fragrant birch and hawthorn hoar
  Twined amorous round the raptured scene.   20
The flow'rs sprang wanton to be prest,
  The birds sang love on every spray,
Till too, too soon the glowing west
  Proclaimed the speed of wingéd day.

Still o'er these scenes my mem'ry wakes,
  And fondly broods with miser care!
Time but th' impression stronger makes,
  As streams their channels deeper wear.
My Mary, dear departed shade!
  Where is thy place of blissful rest?   30
See'st thou thy lover lowly laid?
  Hear'st thou the groans that rend his breast?

                          1790

TAM O' SHANTER

When chapman billies leave the street,
And drouthy neebors neebors meet;
As market-days are wearing late,
An' folk begin to tak the gate;
While we sit bousing at the nappy,
An' getting fou and unco happy,
We think na on the lang Scots miles,
The mosses, waters, slaps, and styles,

---

1. *chapman billies,* peddler fellows.

That lie between us and our hame,
Whare sits our sulky, sullen dame,   10
Gathering her brows like gathering storm,
Nursing her wrath to keep it warm.

This truth fand honest Tam O'Shanter,
As he frae Ayr ae night did canter
(Auld Ayr, wham ne'er a town surpasses,
For honest men and bonie lasses).

O Tam! hadst thou but been sae wise,
As taen thy ain wife Kate's advice!
She tauld thee weel thou was a skellum,
A blethering, blustering, drunken blellum;   20
That frae November till October,
Ae market-day thou was nae sober;
That ilka melder wi' the miller,
Thou sat as lang as thou had siller;
That ev'ry naig was ca'd a shoe on,
The smith an thee gat roaring fou on;
That at the Lord's house, ev'n on Sunday,
Thou drank wi' Kirkton Jean till Monday.
She prophesied that, late or soon,
Thou would be found deep drowned in Doon,   30
Or catched wi' warlocks in the mirk,
By Alloway's auld haunted kirk.

Ah, gentle dames! it gars me greet,
To think how mony counsels sweet,
How mony lengthened, sage advices,
The husband frae the wife despises!

But to our tale: Ae market night,
Tam had got planted unco right,
Fast by an ingle, bleezing finely,
Wi' reaming swats that drank divinely;   40

And at his elbow, Souter Johnny,
His ancient, trusty, drouthy crony—
Tam lo'ed him like a very brither;
Thy had been fou for weeks thegither.
The night drave on wi' sangs and clatter,
And aye the ale was growing better;
The landlady and Tam grew gracious,
Wi' favours secret, sweet, and precious;
The souter tauld his queerest stories;
The landlord's laugh was ready chorus.   50
The storm without might rair and rustle,
Tam did na mind the storm a whistle.

Care, mad to see a man sae happy,
E'en drowned himsel amang the nappy.
As bees flee hame wi' lades o' treasure,
The minutes winged their way wi' pleasure;
Kings may be blest, but Tam was glorious,
O'er a' the ills o' life victorious!

But pleasures are like poppies spread—
You seize the flow'r, its bloom is shed;   60
Or like the snow falls in the river,
A moment white—then melts forever;
Or like the borealis race,
That flit ere you can point their place;
Or like the rainbow's lovely form,
Evanishing amid the storm.—
Nae man can tether time nor tide;
The hour approaches Tam maun ride;
That hour, o' night's black arch the keystane,
That dreary hour he mounts his beast in;   70
And sic a night he taks the road in,
As ne'er poor sinner was abroad in.

The wind blew as 'twad blawn its last;
The rattling show'rs rose on the blast;

The speedy gleams the darkness swallowed;
Loud, deep, and lang the thunder bellowed;
That night, a child might understand,
The Deil had business on his hand.

Weel mounted on his grey mare Meg—
A better never lifted leg—   80
Tam skelpit on thro' dub and mire,
Despising wind, and rain, and fire;
Whyles holding fast his guid blue bonnet,
Whyles crooning o'er some auld Scots sonnet,
Whyles glow'ring round wi' prudent cares,
Lest bogles catch him unawares—
Kirk-Alloway was drawing nigh,
Whare ghaists and houlets nightly cry.

By this time he was cross the ford,
Whare in the snaw the chapman smoored;   90
And past the birks and meikle stane,
Whare drunken Charlie brak's neckbane;
And through the whins, and by the cairn,
Whare hunters fand the murdered bairn;
And near the thorn, aboon the well,
Whare Mungo's mither hanged hersel.
Before him Doon pours all his floods;
The doubling storm roars through the woods;
The lightnings flash from pole to pole;
Near and more near the thunders roll;   100
When, glimmering through the groaning trees,
Kirk-Alloway seemed in a bleeze;
Through ilka bore the beams were glancing,
And loud resounded mirth and dancing.

Inspiring bold John Barleycorn!
What dangers thou canst make us scorn!
Wi' tippenny, we fear nae evil;

Wi' usquabae, we 'll face the Devil!
The swats sae reamed in Tammie's noddle,
Fair play, he cared na deils a boddle.   110
But Maggie stood, right sair astonished,
Till, by the heel and hand admonished,
She ventured forward on the light;
And, wow! Tam saw an unco sight!

Warlocks and witches in a dance!
Nae cotillion, brent new frae France,
But hornpipes, jigs, strathspeys, and reels
Put life and mettle in their heels.
A winnock-bunker in the east,
There sat auld Nick, in shape o' beast,   120
A towzie tyke, black, grim, and large;
To gie them music was his charge.
He screwed the pipes and gart them skirl,
Till roof and rafters a' did dirl.
Coffins stood round, like open presses,
That shawed the dead in their last dresses;
And by some devilish cantraip sleight,
Each in its cauld hand held a light,
By which heroic Tam was able
To note upon the haly table,   130
A murderer's banes in gibbet airns;
Twa span-lang, wee, unchristened bairns;
A thief, new-cutted frae the rape,
Wi' his last gasp his gab did gape;
Five tomahawks, wi' bluid red-rusted;
Five scymitars, wi' murder crusted;
A garter which a babe had strangled;
A knife, a father's throat had mangled,
Whom his ain son o' life bereft—
The grey hairs yet stack to the heft;   140

108. *usquabae*, whisky.
109. *swats sae reamed*, ale so foamed.
110. *boddle*, small copper coin, a trifle.

Wi' mair of horrible and awfu',
Which ev'n to name wad be unlawfu'.

As Tammie glowered, amazed and curious,
The mirth and fun grew fast and furious.
The piper loud and louder blew;
The dancers quick and quicker flew;
They reeled, they set, they crossed, they cleekit,
Till ilka carlin swat and reekit,
And coost her duddies to the wark,
And linket at it in her sark!   150

Now Tam, O Tam! had thae been queans,
A' plump and strapping in their teens,
Their sarks, instead o' creeshie flannen,
Been snaw-white seventeen hunder linen!
Thir breeks o' mine, my only pair,
That ance were plush, o' guid blue hair,
I wad hae gi'en them off my hurdies,
For ae blink o' the bonie burdies!
But withered beldams, auld and droll,
Rigwoodie hags wad spean a foal,   160
Louping an' flinging on a crummock,
I wonder did na turn thy stomach.

But Tam kend what was what fu' brawlie;
There was ae winsome wench and wawlie,
That night enlisted in the core,
Lang after kend on Carrick shore
(For mony a beast to dead she shot,
And perished mony a bonie boat,
And shook baith meikle corn and bear,

147. *cleekit*, linked.
149. *coost*, threw off.
151. *queans*, young women.
153. *creeshie*, greasy.
154. *seventeen hunder*, very fine.

158. *burdies*, girls.
160. *Rigwoodie*, scrawny.
160. *spean*, wean.
165. *core*, troop.

And kept the country-side in fear).   170
Her cutty sark, o' Paisley harn,
That while a lassie she had worn,
In longitude though sorely scanty,
It was her best, and she was vauntie.
Ah! little kend thy reverend grannie,
That sark she coft for her wee Nannie,
Wi' twa pund Scots ('twas a' her riches),
Wad ever graced a dance of witches!
But here my Muse her wing maun cour;
Sic flights are far beyond her power;   180
To sing how Nannie lap and flang
(A souple jade she was and strang),
And how Tam stood, like ane bewitched,
And thought his very een enriched;
Even Satan glowered, and fidged fu' fain,
And hotched and blew wi' might and main
Till first ae caper, syne anither,
Tam tint his reason a' thegither,
And roars out, "Weel done, Cutty sark!"
And in an instant all was dark;   190
And scarcely had he Maggie rallied,
When out the hellish legion sallied.

As bees bizz out wi' angry fyke,
When plundering herds assail their byke;
As open pussie's mortal foes,
When, pop! she starts before their nose;
As eager runs the market-crowd,
When "Catch the thief!" resounds aloud;
So Maggie runs, the witches follow,
Wi' mony an eldritch skriech and hollow.   200

171. *cutty sark*, short skirt.   176. *coft*, bought.
177. *pund Scots*. The Scotch pound was worth only about one-twelfth of
the English pound.   179. *cour*, let down.   188. *tint*, lost.
193. *fyke*, tumult.   194. *byke*, hive.   195. *pussie*, hare.
200. *eldritch*, uncanny.

Ah, Tam! ah, Tam! thou'll get thy fairin'!
In hell they'll roast thee like a herrin'!
In vain thy Kate awaits thy comin'!
Kate soon will be a woefu' woman!
Now, do thy speedy utmost, Meg,
And win the key-stane of the brig;
There, at them thou thy tail may toss—
A running stream they dare na cross;
But ere the key-stane she could make,
The fient a tail she had to shake!   210
For Nannie, far before the rest,
Hard upon noble Maggie pressed,
And flew at Tam wi' furious ettle;
But little wist she Maggie's mettle!
Ae spring brought off her master hale,
But left behind her ain grey tail.
The carlin claught her by the rump,
And left poor Maggie scarce a stump.

Now, wha this tale o' truth shall read,
Ilk man and mother's son take heed: 220
Whene'er to drink you are inclined,
Or cutty sarks run in your mind,
Think, ye may buy the joys o'er dear;
Remember Tam O' Shanter's mare.

1791

AE FOND KISS

Ae fond kiss, and then we sever;
Ae fareweel, alas, forever!
Deep in heart-wrung tears I'll pledge thee;
Warring sighs and groans I'll wage thee!

Who shall say that Fortune grieves him
While the star of hope she leaves him?
Me, nae cheerfu' twinkle lights me;
Dark despair around benights me.

I'll ne'er blame my partial fancy;
Naething could resist my Nancy;   10
But to see her was to love her,
Love but her, and love forever.

Had we never loved sae kindly,
Had we never loved sae blindly,
Never met—or never parted,
We had ne'er been broken-hearted.

Fare thee weel, thou first and fairest!
Fare thee weel, thou best and dearest!
Thine be ilka joy and treasure,
Peace, enjoyment, love, and pleasure!   20

Ae fond kiss, and then we sever!
Ae fareweel, alas, forever!
Deep in heart-wrung tears I'll pledge thee;
Warring sighs and groans I'll wage thee!

1792

SCOTS, WHA HAE

Scots, wha hae wi' Wallace bled,
Scots, wham Bruce has aften led,
Welcome to your gory bed,
    Or to victory!
Now's the day, and now's the hour;
See the front o' battle lour;
See approach proud Edward's power—
    Chains and slavery!

Wha will be a traitor knave?
Wha can fill a coward's grave?   10
Wha sae base as be a slave?
    Let him turn and flee!

Wha for Scotland's king and law
Freedom's sword will strongly draw,
Freeman stand, or Freeman fa',
    Let him follow me!

By oppression's woes and pains!
By your sons in servile chains!
We will drain our dearest veins,
    But they shall be free!   20
Lay the proud usurpers low!
Tyrants fall in every foe!
Liberty's in every blow!—
    Let us do or die!

                                            1794

A MAN'S A MAN FOR A' THAT

Is there, for honest poverty,
    That hings his head, an' a' that?
The coward slave, we pass him by,
    We dare be poor for a' that!
        For a' that, an' a' that,
            Our toils obscure, an' a' that;
        The rank is but the guinea's stamp;
            The man's the gowd for a' that.

What though on hamely fare we dine,
    Wear hodden-grey, an' a' that;   10
Gie fools their silks, and knaves their wine,
    A man's a man for a' that.
        For a' that, an' a' that,
            Their tinsel show, an' a' that;
        The honest man, though e'er sae poor,
            Is king o' men for a' that.

Ye see yon birkie, ca'd a lord,
   Wha struts, an' stares, an' a' that;
Though hundreds worship at his word,
   He's but a coof for a' that.   20
     For a' that, an' a' that,
       His riband, star, an' a' that,
    The man o' independent mind,
       He looks and laughs at a' that.

A prince can mak a belted knight,
   A marquis, duke, an' a' that;
But an honest man's aboon his might,
   Guid faith he mauna fa' that!
     For a' that, an' a' that,
       Their dignities, an' a' that,   30
The pith o' sense, an' pride o' worth,
   Are higher rank than a' that.

Then let us pray that come it may,
   As come it will for a' that,
That sense and worth, o'er a' the earth,
   May bear the gree, an' a' that.
     For a' that, an' a' that,
       It's coming yet, for a' that,
    That man to man, the warld o'er,
       Shall brothers be for a' that.

                         1795

A RED, RED ROSE

O my Luve's like a red, red rose
   That's newly sprung in June;
O my Luve's like the melodie
   That's sweetly played in tune!

So fair art thou, my bonnie lass,
   So deep in luve am I;
And I will luve thee still, my dear,
   Till a' the seas gang dry—

Till a' the seas gang dry, my dear,
   And the rocks melt wi' the sun;   10
I will luve thee still, my dear,
   While the sands o' life shall run.

And fare thee weel, my only Luve,
   And fare thee weel a while!
And I will come again, my Luve,
   Though it were ten thousand mile.

1796

DUNCAN GRAY

Duncan Gray came here to woo,
   Ha, ha, the wooin o't!
On blythe Yule night when we were fou,
   Ha, ha, the wooin o't!
Maggie coost her head fu heigh,
Looked asklent and unco skiegh,
Gart poor Duncan stand abiegh;
   Ha, ha, the wooin o't!

Duncan fleeched, and Duncan prayed;
   Ha, ha, the wooin o't!   10
Meg was deaf as Ailsa Craig,
   Ha, ha, the wooin o't!
Duncan sighed baith out and in,
Grat his een baith bleer't and blin',
Spak o' lowpin owre a linn;
   Ha, ha, the wooin o't!

Time and chance are but a tide,
    Ha, ha, the wooin o't!
Slighted love is sair to bide,
    Ha, ha, the wooin o't!   20
"Shall I, like a fool," quoth he,
"For a haughty hizzie die?
She may gae to—France for me!"
    Ha, ha, the wooin o't!

How it comes let doctors tell,
    Ha, ha, the wooin o't!
Meg grew sick as he grew hale,
    Ha, ha, the wooin o't!
Something in her bosom wrings,
For relief a sigh she brings;   30
And O! her een, they spak sic things!
    Ha, ha, the wooin o't!

Duncan was a lad o' grace,
    Ha, ha, the wooin o't!
Maggie's was a piteous case,
    Ha, ha, the wooin o't!
Duncan could na be her death,
Swelling pity smoored his wrath;
Now they're crouse and cantie baith;
    Ha, ha, the wooin o't!

1798

HIGHLAND MARY

Ye banks and braes and streams around
    The castle o' Montgomery,
Green be your woods, and fair your flowers,
    Your waters never drumlie!
There simmer first unfauld her robes,
    And there the langest tarry;

For there I took the last fareweel
   O' my sweet Highland Mary.

How sweetly bloomed the gay green birk,
   How rich the hawthorn's blossom,   10
As underneath their fragrant shade
   I clasped her to my bosom!
The golden hours on angel wings
   Flew o'er me and my dearie;
For dear to me as light and life
   Was my sweet Highland Mary.

Wi' monie a vow and locked embrace
   Our parting was fu' tender;
And, pledging aft to meet again,
   We tore ourselves asunder;   20
But oh! fell Death's untimely frost,
   That nipped my flower sae early!
Now green's the sod, and cauld's the clay,
   That wraps my Highland Mary!

O pale, pale now, those rosy lips
   I aft hae kissed sae fondly!
And closed for aye the sparkling glance
   That dwelt on me sae kindly!
And mould'ring now in silent dust,
   That heart that lo'ed me dearly!   30
But still within my bosom's core
   Shall live my Highland Mary.

1799

O, WERT THOU IN THE CAULD BLAST

O, wert thou in the cauld blast,
   On yonder lea, on yonder lea,
My plaidie to the angry airt,
   I'd shelter thee, I'd shelter thee.

Or did misfortune's bitter storms
  Around thee blaw, around thee blaw,
Thy bield should be my bosom,
  To share it a', to share it a'.

Or were I in the wildest waste,
  Sae black and bare, sae black and bare,   10
The desert were a paradise,
  If thou wert there, if thou wert there.
Or were I monarch o' the globe,
  Wi' thee to reign, wi' thee to reign,
The brightest jewel in my crown
  Wad be my queen, wad be my queen.

1800

MARY MORISON

O Mary, at thy window be!
  It is the wished, the trysted hour.
Those smiles and glances let me see
  That make the miser's treasure poor.
How blythely wad I bide the stour
  A weary slave frae sun to sun,
Could I the rich reward secure—
  The lovely Mary Morison!

Yestreen, when to the trembling string
  The dance gaed through the lighted ha',   10
To thee my fancy took its wing—
  I sat, but neither heard nor saw.
Though this was fair, and that was braw,
  And yon the toast of a' the town,
I sighed, and said amang them a':
  "Ye are na Mary Morison."

O Mary, canst thou wreck his peace,
　　Wha for thy sake wad gladly die?
Or canst thou break that heart of his,
　　Whase only faut is loving thee? 　　　20
If love for love thou wilt na gie,
　　At least be pity to me shown;
A thought ungentle canna be
　　The thought o' Mary Morison.

1800

NINETEENTH CENTURY

WILLIAM WORDSWORTH (1770–1850)

LINES

COMPOSED A FEW MILES ABOVE TINTERN ABBEY, ON
REVISITING THE BANKS OF THE WYE DURING A TOUR
JULY 13, 1798

Five years have passed; five summers, with the length
Of five long winters! and again I hear
These waters, rolling from their mountain springs
With a soft inland murmur.—Once again
Do I behold these steep and lofty cliffs,
That on a wild, secluded scene impress
Thoughts of more deep seclusion; and connect
The landscape with the quiet of the sky.
The day is come when I again repose
Here, under this dark sycamore, and view   10
These plots of cottage-ground, these orchard-tufts,
Which at this season, with their unripe fruits,
Are clad in one green hue, and lose themselves
'Mid groves and copses. Once again I see
These hedgerows, hardly hedgerows, little lines
Of sportive wood run wild; these pastoral farms,
Green to the very door; and wreaths of smoke
Sent up, in silence, from among the trees!
With some uncertain notice, as might seem
Of vagrant dwellers in the houseless woods,   20
Or of some hermit's cave, where by his fire
The hermit sits alone.
                    These beauteous forms,
Through a long absence, have not been to me
As is a landscape to a blind man's eye;
But oft, in lonely rooms, and 'mid the din

Of towns and cities, I have owed to them
In hours of weariness, sensations sweet,
Felt in the blood, and felt along the heart;
And passing even into my purer mind,
With tranquil restoration—feelings, too,   30
Of unremembered pleasure; such, perhaps,
As have no slight or trivial influence
On that best portion of a good man's life,
His little, nameless, unremembered acts
Of kindness and of love. Nor less, I trust,
To them I may have owed another gift,
Of aspect more sublime; that blessed mood,
In which the burthen of the mystery,
In which the heavy and the weary weight
Of all this unintelligible world,   40
Is lightened—that serene and blessed mood
In which the affections gently lead us on—
Until, the breath of this corporeal frame
And even the motion of our human blood
Almost suspended, we are laid asleep
In body, and become a living soul;
While with an eye made quiet by the power
Of harmony, and the deep power of joy,
We see into the life of things.
                              If this
Be but a vain belief, yet, oh! how oft—   50
In darkness and amid the many shapes
Of joyless daylight; when the fretful stir
Unprofitable, and the fever of the world,
Have hung upon the beatings of my heart—
How oft, in spirit, have I turned to thee,
O silvan Wye! thou wanderer through the woods,
How often has my spirit turned to thee!
    And now, with gleams of half-extinguished thought,
With many recognitions dim and faint,
And somewhat of a sad perplexity,   60

The picture of the mind revives again;
While here I stand, not only with the sense
Of present pleasure, but with pleasing thoughts
That in this moment there is life and food
For future years. And so I dare to hope,
Though changed, no doubt, from what I was when first
I came among these hills; when like a roe
I bounded o'er the mountains, by the sides
Of the deep rivers, and the lonely streams,
Wherever Nature led; more like a man   70
Flying from something that he dreads, than one
Who sought the thing he loved. For Nature then
(The coarser pleasures of my boyish days,
And their glad animal movements all gone by)
To me was all in all.—I cannot paint
What then I was. The sounding cataract
Haunted me like a passion; the tall rock,
The mountain, and the deep and gloomy wood,
Their colours and their forms, were then to me
An appetite; a feeling and a love,   80
That had no need of a remoter charm,
By thought supplied, nor any interest
Unborrowed from the eye.—That time is past,
And all its aching joys are now no more,
And all its dizzy raptures. Not for this
Faint I, nor mourn, nor murmur; other gifts
Have followed; for such loss, I would believe,
Abundant recompense. For I have learned
To look on Nature, not as in the hour
Of thoughtless youth; but hearing oftentimes   90
The still, sad music of humanity,
Nor harsh nor grating, though of ample power
To chasten and subdue. And I have felt
A presence that disturbs me with the joy
Of elevated thoughts; a sense sublime
Of something far more deeply interfused,

Whose dwelling is the light of setting suns,
And the round ocean and the living air,
And the blue sky, and in the mind of man;
A motion and a spirit, that impels   100
All thinking things, all objects of all thought,
And rolls through all things. Therefore am I still
A lover of the meadows and the woods,
And mountains; and of all that we behold
From this green earth; of all the mighty world
Of eye, and ear—both what they half create,
And what perceive; well pleased to recognize
In Nature and the language of the sense,
The anchor of my purest thoughts, the nurse,
The guide, the guardian of my heart, and soul   110
Of all my moral being.
                              Nor perchance,
If I were not thus taught, should I the more
Suffer my genial spirits to decay;
For thou art with me here upon the banks
Of this fair river; thou my dearest friend,
My dear, dear friend; and in thy voice I catch
The language of my former heart, and read
My former pleasures in the shooting lights
Of thy wild eyes. Oh! yet a little while
May I behold in thee what I was once,   120
My dear, dear sister! and this prayer I make,
Knowing that Nature never did betray
The heart that loved her; 'tis her privilege,
Through all the years of this our life, to lead
From joy to joy; for she can so inform
The mind that is within us, so impress
With quietness and beauty, and so feed
With lofty thoughts, that neither evil tongues,
Rash judgments, nor the sneers of selfish men,
Nor greetings where no kindness is, nor all   130
The dreary intercourse of daily life,

Shall e'er prevail against us, or disturb
Our cheerful faith that all which we behold
Is full of blessings. Therefore let the moon
Shine on thee in thy solitary walk;
And let the misty mountain-winds be free
To blow against thee; and in after years,
When these wild ecstasies shall be matured
Into a sober pleasure; when thy mind
Shall be a mansion for all lovely forms   140
Thy memory be as a dwelling-place
For all sweet sounds and harmonies; oh! then,
If solitude, or fear, or pain, or grief,
Should be thy portion, with what healing thoughts
Of tender joy wilt thou remember me,
And these my exhortations! Nor, perchance—
If I should be where I no more can hear
Thy voice, nor catch from thy wild eyes these gleams
Of past existence—wilt thou then forget
That on the banks of this delightful stream   150
We stood together; and that I, so long
A worshiper of Nature, hither came
Unwearied in that service; rather say
With warmer love—oh! with far deeper zeal
Of holier love. Nor wilt thou then forget
That after many wanderings, many years
Of absence, these steep woods and lofty cliffs,
And this green pastoral landscape, were to me
More dear, both for themselves and for thy sake!

                                         1798

THE PRELUDE;
OR, GROWTH OF A POET'S MIND;

An Autobiographical Poem

BOOK FIRST

INTRODUCTION—CHILDHOOD AND SCHOOL–TIME

.   .   .   .

                    Was it for this
That one, the fairest of all rivers, loved   270
To blend his murmurs with my nurse's song,
And, from his alder shades and rocky falls,
And from his fords and shallows, sent a voice
That flowed along my dreams? For this, didst thou,   .
O Derwent! winding among grassy holms
Where I was looking on, a babe in arms,
Make ceaseless music that composed my thoughts
To more than infant softness, giving me
Amid the fretful dwellings of mankind
A foretaste, a dim earnest, of the calm   280
That Nature breathes among the hills and groves.

    When he had left the mountains and received
On his smooth breast the shadow of those towers
That yet survive, a shattered monument
Of feudal sway, the bright blue river passed
Along the margin of our terrace walk;
A tempting playmate whom we dearly loved.
Oh, many a time have I, a five years' child,
In a small mill-race severed from his stream,
Made one long bathing of a summer's day;   290
Basked in the sun, and plunged and basked again
Alternate, all a summer's day, or scoured
The sandy fields, leaping through flowery groves
Of yellow ragwort; or, when rock and hill,
The woods, and distant Skiddaw's lofty height,

Were bronzed with deepest radiance, stood alone
Beneath the sky, as if I had been born
On Indian plains, and from my mother's hut
Had run abroad in wantonness, to sport
A naked savage, in the thunder shower.   300

    Fair seed-time had my soul, and I grew up
Fostered alike by beauty and by fear:
Much favoured in my birth-place, and no less
In that belovéd Vale to which erelong
We were transplanted;—there were we let loose
For sports of wider range. Ere I had told
Ten birthdays, when among the mountain slopes
Frost, and the breath of frosty wind, had snapped
The last autumnal crocus, 'twas my joy
With store of springes o'er my shoulder hung   310
To range the open heights where woodcocks run
Along the smooth green turf. Through half the night,
Scudding away from snare to snare, I plied
That anxious visitation;—moon and stars
Were shining o'er my head. I was alone,
And seemed to be a trouble to the peace
That dwelt among them. Sometimes it befell
In these night wanderings, that a strong desire
O'erpowered my better reason, and the bird
Which was the captive of another's toil   320
Became my prey; and when the deed was done
I heard among the solitary hills
Low breathings coming after me, and sounds
Of undistinguishable motion, steps
Almost as silent as the turf they trod.

    Nor less, when spring had warmed the cultured Vale,
Moved we as plunderers where the mother-bird
Had in high places built her lodge; though mean
Our object and inglorious, yet the end

Was not ignoble. Oh! when I have hung   330
Above the raven's nest, by knots of grass
And half-inch fissures in the slippery rock
But ill sustained, and almost (so it seemed)
Suspended by the blast that blew amain,
Shouldering the naked crag, oh, at that time
While on the perilous ridge I hung alone,
With what strange utterance did the loud dry wind
Blow through my ear! the sky seemed not a sky
Of earth—and with what motion moved the clouds!

Dust as we are, the immortal spirit grows   340
Like harmony in music; there is a dark
Inscrutable workmanship that reconciles
Discordant elements, makes them cling together
In one society. How strange, that all
The terrors, pains, and early miseries,
Regrets, vexations, lassitudes interfused
Within my mind, should e'er have borne a part,
And that a needful part, in making up
The calm existence that is mine when I
Am worthy of myself! Praise to the end!   350
Thanks to the means which Nature deigned to employ;
Whether her fearless visitings, or those
That came with soft alarm, like hurtless light
Opening the peaceful clouds; or she would use
Severer interventions, ministry
More palpable, as best might suit her aim.

One summer evening (led by her) I found
A little boat tied to a willow tree
Within a rocky cave, its usual home.
Straight I unloosed her chain, and stepping in   360
Pushed from the shore. It was an act of stealth
And troubled pleasure, nor without the voice
Of mountain-echoes did my boat move on;
Leaving behind her still, on either side,

Small circles glittering idly in the moon,
Until they melted all into one track
Of sparkling light. But now, like one who rows,
Proud of his skill, to reach a chosen point
With an unswerving line, I fixed my view
Upon the summit of a craggy ridge,   370
The horizon's utmost boundary; far above
Was nothing but the stars and the grey sky.
She was an elfin pinnace; lustily
I dipped my oars into the silent lake,
And, as I rose upon the stroke, my boat
Went heaving through the water like a swan;
When, from behind that craggy steep till then
The horizon's bound, a huge peak, black and huge,
As if with voluntary power instinct,
Upreared its head. I struck and struck again,   380
And growing still in stature the grim shape
Towered up between me and the stars, and still,
For so it seemed, with purpose of its own
And measured motion like a living thing
Strode after me. With trembling oars I turned,
And through the silent water stole my way
Back to the covert of the willow tree;
There in her mooring-place I left my bark,—
And through the meadows homeward went, in grave
And serious mood; but after I had seen   390
That spectacle, for many days, my brain
Worked with a dim and undetermined sense
Of unknown modes of being; o'er my thoughts
There hung a darkness, call it solitude
Or blank desertion. No familiar shapes
Remained, no pleasant images of trees,
Of sea or sky, no colours of green fields;
But huge and mighty forms, that do not live
Like living men, moved slowly through the mind
By day, and were a trouble to my dreams.   400

Wisdom and Spirit of the universe!
Thou Soul that art the eternity of thought
That givest to forms and images a breath
And everlasting motion, not in vain
By day or star-light thus from my first dawn
Of childhood didst thou intertwine for me
The passions that build up our human soul;
Not with the mean and vulgar works of man,
But with high objects, with enduring things—
With life and nature—purifying thus   410
The elements of feeling and of thought,
And sanctifying, by such discipline,
Both pain and fear, until we recognize
A grandeur in the beatings of the heart.
Nor was this fellowship vouchsafed to me
With stinted kindness. In November days,
When vapors rolling down the valley made
A lonely scene more lonesome, among woods,
At noon and 'mid the calm of summer nights,
When, by the margin of the trembling lake,   420
Beneath the gloomy hills homeward I went
In solitude, such intercourse was mine;
Mine was it in the fields both day and night,
And by the waters, all the summer long.

And in the frosty season, when the sun
Was set, and visible for many a mile
The cottage windows blazed through twilight gloom,
I heeded not their summons: happy time
It was indeed for all of us—for me
It was a time of rapture! Clear and loud   430
The village clock tolled six,—I wheeled about,
Proud and exulting like an untired horse
That cares not for his home. All shod with steel,
We hissed along the polished ice in games
Confederate, imitative of the chase

And woodland pleasures,—the resounding horn,
The pack loud chiming, and the hunted hare.
So through the darkness and the cold we flew,
And not a voice was idle; with the din
Smitten, the precipices rang aloud;   440
The leafless trees and every icy crag
Tinkled like iron; while far distant hills
Into the tumult sent an alien sound
Of melancholy not unnoticed, while the stars
Eastward were sparkling clear, and in the west
The orange sky of evening died away.
Not seldom from the uproar I retired
Into a silent bay, or sportively
Glanced sideway, leaving the tumultuous throng,
To cut across the reflex of a star   450
That fled, and, flying still before me, gleamed
Upon the glassy plain; and oftentimes,
When we had given our bodies to the wind,
And all the shadowy banks on either side
Came sweeping through the darkness, spinning still
The rapid line of motion, then at once
Have I, reclining back upon my heels,
Stopped short; yet still the solitary cliffs
Wheeled by me—even as if the earth had rolled
With visible motion her diurnal round!   460
Behind me did they stretch in solemn train,
Feebler and feebler, and I stood and watched
Till all was tranquil as a dreamless sleep.

Ye Presences of Nature in the sky
And on the earth! Ye Visions of the hills!
And Souls of lonely places! can I think
A vulgar hope was yours when ye employed
Such ministry, when ye, through many a year
Haunting me thus among my boyish sports,
On caves and trees, upon the woods and hills,   470

Impressed, upon all forms, the characters
Of danger or desire; and thus did make
The surface of the universal earth,
With triumph and delight, with hope and fear,
Work like a sea?
           Not uselessly employed,
Might I pursue this theme through every change
Of exercise and play, to which the year
Did summon us in his delightful round.

   .   .   .   .

  Nor, sedulous as I have been to trace
How Nature by extrinsic passion first
Peopled the mind with forms sublime or fair,
And made me love them, may I here omit
How other pleasures have been mine, and joys
Of subtler origin; how I have felt,
Not seldom even in that tempestuous time,   550
Those hallowed and pure motions of the sense
Which seem, in their simplicity, to own
An intellectual charm; that calm delight
Which, if I err not, surely must belong
To those first-born affinities that fit
Our new existence to existing things,
And, in our dawn of being, constitute
The bond of union between life and joy.

  Yes, I remember when the changeful earth,
And twice five summers on my mind had stamped 560
The faces of the moving year, even then
I held unconscious intercourse with beauty
Old as creation, drinking in a pure
Organic pleasure from the silver wreaths
Of curling mist, or from the level plain
Of waters coloured by impending clouds.

The sands of Westmoreland, the creeks and bays
Of Cumbria's rocky limits, they can tell
How, when the Sea threw off his evening shade,
And to the shepherd's hut on distant hills   570
Sent welcome notice of the rising moon,
How I have stood, to fancies such as these
A stranger, linking with the spectacle
No conscious memory of a kindred sight,
And bringing with me no peculiar sense
Of quietness or peace; yet have I stood,
Even while mine eye hath moved o'er many a league
Of shining water, gathering as it seemed,
Through every hair-breadth in that field of light,
New pleasure like a bee among the flowers.   580

Thus oft amid those fits of vulgar joy
Which, through all seasons, on a child's pursuits
Are prompt attendants, 'mid that giddy bliss
Which, like a tempest, works along the blood
And is forgotten; even then I felt
Gleams like the flashing of a shield;—the earth
And common face of Nature spake to me
Rememberable things; sometimes, 'tis true,
By chance collisions and quaint accidents
(Like those ill-sorted unions, work supposed   590
Of evil-minded fairies), yet not vain
Nor profitless, if haply they impressed
Collateral objects and appearances,
Albeit lifeless then, and doomed to sleep
Until maturer seasons call them forth
To impregnate and to elevate the mind.
—And if the vulgar joy by its own weight
Wearied itself out of the memory,
The scenes which were a witness of that joy
Remained in their substantial lineaments   600
Depicted on the brain, and to the eye

Were visible, a daily sight; and thus
By the impressive discipline of fear,
By pleasure and repeated happiness,
So frequently repeated, and by force
Of obscure feelings representative
Of things forgotten, these same scenes so bright,
So beautiful, so majestic in themselves,
Though yet the day was distant, did become
Habitually dear, and all their forms   610
And changeful colours by invisible links
Were fastened to the affections.

                                        (1799–1805) 1850

SHE DWELT AMONG THE UNTRODDEN WAYS

She dwelt among the untrodden ways
    Beside the springs of Dove,
A maid whom there were none to praise
    And very few to love;

A violet by a mossy stone
    Half hidden from the eye!
Fair as a star, when only one
    Is shining in the sky.

She lived unknown, and few could know
    When Lucy ceased to be;   10
But she is in her grave, and, oh!
    The difference to me!

                                                          1800

THREE YEARS SHE GREW IN SUN AND SHOWER

Three years she grew in sun and shower.
Then Nature said, "A lovelier flower

On earth was never sown;
This child I to myself will take;
She shall be mine, and I will make
A lady of my own.

"Myself will to my darling be
Both law and impulse; and with me
The girl, in rock and plain,
In earth and heaven, in glade and bower,   10
Shall feel an overseeing power
To kindle or restrain.

"She shall be sportive as the fawn
That wild with glee across the lawn
Or up the mountain springs;
And hers shall be the breathing balm,
And hers the silence and the calm
Of mute, insensate things.

"The floating clouds their state shall lend
To her; for her the willow bend;   20
Nor shall she fail to see,
Even in the motions of the storm,
Grace that shall mould the maiden's form
By silent sympathy.

"The stars of midnight shall be dear
To her; and she shall lean her ear
In many a secret place
Where rivulets dance their wayward round,
And beauty born of murmuring sound
Shall pass into her face.   30

"And vital feelings of delight
Shall rear her form to stately height,
Her virgin bosom swell;

Such thoughts to Lucy I will give
While she and I together live
Here in this happy dell.''

Thus Nature spake.—The work was done.—
How soon my Lucy's race was run!
She died, and left to me
This heath, this calm and quiet scene;   40
The memory of what has been,
And never more will be.

                                                    1800

LUCY GRAY; OR, SOLITUDE

Oft I had heard of Lucy Gray—
And, when I crossed the wild,
I chanced to see at break of day
The solitary child.

No mate, no comrade Lucy knew;
She dwelt on a wide moor—
The sweetest thing that ever grew
Beside a human door!

You yet may spy the fawn at play,
The hare upon the green;   10
But the sweet face of Lucy Gray
Will never more be seen.

"Tonight will be a stormy night—
You to the town must go;
And take a lantern, child, to light
Your mother through the snow."

"That, father, will I gladly do.
'Tis scarcely afternoon—
The minster-clock has just struck two,
And yonder is the moon!"   20

At this the father raised his hook,
And snapped a fagot-band;
He plied his work—and Lucy took
The lantern in her hand.

Not blither is the mountain roe;
With many a wanton stroke
Her feet disperse the powdery snow,
That rises up like smoke.

The storm came on before its time;
She wandered up and down;   30
And many a hill did Lucy climb,
But never reached the town.

The wretched parents all that night
Went shouting far and wide;
But there was neither sound nor sight
To serve them for a guide.

At daybreak on a hill they stood
That overlooked the moor;
And thence they saw the bridge of wood
A furlong from their door.   40

They wept—and, turning homeward, cried,
"In heaven we all shall meet";
—When in the snow the mother spied
The print of Lucy's feet.

Then downward from the steep hill's edge
They tracked the footmarks small;
And through the broken hawthorn hedge,
And by the long stone wall;

And then an open field they crossed;
The marks were still the same.   50
They tracked them on, nor ever lost;
And to the bridge they came.

They followed from the snowy bank
Those footmarks, one by one,
Into the middle of the plank;
And further there were none!

—Yet some maintain that to this day
She is a living child,
That you may see sweet Lucy Gray
Upon the lonesome wild.   60

O'er rough and smooth she trips along,
And never looks behind;
And sings a solitary song
That whistles in the wind.

                                    1800

THE SOLITARY REAPER

Behold her, single in the field,
Yon solitary Highland lass!
Reaping and singing by herself;
Stop here, or gently pass!
Alone she cuts and binds the grain,
And sings a melancholy strain;
O listen! for the Vale profound
Is overflowing with the sound.

No nightingale did ever chaunt
More welcome notes to weary bands   10
Of travelers in some shady haunt,
Among Arabian sands.
A voice so thrilling ne'er was heard
In springtime from the cuckoo-bird,
Breaking the silence of the seas
Among the farthest Hebrides.

Will no one tell me what she sings?—
Perhaps the plaintive numbers flow
For old, unhappy, far-off things,
And battles long ago.   20
Or is it some more humble lay,
Familiar matter of today?
Some natural sorrow, loss, or pain,
That has been, and may be again?

Whate'er the theme, the maiden sang
As if her song could have no ending;
I saw her singing at her work,
And o'er the sickle bending—
I listened, motionless and still;
And, as I mounted up the hill,   30
The music in my heart I bore,
Long after it was heard no more.

1807

SHE WAS A PHANTOM OF DELIGHT

She was a phantom of delight
When first she gleamed upon my sight;
A lovely apparition, sent
To be a moment's ornament;
Her eyes as stars of twilight fair;
Like twilight's, too, her dusky hair;
But all things else about her drawn
From Maytime and the cheerful dawn;
A dancing shape, an image gay,
To haunt, to startle, and waylay.   10

I saw her upon nearer view,
A spirit, yet a woman, too!
Her household motions light and free,
And steps of virgin liberty;

A countenance in which did meet
Sweet records, promises as sweet;
A creature not too bright or good
For human nature's daily food;
For transient sorrows, simple wiles,
Praise, blame, love, kisses, tears, and smiles.   20

And now I see with eyes serene
The very pulse of the machine:
A being breathing thoughtful breath,
A traveler between life and death;
The reason firm, the temperate will,
Endurance, foresight, strength, and skill;
A perfect woman, nobly planned,
To warn, to comfort, and command;
And yet a spirit still, and bright
With something of angelic light.

1807

I WANDERED LONELY AS A CLOUD

I wandered lonely as a cloud
That floats on high o'er vales and hills,
When all at once I saw a crowd,
A host of golden daffodils,
Beside the lake, beneath the trees,
Fluttering and dancing in the breeze.

Continuous as the stars that shine
And twinkle on the milky way,
They stretched in never-ending line
Along the margin of a bay;   10
Ten thousand saw I at a glance,
Tossing their heads in sprightly dance.

The waves beside them danced, but they
Outdid the sparkling waves in glee—

A poet could not but be gay
In such a jocund company.
I gazed—and gazed—but little thought
What wealth the show to me had brought.

For oft when on my couch I lie
In vacant or in pensive mood,   20
They flash upon that inward eye
Which is the bliss of solitude,
And then my heart with pleasure fills,
And dances with the daffodils.

1807

I TRAVELED AMONG UNKNOWN MEN

I traveled among unknown men,
    In lands beyond the sea;
Nor, England! did I know till then
    What love I bore to thee.

'Tis past, that melancholy dream!
    Nor will I quit thy shore
A second time; for still I seem
    To love thee more and more.

Among thy mountains did I feel
    The joy of my desire;   10
And she I cherished turned her wheel
    Beside an English fire.

Thy mornings showed, thy nights concealed,
    The bowers where Lucy played;
And thine, too, is the last green field
    That Lucy's eyes surveyed.

1807

ODE

INTIMATIONS OF IMMORTALITY FROM RECOLLECTIONS OF EARLY CHILDHOOD

The Child is Father of the Man;
And I could wish my days to be
Bound each to each by natural piety.

There was a time when meadow, grove, and stream,
The earth, and every common sight,
  To me did seem
  Appareled in celestial light,
The glory and the freshness of a dream.
It is not now as it hath been of yore—
  Turn wheresoe'er I may,
   By night or day,
The things which I have seen I now can see no more.

  The rainbow comes and goes,   10
  And lovely is the rose;
  The moon doth with delight
 Look round her when the heavens are bare;
  Waters on a starry night
  Are beautiful and fair;
 The sunshine is a glorious birth;
 But yet I know, where'er I go,
That there hath passed away a glory from the earth.

Now, while the birds thus sing a joyous song,
 And while the young lambs bound,   20
  As to the tabor's sound,
To me alone there came a thought of grief;
A timely utterance gave that thought relief,
 And I again am strong.
The cataracts blow their trumpets from the steep;
No more shall grief of mine the season wrong;
I hear the echoes through the mountains throng,

The winds come to me from the fields of sleep,
    And all the earth is gay;
        Land and sea   30
    Give themselves up to jollity,
        And with the heart of May
    Doth every beast keep holiday—
        Thou child of joy,
Shout round me, let me hear thy shouts, thou happy
    shepherd-boy!

Ye blesséd creatures, I have heard the call
    Ye to each other make; I see
The heavens laugh with you in your jubilee.
    My heart is at your festival,
    My head hath its coronal,   40
The fullness of your bliss, I feel—I feel it all.
    O evil day! if I were sullen
    While Earth herself is adorning,
        This sweet May-morning,
    And the children are culling
        On every side,
    In a thousand valleys far and wide,
    Fresh flowers; while the sun shines warm,
And the babe leaps up on his mother's arm—
    I hear, I hear, with joy I hear!   50
    —But there 's a tree, of many, one,
A single field which I have looked upon;
Both of them speak of something that is gone.
    The pansy at my feet
    Doth the same tale repeat:
Whither is fled the visionary gleam?
Where is it now, the glory and the dream?

Our birth is but a sleep and a forgetting:
The soul that rises with us, our life's star,
    Hath had elsewhere its setting,   60
        And cometh from afar;

Not in entire forgetfulness,
    And not in utter nakedness,
But trailing clouds of glory do we come
    From God, who is our home.
Heaven lies about us in our infancy!
Shades of the prison-house begin to close
    Upon the growing boy,
But he beholds the light, and whence it flows,
    He sees it in his joy;   70
The youth, who daily farther from the east
    Must travel, still is Nature's priest,
    And by the vision splendid
    Is on his way attended;
At length the man perceives it die away,
And fade into the light of common day.

Earth fills her lap with pleasures of her own;
Yearnings she hath in her own natural kind,
And, even with something of a mother's mind,
    And no unworthy aim,   80
    The homely nurse doth all she can
To make her foster-child, her inmate man,
    Forget the glories he hath known,
And that imperial palace whence he came.

Behold the child among his new-born blisses,
A six years' darling of a pygmy size!
See, where 'mid work of his own hand he lies,
Fretted by sallies of his mother's kisses,
With light upon him from his father's eyes!
See, at his feet, some little plan or chart,   90
Some fragment from his dream of human life,
Shaped by himself with newly-learnéd art;
        A wedding or a festival,
        A mourning or a funeral;
        And this hath now his heart,

And unto this he frames his song;
    Then will he fit his tongue
To dialogues of business, love, or strife
    But it will not be long
    Ere this be thrown aside,   100
    And with new joy and pride
The little actor cons another part;
Filling from time to time his "humorous stage"
With all the persons, down to palsied Age,
That Life brings with her in her equipage;
    As if his whole vocation
    Were endless imitation.

Thou whose exterior semblance doth belie
    Thy soul's immensity;
Thou best philosopher, who yet dost keep   110
Thy heritage, thou eye among the blind,
That, deaf and silent, read'st the eternal deep,
Haunted forever by the eternal mind—
    Mighty prophet! Seer blest!
    On whom those truths do rest,
Which we are toiling all our lives to find,
In darkness lost, the darkness of the grave;
Thou, over whom thy immortality
Broods like the day, a master o'er a slave,
A presence which is not to be put by;   120
Thou little child, yet glorious in the might
Of heaven-born freedom on thy being's height,
Why with such earnest pains dost thou provoke
The years to bring the inevitable yoke,
Thus blindly with thy blessedness at strife?
Full soon thy soul shall have her earthly freight,
And custom lie upon thee with a weight,
Heavy as frost, and deep almost as life!

    O joy! that in our embers
    Is something that doth live,   130

     That Nature yet remembers
     What was so fugitive!
The thought of our past years in me doth breed
Perpetual benediction; not indeed
For that which is most worthy to be blest—
Delight and liberty, the simple creed
Of childhood, whether busy or at rest,
With new-fledged hope still fluttering in his
       breast—
     Not for these I raise
     The song of thanks and praise;   140
  But for those obstinate questionings
  Of sense and outward things,
  Fallings from us, vanishings;
  Blank misgivings of a creature
Moving about in worlds not realized,
High instincts before which our mortal nature
Did tremble like a guilty thing surprised.
     But for those first affections,
     Those shadowy recollections,
  Which, be they what they may,   150
Are yet the fountain light of all our day,
Are yet a master light of all our seeing;
Uphold us, cherish, and have power to make
Our noisy years seem moments in the being
Of the eternal Silence: truths that wake,
     To perish never;
Which neither listlessness, nor mad endeavor,
     Nor man nor boy,
Nor all that is at enmity with joy,
Can utterly abolish or destroy!   160
     Hence in a season of calm weather
     Though inland far we be,
Our souls have sight of that immortal sea
     Which brought us hither,
     Can in a moment travel thither,

And see the children sport upon the shore,
And hear the mighty waters rolling evermore.

Then sing, ye birds, sing, sing a joyous song!
    And let the young lambs bound
    As to the tabor's sound!   170
We in thought will join your throng,
    Ye that pipe and ye that play,
    Ye that through your hearts today
    Feel the gladness of the May!
What though the radiance which was once so bright
Be now forever taken from my sight,
    Though nothing can bring back the hour
Of splendor in the grass, of glory in the flower;
    We will grieve not, rather find
    Strength in what remains behind;   180
    In the primal sympathy
    Which having been must ever be;
    In the soothing thoughts that spring
    Out of human suffering;
    In the faith that looks through death,
In years that bring the philosophic mind.

And O ye fountains, meadows, hills, and groves,
Forebode not any severing of our loves!
Yet in my heart of hearts I feel your might;
I only have relinquished one delight   190
To live beneath your more habitual sway.
I love the brooks which down their channels fret,
Even more than when I tripped lightly as they;
The innocent brightness of a new-born day
        Is lovely yet;
The clouds that gather round the setting sun
Do take a sober coloring from an eye
That hath kept watch o'er man's mortality;
Another race hath been, and other palms are won.

Thanks to the human heart by which we live,   200
Thanks to its tenderness, its joys, and fears,
To me the meanest flower that blows can give
Thoughts that do often lie too deep for tears.

1807

ODE TO DUTY

Stern Daughter of the Voice of God!
O Duty! if that name thou love
Who art a light to guide, a rod
To check the erring, and reprove;
Thou, who art victory and law
When empty terrors overawe;
From vain temptations dost set free;
And calm'st the weary strife of frail humanity!

There are who ask not if thine eye
Be on them; who, in love and truth,   10
Where no misgiving is, rely
Upon the genial sense of youth:
Glad Hearts! without reproach or blot;
Who do thy work, and know it not:
Oh! if through confidence misplaced
They fail, thy saving arms, dread Power! around them cast.

Serene will be our days and bright,
And happy will our nature be,
When love is an unerring light,
And joy its own security.   20
And they a blissful course may hold
Even now, who, not unwisely bold,
Live in the spirit of this creed;
Yet seek thy firm support, according to their need.

I, loving freedom, and untried;
No sport of every random gust,
Yet being to myself a guide,
Too blindly have reposed my trust:
And oft, when in my heart was heard
Thy timely mandate, I deferred   30
The task, in smoother walks to stray;
But thee I now would serve more strictly, if I may.

Through no disturbance of my soul,
Or strong compunction in me wrought,
I supplicate for thy control;
But in the quietness of thought:
Me this unchartered freedom tires;
I feel the weight of chance-desires:
My hopes no more must change their name,
I long for a repose that ever is the same.   40

Stern Lawgiver! yet thou dost wear
The Godhead's most benignant grace;
Nor know we anything so fair
As is the smile upon thy face:
Flowers laugh before thee on their beds
And fragrance in thy footing treads;
Thou dost preserve the stars from wrong;
And the most ancient heavens, through Thee, are fresh
     and strong.

To humbler functions, awful Power!
I call thee: I myself commend   50
Unto thy guidance from this hour;
Oh, let my weakness have an end!
Give unto me, made lowly wise,
The spirit of self-sacrifice;
The confidence of reason give;
And in the light of truth thy Bondman let me live!

1807

CHARACTER OF THE HAPPY WARRIOR

Who is the Happy Warrior? Who is he
That every man in arms should wish to be?
—It is the generous Spirit, who, when brought
Among the tasks of real life, hath wrought
Upon the plan that pleased his boyish thought:
Whose high endeavors are an inward light
That makes the path before him always bright:
Who, with a natural instinct to discern
What knowledge can perform, is diligent to learn;
Abides by this resolve, and stops not there,   10
But makes his moral being his prime care;
Who, doomed to go in company with Pain,
And Fear, and Bloodshed, miserable train!
Turns his necessity to glorious gain;
In face of these doth exercise a power
Which is our human nature's highest dower;
Controls them and subdues, transmutes, bereaves
Of their bad influence, and their good receives:
By objects, which might force the soul to abate
Her feeling, rendered more compassionate;   20
Is placable—because occasions rise
So often that demand such sacrifice;
More skilful in self-knowledge, even more pure,
As tempted more; more able to endure,
As more exposed to suffering and distress;
Thence, also, more alive to tenderness.
—'Tis he whose law is reason; who depends
Upon that law as on the best of friends;
Whence, in a state where men are tempted still
To evil for a guard against worse ill,   30
And what in quality or act is best
Doth seldom on a right foundation rest,
He labours good on good to fix, and owes
To virtue every triumph that he knows:

—Who, if he rise to station of command,
Rises by open means; and there will stand
On honourable terms, or else retire,
And in himself possess his own desire;
Who comprehends his trust, and to the same
Keeps faithful with a singleness of aim; 40
And therefore does not stoop, nor lie in wait
For wealth, or honours, or for worldly state;
Whom they must follow; on whose head must fall,
Like showers of manna, if they come at all:
Whose powers shed round him in the common strife,
Or mild concerns of ordinary life,
A constant influence, a peculiar grace;
But who, if he be called upon to face
Some awful moment to which Heaven has joined
Great issues, good or bad for human kind, 50
Is happy as a Lover; and attired
With sudden brightness, like a Man inspired;
And, through the heat of conflict, keeps the law
In calmness made, and sees what he foresaw;
Or if an unexpected call succeed,
Come when it will, is equal to the need:
—He who, though thus endued as with a sense
And faculty for storm and turbulence,
Is yet a Soul whose master-bias leans
To homefelt pleasures and to gentle scenes; 60
Sweet images! which, wheresoe'er he be,
Are at his heart; and such fidelity
It is his darling passion to approve;
More brave for this, that he hath much to love:—
'Tis, finally, the Man, who, lifted high,
Conspicuous object in a Nation's eye,
Or left unthought-of in obscurity,—
Who, with a toward or untoward lot,
Prosperous or adverse, to his wish or not—
Plays, in the many games of life, that one 70

Where what he most doth value must be won:
Whom neither shape of danger can dismay,
Nor thought of tender happiness betray;
Who, not content that former worth stand fast,
Looks forward, persevering to the last,
From well to better, daily self-surpast:
Who, whether praise of him must walk the earth
Forever, and to noble deeds give birth,
Or he must fall, to sleep without his fame,
And leave a dead unprofitable name—   80
Finds comfort in himself and in his cause;
And, while the mortal mist is gathering, draws
His breath in confidence of Heaven's applause:
This is the happy Warrior; this is He
That every Man in arms should wish to be.

1807

COMPOSED UPON WESTMINSTER BRIDGE, SEPTEMBER 3, 1802

Earth has not anything to show more fair;
Dull would he be of soul who could pass by
A sight so touching in its majesty:
This city now doth like a garment wear
The beauty of the morning; silent, bare,
Ships, towers, domes, theaters, and temples lie
Open unto the fields, and to the sky;
All bright and glittering in the smokeless air.
Never did sun more beautifully steep
In his first splendor valley, rock, or hill;   10
Ne'er saw I, never felt, a calm so deep!
The river glideth at his own sweet will.
Dear God! the very houses seem asleep;
And all that mighty heart is lying still!

1807

IT IS A BEAUTEOUS EVENING,
CALM AND FREE

It is a beauteous evening, calm and free.
The holy time is quiet as a nun
Breathless with adoration; the broad sun
Is sinking down in its tranquillity;
The gentleness of heaven broods o'er the sea;
Listen! the mighty Being is awake,
And doth with his eternal motion make
A sound like thunder—everlastingly.
Dear Child! dear Girl! that walkest with me here,
If thou appear untouched by solemn thought,   10
Thy nature is not therefore less divine;
Thou liest in Abraham's bosom all the year,
And worship'st at the Temple's inner shrine,
God being with thee when we know it not.

1807

LONDON, 1802

Milton! thou shouldst be living at this hour:
England hath need of thee; she is a fen
Of stagnant waters; altar, sword, and pen,
Fireside, the heroic wealth of hall and bower,
Have forfeited their ancient English dower
Of inward happiness. We are selfish men;
Oh! raise us up, return to us again;
And give us manners, virtue, freedom, power.
Thy Soul was like a Star, and dwelt apart;
Thou hadst a voice whose sound was like the sea; 10
Pure as the naked heavens, majestic, free,
So didst thou travel on life's common way,
In cheerful godliness; and yet thy heart
The lowliest duties on herself did lay.

1807

THE WORLD IS TOO MUCH WITH US

The world is too much with us: late and soon,
Getting and spending, we lay waste our powers.
Little we see in nature that is ours;
We have given our hearts away, a sordid boon!
This sea that bares her bosom to the moon,
The winds that will be howling at all hours,
And are up-gathered now like sleeping flowers,
For this, for everything, we are out of tune;
It moves us not.—Great God! I 'd rather be
A pagan suckled in a creed outworn;   10
So might I, standing on this pleasant lea,
Have glimpses that would make me less forlorn;
Have sight of Proteus rising from the sea;
Or hear old Triton blow his wreathéd horn.

1807

THOUGHT OF A BRITON ON THE SUBJUGATION OF SWITZERLAND

Two Voices are there; one is of the sea,
One of the mountains; each a mighty Voice.
In both from age to age thou didst rejoice;
They were thy chosen music, Liberty!
There came a Tyrant, and with holy glee
Thou fought'st against him; but hast vainly striven.
Thou from thy Alpine holds at length art driven,
Where not a torrent murmurs heard by thee.
Of one deep bliss thine ear hath been bereft;
Then cleave, O cleave to that which still is left;   10
For, high-souled Maid, what sorrow would it be
That mountain floods should thunder as before,
And ocean bellow from his rocky shore,
And neither awful voice be heard by thee!

1807

ON THE EXTINCTION OF THE
VENETIAN REPUBLIC

Once did She hold the gorgeous east in fee;
And was the safeguard of the west: the worth
Of Venice did not fall below her birth,
Venice, the eldest Child of Liberty.
She was a maiden City, bright and free;
No guile seduced, no force could violate;
And, when she took unto herself a Mate,
She must espouse the everlasting Sea.
And what if she had seen those glories fade,
Those titles vanish, and that strength decay;   10
Yet shall some tribute of regret be paid
When her long life hath reached its final day:
Men are we, and must grieve when even the Shade
Of that which once was great, is passed away.

1807

INSIDE OF KING'S COLLEGE CHAPEL,
CAMBRIDGE

Tax not the royal Saint with vain expense,
With ill-matched aims the Architect who planned—
Albeit labouring for a scanty band
Of white robed Scholars only—this immense
And glorious Work of fine intelligence!
Give all thou canst; high Heaven rejects the lore
Of nicely-calculated less or more;
So deemed the man who fashioned for the sense
These lofty pillars, spread that branching roof
Self-poised, and scooped into ten thousand cells,   10
Where light and shade repose, where music dwells
Lingering—and wandering on as loth to die;
Like thoughts whose very sweetness yieldeth proof
That they were born for immortality.

1822

TO A SKY–LARK

Ethereal minstrel! pilgrim of the sky!
Dost thou despise the earth where cares abound?
Or, while the wings aspire, are heart and eye
Both with thy nest upon the dewy ground?
Thy nest which thou canst drop into at will,
Those quivering wings composed, that music still!

Leave to the nightingale her shady wood;
A privacy of glorious light is thine;
Whence thou dost pour upon the world a flood
Of harmony, with instinct more divine;   10
Type of the wise who soar, but never roam;
True to the kindred points of heaven and home!

                                        1827

SCORN NOT THE SONNET

Scorn not the Sonnet; Critic, you have frowned,
Mindless of its just honours; with this key
Shakespeare unlocked his heart; the melody
Of this small lute gave ease to Petrarch's wound;
A thousand times this pipe did Tasso sound;
With it Camöens soothed an exile's grief;
The Sonnet glittered a gay myrtle leaf
Amid the cypress with which Dante crowned
His visionary brow: a glow-worm lamp,
It cheered mild Spenser, called from Faëryland   10
To struggle through dark ways; and, when a damp
Fell round the path of Milton, in his hand
The Thing became a trumpet; whence he blew
Soul-animating strains—alas, too few!

                                        1827

THE TROSSACHS

There's not a nook within this solemn Pass,
But were an apt confessional for one
Taught by his summer spent, his autumn gone,
That life is but a tale of morning grass
Withered at eve. From scenes of art which chase
That thought away, turn, and with watchful eyes
Feed it 'mid Nature's old felicities,
Rocks, rivers, and smooth lakes more clear than glass
Untouched, unbreathed upon. Thrice-happy quest,
If from a golden perch of aspen spray   10
(October's workmanship to rival May)
The pensive warbler of the ruddy breast
That moral sweeten by a heaven-taught lay,
Lulling the year, with all its cares, to rest!

1835

SAMUEL TAYLOR COLERIDGE
(1772–1834)

THE RIME OF THE ANCIENT MARINER

IN SEVEN PARTS

ARGUMENT

How a Ship having passed the Line was driven by storms to the cold Country
toward the South Pole; and how from thence she made her course to the
tropical Latitude of the Great Pacific Ocean; and of the strange things
that befell; and in what manner the Ancyent Marinere came back to his
own Country.

PART I

It is an ancient Mariner,
And he stoppeth one of three.
"By thy long gray beard and glittering eye,
Now wherefore stopp'st thou me?

An ancient
Mariner meeteth
three Gallants
bidden to a
wedding-feast,
and detaineth
one.

The Bridegroom's doors are opened wide,
And I am next of kin;
The guests are met, the feast is set—
May'st hear the merry din."

He holds him with his skinny hand,
"There was a ship," quoth he.   10
"Hold off! unhand me, gray-beard loon!"
Eftsoons his hand dropped he.

The Wedding-Guest is spell-bound by the eye of the old seafaring man, and constrained to hear his tale.

He holds him with his glittering eye;
The Wedding-Guest stood still,
And listens like a three years' child—
The Mariner hath his will.

The Wedding-Guest sat on a stone—
He cannot choose but hear;
And thus spake on that ancient man,
The bright-eyed Mariner: 20

"The ship was cheered, the harbor cleared;
Merrily did we drop
Below the kirk, below the hill,
Below the lighthouse top.

The Mariner tells how the ship sailed southward with a good wind and fair weather till it reached the Line.

The sun came up upon the left;
Out of the sea came he!
And he shone bright, and on the right
Went down into the sea.

Higher and higher every day,
Till over the mast at noon—"   30
The Wedding-Guest here beat his breast,
For he heard the loud bassoon.

The Wedding-Guest heareth the bridal music; but the Mariner continueth his tale.

The bride hath paced into the hall,
Red as a rose is she;
Nodding their heads before her goes
The merry minstrelsy.

The Wedding-Guest he beat his breast,
Yet he cannot choose but hear;
And thus spake on that ancient man,
The bright-eyed Mariner.   40

"And now the Storm-blast came, and he
Was tyrannous and strong;
He struck with his o'ertaking wings,
And chased us south along.

The ship drawn
by a storm
toward the
South Pole.

With sloping masts and dipping prow,
As who pursued with yell and blow
Still treads the shadow of his foe,
And forward bends his head,
The ship drove fast, loud roared the blast,
And southward aye we fled.   50

And now there came both mist and snow,
And it grew wondrous cold;
And ice, mast-high, came floating by
As green as emerald.

And through the drifts the snowy clifts
Did send a dismal sheen;
Nor shapes of men nor beasts we ken—
The ice was all between.

The land of ice,
and of fearful
sounds, where
no living thing
was to be seen;

The ice was here, the ice was there,
The ice was all around;   60
It cracked and growled, and roared and
        howled,
Like noises in a swound!

At length did cross an Albatross;
Thorough the fog it came;
As if it had been a Christian soul,
We hailed it in God's name.

Till a great
sea-bird called
the Albatross,
came through
the snow-fog,
and was received
with great joy
and hospitality.

It ate the food it ne'er had eat,
And round and round it flew.
The ice did split with a thunder-fit;
The helmsman steered us through!   70

And a good south wind sprung up behind;
The Albatross did follow,
And every day, for food or play,
Came to the mariners' hollo!

In mist or cloud, on mast or shroud,
It perched for vespers nine;
Whiles all the night, through fog-smoke white
Glimmered the white moonshine."

"God save thee, ancient Mariner,
From the fiends that plague thee thus!— 80
Why look'st thou so?"—"With my cross-bow
I shot the Albatross.

PART II

"The sun now rose upon the right;
Out of the sea came he,
Still hid in mist, and on the left
Went down into the sea.

And the good south wind still blew behind,
But no sweet bird did follow,
Nor any day, for food or play,
Came to the mariners' hollo!   90

And I had done an hellish thing,
And it would work 'em woe;
For all averred I had killed the bird
That made the breeze to blow.
'Ah, wretch!' said they, 'the bird to slay,
That made the breeze to blow!'

Nor dim nor red, like God's own head,
The glorious sun uprist;
Then all averred, I had killed the bird
That brought the fog and mist.   100
''Twas right,' said they, 'such birds to slay,
That bring the fog and mist.'

But when the fog cleared off, they justify the same, and thus make themselves accomplices in the crime.

The fair breeze blew, the white foam flew,
The furrow followed free;
We were the first that ever burst
Into that silent sea.

The fair breeze continues; the ship enters the Pacific Ocean and sails northward, even till it reaches the Line.

Down dropped the breeze, the sails dropped down,
'Twas sad as sad could be;
And we did speak only to break
The silence of the sea!   110

The ship hath been suddenly becalmed.

All in a hot and copper sky,
The bloody sun, at noon,
Right up above the mast did stand,
No bigger than the moon.

Day after day, day after day,
We stuck, nor breath nor motion;
As idle as a painted ship
Upon a painted ocean.

Water, water, everywhere,
And all the boards did shrink;   120
Water, water, everywhere,
Nor any drop to drink.

And the Albatross begins to be avenged

The very deep did rot—O Christ!
That ever this should be!
Yea, slimy things did crawl with legs
Upon the slimy sea.

About, about, in reel and rout
The death-fires danced at night;
The water, like a witch's oils,
Burned green, and blue, and white.   130

A Spirit had
followed them;
one of the in-
visible inhabit-
ants of this
planet, neither
departed souls
nor angels:

And some in dreams assuréd were
Of the Spirit that plagued us so;
Nine fathom deep he had followed us
From the land of mist and snow.

concerning whom the learned Jew Josephus and the Platonic Constantinopolitan,
Michael Psellus, may be consulted. They are very numerous, and there is no climate
or element without one or more.

The shipmates
in their sore
distress would
fain throw the
whole guilt on
the ancient
Mariner; in
sign whereof
they hang the
dead sea-bird
round his neck.

And every tongue, through utter drought,
Was withered at the root;
We could not speak, no more than if
We had been choked with soot.

Ah! well-a-day!—what evil looks
Had I from old and young!   140
Instead of the cross, the Albatross
About my neck was hung.

PART III

"There passed a weary time. Each throat
Was parched, and glazed each eye.

The ancient
Mariner be-
holdeth a sign
in the element
afar off.

A weary time! a weary time!
How glazed each weary eye!
When looking westward, I beheld
A something in the sky.

At first it seemed a little speck,
And then it seemed a mist;   150
It moved, and moved, and took at last
A certain shape, I wist.

A speck, a mist, a shape, I wist!
And still it neared and neared;
As if it dodged a water-sprite,
It plunged and tacked and veered.

With throats unslaked, with black lips
    baked,
We could nor laugh nor wail;
Through utter drought all dumb we stood!
I bit my arm, I sucked the blood,   160
And cried, 'A sail! a sail!'

At its nearer approach, it seemeth him to be a ship; and at a dear ransom he freeth his speech from the bonds of thirst.

With throats unslaked, with black lips
    baked,
Agape they heard me call;
Gramercy! they for joy did grin,
And all at once their breath drew in,
As they were drinking all.

A flash of joy;

'See! see!' (I cried) 'She tacks no more!
Hither to work us weal;
Without a breeze, without a tide,
She steadies with upright keel!'   170

And horror follows. For can it be a ship that comes onward without wind or tide?

The western wave was all aflame;
The day was well-nigh done!
Almost upon the western wave
Rested the broad bright sun;
When that strange shape drove suddenly
Betwixt us and the sun.

And straight the sun was flecked with bars
(Heaven's Mother send us grace!)
As if through a dungeon-grate he peered
With broad and burning face.   180

It seemeth him but the skeleton of a ship.

Alas! (thought I, and my heart beat loud)
How fast she nears and nears!
Are those her sails that glance in the sun,
Like restless gossameres?

Are those her ribs through which the sun
Did peer, as through a grate?
And is that Woman all her crew?
Is that a Death? and are there two?
Is Death that Woman's mate?

Her lips were red, her looks were free,   190
Her locks were yellow as gold;
Her skin was as white as leprosy;
The Nightmare Life-in-Death was she,
Who thicks man's blood with cold.

The naked hulk alongside came,
And the twain were casting dice;
'The game is done! I've won! I've won!'
Quoth she, and whistles thrice.

The sun's rim dips; the stars rush out;
At one stride comes the dark;   200
With far-heard whisper, o'er the sea,
Off shot the specter-bark.

We listened and looked sideways up!
Fear at my heart, as at a cup,
My lifeblood seemed to sip!
The stars were dim, and thick the night;
The steersman's face by his lamp gleamed
        white;

From the sails the dew did drip—
Till clomb above the eastern bar
The hornéd moon, with one bright star   210
Within the nether tip.

One after one, by the star-dogged moon, One after
Too quick for groan or sigh, another
Each turned his face with a ghastly pang,
And cursed me with his eye.

Four times fifty living men His shipmates
(And I heard nor sigh nor groan) drop down dead,
With heavy thump, a lifeless lump,
They dropped down one by one.

The souls did from their bodies fly— 220 But Life-in-
They fled to bliss or woe! Death begins
And every soul, it passed me by, her work on the
Like the whizz of my crossbow!" ancient Mariner.

PART IV

"I fear thee, ancient Mariner! The Wedding-
I fear thy skinny hand! Guest feareth
And thou art long, and lank, and brown, that a spirit is
As is the ribbed sea-sand. talking to him;

I fear thee and thy glittering eye, But the ancient
And thy skinny hand, so brown"— Mariner as-
"Fear not, fear not, thou Wedding-Guest! sureth him of
This body dropped not down. 231 his bodily life,
and proceedeth
to relate his
horrible
penance.

Alone, alone, all, all alone,
Alone on a wide, wide sea!
And never a saint took pity on
My soul in agony.

The many men, so beautiful!
And they all dead did lie; He despiseth
And a thousand thousand slimy things the creatures
Lived on; and so did I. of the calm,

And envieth
that they should
live, and so
many lie dead.

I looked upon the rotting sea,   240
And drew my eyes away;
I looked upon the rotting deck,
And there the dead men lay.

I looked to Heaven, and tried to pray;
But or ever a prayer had gusht,
A wicked whisper came, and made
My heart as dry as dust.

I closed my lids, and kept them close,
And the balls like pulses beat;
For the sky and the sea, and the sea and
    the sky   250
Lay like a load on my weary eye,
And the dead were at my feet.

But the curse
liveth for him
in the eye of
the dead men.

The cold sweat melted from their limbs,
Nor rot nor reek did they;
The look with which they looked on me
Had never passed away.

An orphan's curse would drag to hell
A spirit from on high,
But oh! more horrible than that
Is a curse in a dead man's eye!   260
Seven days, seven nights, I saw that curse
And yet I could not die.

In his loneliness
and fixedness
he yearneth
toward the
journeying
moon, and the
stars that still
sojourn, yet
still move on-
ward; and every-
where the blue
sky belongs to
them, and is
their appointed
rest and their
native country
and their own

The moving moon went up the sky,
And nowhere did abide;
Softly she was going up
And a star or two beside—

Her beams bemocked the sultry main,
Like April hoarfrost spread;
But where the ship's huge shadow lay,
The charméd water burned alway   270
A still and awful red.

Beyond the shadow of the ship,
I watched the water-snakes;
They moved in tracks of shining white,
And when they reared, the elfish light
Fell off in hoary flakes.

natural homes, which they enter unannounced, as lords that are certainly expected and yet there is a silent joy at their arrival.

Within the shadow of the ship
I watched their rich attire;
Blue, glossy green, and velvet black,
They coiled and swam; and every track 280
Was a flash of golden fire.

By the light of the moon he beholdeth God's creatures of the great calm,

O happy living things! no tongue
Their beauty might declare;
A spring of love gushed from my heart,
And I blessed them unaware!
Sure my kind saint took pity on me,
And I blessed them unaware.

Their beauty and their happiness.

He blesseth them in his heart.

The selfsame moment I could pray;
And from my neck so free
The Albatross fell off, and sank   290
Like lead into the sea.

The spell begins to break.

PART V

"Oh sleep! it is a gentle thing,
Beloved from pole to pole!
To Mary Queen the praise be given!
She sent the gentle sleep from heaven,
That slid into my soul.

The silly buckets on the deck,
That had so long remained,
I dreamt that they were filled with dew;
And when I awoke, it rained.   300

By grace of the holy Mother, the ancient Mariner is refreshed with rain.

My lips were wet, my throat was cold,
My garments all were dank;
Sure I had drunken in my dreams,
And still my body drank.

I moved, and could not feel my limbs,
I was so light—almost
I thought that I had died in sleep,
And was a blessed ghost.

He heareth sounds, and seeth strange sights and commotions in the sky and the element.

And soon I heard a roaring wind;
It did not come anear;   310
But with its sound it shook the sails
That were so thin and sear.

The upper air burst into life!
And a hundred fire-flags sheen;
To and fro they were hurried about;
And to and fro, and in and out,
The wan stars danced between.

And the coming wind did roar more loud,
And the sails did sigh like sedge;
And the rain poured down from one black
      cloud;   320
The moon was at its edge.

The thick, black cloud was cleft, and still
The moon was at its side;
Like waters shot from some high crag,
The lightning fell with never a jag,
A river steep and wide.

The bodies of the ship's crew are inspired, and the ship moves on;

The loud wind never reached the ship,
Yet now the ship moved on!
Beneath the lightning and the moon
The dead men gave a groan.   330

They groaned, they stirred, they all uprose,
Nor spake, nor moved their eyes;
It had been strange, even in a dream,
To have seen those dead men rise.

The helmsman steered, the ship moved on;
Yet never a breeze up-blew.
The mariners all 'gan work the ropes,
Where they were wont to do;
They raised their limbs like lifeless tools—
We were a ghastly crew.   340

The body of my brother's son
Stood by me, knee to knee;
The body and I pulled at one rope,
But he said naught to me."

"I fear thee, ancient Mariner!"
"Be calm, thou Wedding-Guest!
'Twas not those souls that fled in pain,
Which to their corses came again,
But a troop of spirits blest;

For when it dawned—they dropped their
        arms   350
And clustered round the mast;
Sweet sounds rose slowly through their
        mouths,
And from their bodies passed.

Around, around, flew each sweet sound,
Then darted to the sun;
Slowly the sounds came back again,
Now mixed, now one by one.

Sometimes a-dropping from the sky
I heard the skylark sing;
Sometimes all little birds that are,   360

But not by the souls of the men, nor by demons of earth or middle air, but by a blessed troop of angelic spirits, sent down by the invocation of the guardian saint.

How they seemed to fill the sea and air
With their sweet jargoning!

And now 'twas like all instruments,
Now like a lonely flute;
And now it is an angel's song,
That makes the heavens be mute.

It ceased; yet still the sails made on
A pleasant noise till noon,
A noise like of a hidden brook
In the leafy month of June,   370
That to the sleeping woods all night
Singeth a quiet tune.

Till noon we quietly sailed on,
Yet never a breeze did breathe;
Slowly and smoothly went the ship,
Moved onward from beneath.

The lonesome Spirit from the South Pole carries on the ship as far as the Line, in obedience to the angelic troop, but still requireth vengeance.

Under the keel nine fathom deep,
From the land of mist and snow,
The Spirit slid; and it was he
That made the ship to go.   380
The sails at noon left off their tune,
And the ship stood still also.

The sun, right up above the mast,
Had fixed her to the ocean;
But in a minute she 'gan stir,
With a short, uneasy motion—
Backwards and forwards half her length
With a short, uneasy motion.

Then like a pawing horse let go,
She made a sudden bound;   390
It flung the blood into my head,
And I fell down in a swound.

How long in that same fit I lay,
I have not to declare;
But ere my living life returned,
I heard and in my soul discerned
Two voices in the air.

'Is it he?' quoth one, 'Is this the man?
By Him who died on cross,
With his cruel bow he laid full low   400
The harmless Albatross.

The Spirit who bideth by himself
In the land of mist and snow,
He loved the bird that loved the man
Who shot him with his bow.'

The other was a softer voice,
As soft as honey-dew;
Quoth he, 'The man hath penance done,
And penance more will do.'

The Polar Spirit's fellow demons, the invisible inhabitants of the element, take part in his wrong; and two of them relate, one to the other, that penance long and heavy for the ancient Mariner hath been accorded to the Polar Spirit, who returneth southward.

PART VI

First Voice

"'But tell me, tell me! speak again,   410
Thy soft response renewing—
What makes that ship drive on so fast?
What is the ocean doing?'

Second Voice

'Still as a slave before his lord,
The ocean hath no blast;
His great bright eye most silently
Up to the moon is cast—

If he may know which way to go;
For she guides him smooth or grim.
See, brother, see! how graciously   420
She looketh down on him.'

The Mariner hath been cast into a trance; for the angelic power causeth the vessel to drive northward faster than human life could endure.

First Voice

'But why drives on that ship so fast,
Without or wave or wind?'

Second Voice

'The air is cut away before,
And closes from behind.

Fly, brother, fly! more high, more high!
Or we shall be belated;
For slow and slow that ship will go,
When the Mariner's trance is abated.'

The super-
natural motion
is retarded; the
Mariner awakes,
and his penance
begins anew.

I woke, and we were sailing on   430
As in a gentle weather.
'Twas night, calm night, the moon was high;
The dead men stood together.

All stood together on the deck,
For a charnel-dungeon fitter;
All fixed on me their stony eyes,
That in the moon did glitter.

The pang, the curse, with which they died,
Had never passed away;
I could not draw my eyes from theirs,   440
Nor turn them up to pray.

The curse
is finally
expiated.

And now this spell was snapped; once more
I viewed the ocean green,
And looked far forth, yet little saw
Of what had else been seen—

Like one that on a lonesome road
Doth walk in fear and dread,

And having once turned round, walks on,
And turns no more his head,
Because he knows a frightful fiend   450
Doth close behind him tread.

But soon there breathed a wind on me,
Nor sound nor motion made;
Its path was not upon the sea,
In ripple or in shade.

It raised my hair, it fanned my cheek
Like a meadow-gale of spring—
It mingled strangely with my fears,
Yet it felt like a welcoming.

Swiftly, swiftly flew the ship,   460
Yet she sailed softly, too;
Sweetly, sweetly blew the breeze—
On me alone it blew.

Oh! dream of joy! is this indeed
The lighthouse top I see?
Is this the hill? Is this the kirk?
Is this mine own countree?

And the ancient Mariner beholdeth his native country.

We drifted o'er the harbor-bar,
And I with sobs did pray—
'O let me be awake, my God!   470
Or let me sleep alway.'

The harbor-bay was clear as glass,
So smoothly it was strewn!
And on the bay the moonlight lay,
And the shadow of the moon.

The rock shone bright, the kirk no less,
That stands above the rock;
The moonlight steeped in silentness
The steady weathercock.

The angelic
spirits leave the
dead bodies.

And the bay was white with silent light, 480
Till rising from the same,
Full many shapes, that shadows were,
In crimson colours came.

And appear in
their own forms
of light.

A little distance from the prow
Those crimson shadows were;
I turned my eyes upon the deck—
O Christ! what saw I there!

Each corse lay flat, lifeless and flat,
And by the holy rood!
A man all light, a seraph-man,   490
On every corse there stood.

This seraph-band, each waved his hand—
It was a heavenly sight!
They stood as signals to the land,
Each one a lovely light;

This seraph-band, each waved his hand;
No voice did they impart—
No voice; but oh! the silence sank
Like music on my heart.

But soon I heard the dash of oars,   500
I heard the Pilot's cheer;
My head was turned perforce away,
And I saw a boat appear.

The Pilot, and the Pilot's boy,
I heard them coming fast;
Dear Lord in heaven! it was a joy
The dead men could not blast.

I saw a third—I heard his voice;
It is the Hermit good!

He singeth loud his godly hymns   510
That he makes in the wood.
He'll shrieve my soul, he'll wash away
The Albatross's blood.

PART VII

"This Hermit good lives in that wood
Which slopes down to the sea;
How loudly his sweet voice he rears!
He loves to talk with marineres
That come from a far countree.

*The Hermit
of the wood*

He kneels at morn, and noon, and eve—
He hath a cushion plump;   520
It is the moss that wholly hides
The rotted old oak-stump.

The skiff-boat neared; I head them talk,
'Why this is strange, I trow!
Where are those lights so many and fair
That signal made but now?'

'Strange, by my faith!' the Hermit said—
'And they answered not our cheer!
The planks look warped! and see those sails
How thin they are and sear!   530
I never saw aught like to them,
Unless perchance it were

*Approacheth
the ship with
wonder.*

Brown skeletons of leaves that lag
My forest-brook along;
When the ivy-tod is heavy with snow,
And the owlet whoops to the wolf below
That eats the she-wolf's young.'

'Dear Lord! it hath a fiendish look'—
(The Pilot made reply)
'I am a-feared'—'Push on, push on!'   540
Said the Hermit cheerily.

The boat came closer to the ship,
But I nor spake nor stirred;
The boat came close beneath the ship,
And straight a sound was heard.

The ship sud-
denly sinketh.

Under the water it rumbled on,
Still louder and more dread;
It reached the ship, it split the bay;
The ship went down like lead.

The ancient
Mariner is saved
in the Pilot's
boat.

Stunned by that loud and dreadful sound,
Which sky and ocean smote,   551
Like one that hath been seven days drowned
My body lay afloat;
But swift as dreams, myself I found
Within the Pilot's boat.

Upon the whirl, where sank the ship,
The boat spun round and round;
And all was still, save that the hill
Was telling of the sound.

I moved my lips—the Pilot shrieked   560
And fell down in a fit;
The holy Hermit raised his eyes
And prayed where he did sit.

I took the oars; the Pilot's boy,
Who now doth crazy go,
Laughed loud and long, and all the while
His eyes went to and fro.

'Ha! ha!' quoth he, 'full plain I see,
The Devil knows how to row.'

And now, all in my own countree,   570
I stood on the firm land!
The Hermit stepped forth from the boat,
And scarcely he could stand.

'O shrieve me, shrieve me, holy man!'
The Hermit crossed his brow.
'Say quick,' quoth he, 'I bid thee say—
What manner of man art thou?'

Forthwith this frame of mine was wrenched
With a woeful agony,
Which forced me to begin my tale;   580
And then it left me free.

Since then, at an uncertain hour,
That agony returns;
And till my ghastly tale is told,
This heart within me burns.

I pass, like night, from land to land;
I have strange power of speech;
That moment that his face I see,
I know the man that must hear me—
To him my tale I teach.   590

What loud uproar bursts from that door!
The wedding-guests are there;
But in the garden-bower the bride
And bride-maids singing are;
And hark the little vesper bell,
Which biddeth me to prayer!

O Wedding-Guest! this soul hath been
Alone on a wide, wide sea;
So lonely 'twas that God himself
Scarce seemèd there to be.   600

O sweeter than the marriage feast,
'Tis sweeter far to me,
To walk together to the kirk
With a goodly company!—

And to teach,
by his own
example, love
and reverence
to all things
that God made
and loveth.

To walk together to the kirk,
And all together pray,
While each to his great Father bends,
Old men, and babes, and loving friends,
And youths and maidens gay!

Farewell, farewell! but this I tell   610
To thee, thou Wedding-Guest!
He prayeth well, who loveth well,
Both man and bird and beast.

He prayeth best, who loveth best
All things both great and small;
For the dear God who loveth us,
He made and loveth all."

The Mariner, whose eye is bright,
Whose beard with age is hoar,
Is gone; and now the Wedding-Guest   620
Turned from the bridegroom's door.

He went like one that hath been stunned,
And is of sense forlorn;
A sadder and a wiser man
He rose the morrow morn.

1798, 1800

KUBLA KHAN

In Xanadu did Kubla Khan
   A stately pleasure-dome decree;
Where Alph, the sacred river, ran
   Through caverns measureless to man
Down to a sunless sea.
So twice five miles of fertile ground
With walls and towers were girdled round;
And there were gardens bright with sinuous rills
Where blossomed many an incense-bearing tree;
And here were forests ancient as the hills,   10
Enfolding sunny spots of greenery.

But O, that deep romantic chasm which slanted
Down the green hill athwart a cedarn cover!
A savage place! as holy and enchanted
As e'er beneath a waning moon was haunted
By woman wailing for her demon-lover!
And from this chasm, with ceaseless turmoil seething,
As if this earth in fast thick pants were breathing,
A mighty fountain momently was forced;
Amid whose swift, half-intermitted burst   20
Huge fragments vaulted like rebounding hail,
Or chaffy grain beneath the thresher's flail.
And 'mid these dancing rocks at once and ever
It flung up momently the sacred river.
Five miles meandering with a mazy motion
Through wood and dale the sacred river ran,
Then reached the caverns measureless to man,
And sank in tumult to a lifeless ocean;
And 'mid this tumult Kubla heard from far
Ancestral voices prophesying war!   30

   The shadow of the dome of pleasure
      Floated midway on the waves;

Where was heard the mingled measure
   From the fountain and the caves.
It was a miracle of rare device,
A sunny pleasure-dome with caves of ice!

   A damsel with a dulcimer
     In a vision once I saw.
   It was an Abyssinian maid,
     And on her dulcimer she played,   40
   Singing of Mount Abora.
   Could I revive within me
   Her symphony and song,
To such a deep delight 'twould win me
That with music loud and long,
I would build that dome in air,
That sunny dome! those caves of ice!
And all who heard should see them there,
And all should cry, Beware! Beware!
His flashing eyes, his floating hair!   50
Weave a circle round him thrice,
   And close your eyes with holy dread,
   For he on honey-dew hath fed,
And drunk the milk of Paradise.

                              1816

WALTER SAVAGE LANDOR
(1775–1864)

ROSE AYLMER

Ah, what avails the sceptered race!
   Ah, what the form divine!
What every virtue, every grace!
   Rose Aylmer, all were thine.

Rose Aylmer, whom these wakeful eyes
   May weep, but never see,
A night of memories and of sighs
   I consecrate to thee.

1806

TO ROBERT BROWNING

There is delight in singing, tho' none hear
Beside the singer: and there is delight
In praising, tho' the praiser sit alone
And see the praised far off him, far above.
Shakespeare is not our poet, but the world's,
Therefore on him no speech! and brief for thee,
Browning! Since Chaucer was alive and hale,
No man hath walked along our roads with step
So active, so inquiring eye, or tongue
So varied in discourse. But warmer climes   10
Give brighter plumage, stronger wing: the breeze
Of Alpine heights thou playest with, borne on
Beyond Sorrento and Amalfi, where
The Siren waits thee, singing song for song.

1846

ON HIS SEVENTY-FIFTH BIRTHDAY

I strove with none, for none was worth my strife;
   Nature I loved, and next to Nature, Art;
I warmed both hands before the fire of life;
   It sinks, and I am ready to depart.

1853

ON DEATH

Death stands above me, whispering low
   I know not what into my ear;
Of his strange language all I know
   Is, there is not a word of fear.

1853

GEORGE NOEL GORDON, LORD BYRON (1788–1824)

MAID OF ATHENS, ERE WE PART

Ζωη μου, σας αγαπω.*

Maid of Athens, ere we part,
Give, oh, give me back my heart!
Or, since that has left my breast,
Keep it now, and take the rest!
Hear my vow before I go,
Ζωη μου, σας αγαπω.

By those tresses unconfined,
Wooed by each Aegean wind;
By those lids whose jetty fringe
Kiss thy soft cheeks' blooming tinge;   10
By those wild eyes like the roe,
Ζωη μου, σας αγαπω.

By that lip I long to taste;
By that zone-encircled waist;
By all the token-flowers that tell
What words can never speak so well;
By love's alternate joy and woe,
Ζωη μου, σας αγαπω.

Maid of Athens! I am gone:
Think of me, sweet! when alone.   20
Though I fly to Istambol,
Athens holds my heart and soul;
Can I cease to love thee? No!
Ζωη μου, σας αγαπω.

1812

* My life, I love you.

SHE WALKS IN BEAUTY

She walks in beauty, like the night
  Of cloudless climes and starry skies;
And all that's best of dark and bright
  Meet in her aspect and her eyes:
Thus mellow'd to that tender light
  Which heaven to gaudy day denies.

One shade the more, one ray the less,
  Had half impair'd the nameless grace
Which waves in every raven tress,
  Or softly lightens o'er her face;   10
Where thoughts serenely sweet express
  How pure, how dear their dwelling-place.

And on that cheek, and o'er that brow,
  So soft, so calm, yet eloquent,
The smiles that win, the tints that glow,
  But tell of days in goodness spent,
A mind at peace with all below,
  A heart whose love is innocent!

1815

SONNET ON CHILLON

Eternal Spirit of the chainless Mind!
Brightest in dungeons, Liberty! thou art,
For there thy habitation is the heart—
The heart which love of thee alone can bind;
And when thy sons to fetters are consigned—
To fetters, and the damp vault's dayless gloom,
Their country conquers with their martyrdom,
And Freedom's fame finds wings on every wind.
Chillon! thy prison is a holy place,

And thy sad floor an altar—for 'twas trod,   10
Until his very steps have left a trace
Worn, as if thy cold pavement were a sod,
By Bonnivard! May none those marks efface!
For they appeal from tyranny to God.

1816

TO THOMAS MOORE *

My boat is on the shore,
   And my bark is on the sea;
But, before I go, Tom Moore,
   Here's a double health to thee!

Here's a sigh to those who love me,
   And a smile to those who hate;
And, whatever sky's above me,
   Here's a heart for every fate.

Though the ocean roar around me,
   Yet it still shall bear me on;   10
Though a desert should surround me,
   It hath springs that may be won.

Were't the last drop in the well,
   As I gasped upon the brink,
Ere my fainting spirit fell,
   'Tis to thee that I would drink.

With that water, as this wine,
   The libation I would pour
Should be—peace with thine and mine,
   And a health to thee, Tom Moore.

1821

* Begun in 1816, when Byron left England for the last time.

From DON JUAN

Canto III

.   .   .   .

The isles of Greece, the isles of Greece!
   Where burning Sappho loved and sung,
Where grew the arts of war and peace,—
   Where Delos rose, and Phoebus sprung!
Eternal summer gilds them yet,
But all, except their sun, is set.

The Scian and the Teian muse,
   The hero's harp, the lover's lute,
Have found the fame your shores refuse:
   Their place of birth alone is mute   10
To sounds which echo further west
Than your sires' "Islands of the Blest."

The mountains look on Marathon—
   And Marathon looks on the sea;
And musing there an hour alone,
   I dreamed that Greece might still be free;
For standing on the Persian's grave,
I could not deem myself a slave.

A king sate on the rocky brow
   Which looks o'er sea-born Salamis;   20
And ships, by thousands, lay below,
   And men in nations;—all were his!
He counted them at break of day—
And when the sun set, where were they?

And where are they? and where art thou,
   My country? On thy voiceless shore
The heroic lay is tuneless now—
   The heroic bosom beats no more!

And must thy lyre, so long divine,
Degenerate into hands like mine?   30

'Tis something, in the dearth of fame,
    Though linked among a fettered race,
To feel at least a patriot's shame,
    Even as I sing, suffuse my face;
For what is left the poet here?
For Greeks a blush—for Greece a tear.

Must *we* but weep o'er days more blest?
    Must *we* but blush?—Our fathers bled.
Earth! render back from out thy breast
    A remnant of our Spartan dead!   40
Of the three hundred grant but three,
To make a new Thermopylae!

What, silent still? and silent all?
    Ah! no;—the voices of the dead
Sound like a distant torrent's fall,
    And answer, "Let one living head,
But one arise,—we come, we come!"
'Tis but the living who are dumb.

In vain—in vain: strike other chords:
    Fill high the cup with Samian wine!   50
Leave battles to the Turkish hordes,
    And shed the blood of Scio's vine!
Hark! rising to the ignoble call—
How answers each bold Bacchanal!

You have the Pyrrhic dance as yet:
    Where is the Pyrrhic phalanx gone?
Of two such lessons, why forget
    The nobler and the manlier one?
You have the letters Cadmus gave—
Think ye he meant them for a slave?   60

Fill high the bowl with Samian wine!
  We will not think of themes like these!
It made Anacreon's song divine;
  He served—but served Polycrates—
A tyrant; but our masters then
Were still, at least, our countrymen.

The tyrant of the Chersonese
  Was freedom's best and bravest friend;
That tyrant was Miltiades!
  Oh! that the present hour would lend   70
Another despot of the kind!
Such chains as his were sure to bind.

Fill high the bowl with Samian wine!
  On Suli's rock, and Parga's shore,
Exists the remnant of a line
  Such as the Doric mothers bore;
And there, perhaps, some seed is sown,
The Heracleidan blood might own.

Trust not for freedom to the Franks,
  They have a king who buys and sells;   80
In native swords and native ranks,
  The only hope of courage dwells:
But Turkish force and Latin fraud
Would break your shield, however broad.

Fill high the bowl with Samian wine!
  Our virgins dance beneath the shade—
I see their glorious black eyes shine;
  But gazing on each glowing maid,
My own the burning tear-drop laves,
To think such breasts must suckle slaves.   90

Place me on Sunium's marbled steep,
  Where nothing, save the waves and I,

May hear our mutual murmurs sweep;
   There, swan-like, let me sing and die:
A land of slaves shall ne'er be mine—
Dash down yon cup of Samian wine!

Thus sung, or would, or could, or should have sung,
   The modern Greek, in tolerable verse:
If not like Orpheus quite, when Greece was young,
   Yet in these times he might have done much worse: 100
His strain displayed some feeling—right or wrong;
   And feeling, in a poet, is the source
Of others' feeling; but they are such liars,
And take all colours—like the hands of dyers.

But words are things, and a small drop of ink,
   Falling like dew, upon a thought, produces
That which makes thousands, perhaps millions, think;
   'Tis strange, the shortest letter which man uses
Instead of speech, may form a lasting link
   Of ages; to what straits old Time reduces   110
Frail man when paper—even a rag like this,
Survives himself, his tomb, and all that's his!

And when his bones are dust, his grave a blank,
   His station, generation, even his nation,
Become a thing, or nothing, save to rank
   In chronological commemoration,
Some dull MS. oblivion long has sank.
   Or graven stone found in a barrack's station
In digging the foundation of a closet,
May turn his name up, as a rare deposit.   120

And glory long has made the sages smile;
   'Tis something, nothing, words, illusion, wind—
Depending more upon the historian's style
   Than on the name a person leaves behind:

Troy owes to Homer what whist owes to Hoyle:
    The present century was growing blind
To the great Marlborough's skill in giving knocks,
Until his late Life by Archdeacon Coxe.

Milton's the prince of poets—so we say;
    A little heavy, but no less divine: 130
An independent being in his day—
    Learned, pious, temperate in love and wine;
But his life falling into Johnson's way,
    We're told this great high priest of all the Nine
Was whipt at college—a harsh sire—odd spouse,
For the first Mrs. Milton left his house.

All these are, *certes*, entertaining facts,
    Like Shakspere's stealing deer, Lord Bacon's bribes;
Like Titus' youth, and Caesar's earliest acts;
    Like Burns (whom Doctor Currie well describes);   140
Like Cromwell's pranks:—But although truth exacts
    These amiable descriptions from the scribes,
As most essential to their hero's story,
They do not much contribute to his glory.

All are not moralists, like Southey, when
    He prated to the world of "Pantisocracy:"
Or Wordsworth unexcised, unhired, who then
    Seasoned his peddler poems with democracy;
Or Coleridge, long before his flighty pen
    Let to the Morning Post its aristocracy;   150
When he and Southey, following the same path,
Espoused two partners (milliners of Bath).

Such names at present cut a convict figure,
    The very Botany Bay in moral geography:
Their royal treason, renegado rigor,
    Are good manure for their more bare biography.

Wordsworth's last quarto, by the way, is bigger
　　Than any since the birthday of typography:
A drowsy frowzy poem, called the "Excursion,"
Writ in a manner which is my aversion.　　　　　　160

　　.　　.　　.　　.　　.　　.　　.

T'our tale.—The feast was over, the slaves gone,
　　The dwarfs and dancing girls had all retired;
The Arab lore and poet's song were done,
　　And every sound of revelry expired;
The lady and her lover, left alone.
　　The rosy flood of twilight's sky admired:
Ave Maria! o'er the earth and sea,
That heavenliest hour of Heaven is worthiest thee!

Ave Maria! blessed be the hour!
　　The time, the clime, the spot, where I so oft　　170
Have felt that moment in its fullest power
　　Sink o'er the earth so beautiful and soft,
While swung the deep bell in the distant tower,
　　Or the faint dying day-hymn stole aloft,
And not a breath crept through the rosy air,
And yet the forest leaves seemed stirred with prayer.

Ave Maria! 'tis the hour of prayer!
　　Ave Maria! 'tis the hour of love!
Ave Maria! may our spirits dare
　　Look up to thine and to thy Son's above!　　180
Ave Maria! oh, that face so fair!
　　Those downcast eyes beneath the Almighty dove—
What though 'tis but a pictured image strike,
That painting is no idol,—'tis too like.

Some kinder casuists are pleased to say,
　　In nameless print—that I have no devotion;
But set those persons down with me to pray,
　　And you shall see who has the properest notion

Of getting into heaven the shortest way;
 My altars are the mountains and the ocean,   190
Earth, air, stars,—all that springs from the great Whole,
Who hath produced, and will receive the soul.

Sweet hour of twilight!—in the solitude
 Of the pine forest and the silent shore
Which bounds Ravenna's immemorial wood,
 Rooted where once the Adrian wave flowed o'er,
To where the last Caesarean fortress stood,
 Evergreen forest! which Boccaccio's lore
And Dryden's lay made haunted ground to me,
How have I loved the twilight hour and thee!   200

The shrill cicalas, people of the pine,
 Making their summer lives one ceaseless song,
Were the sole echoes, save my steed's and mine,
 And vesper bell's that rose the boughs along;
The specter huntsman of Onesti's line,
 His hell-dogs, and their chase, and the fair throng
Which learned from this example not to fly
From a true lover, shadowed my mind's eye.

O Hesperus! thou bringest all good things—
 Home to the weary, to the hungry cheer,   210
To the young bird the parent's brooding wings,
 The welcome stall to the o'erlaboured steer;
Whate'er of peace about our hearthstone clings,
 Whate'er our household gods protect of dear,
Are gathered round us by thy look of rest;
Thou bring'st the child, too, to the mother's breast.

Soft hour! which wakes the wish and melts the heart
 Of those who sail the seas, on the first day
When they from their sweet friends are torn apart;
 Or fills with love the pilgrim on his way   220

As the far bell of vesper makes him start,
  Seeming to weep the dying day's decay;
Is this a fancy which our reason scorns?
Ah! surely nothing dies but something mourns!

When Nero perished by the justest doom
  Which ever the destroyer yet destroyed,
Amidst the roar of liberated Rome,
  Of nations freed, and the world overjoyed,
Some hands unseen strewed flowers upon his tomb:
  Perhaps the weakness of a heart not void   230
Of feeling for some kindness done, when power
Had left the wretch an uncorrupted hour.

But I'm digressing; what on earth has Nero,
  Or any such like sovereign buffoons,
To do with the transactions of my hero,
  More than such madmen's fellow man—the moon's?
Sure my invention must be down at zero;
  And I grown one of many "wooden spoons"
Of verse (the name with which we Cantabs please
To dub the last of honors in degrees).   240

    .   .   .   .

           1821

PERCY BYSSHE SHELLEY
(1792–1822)

HYMN TO INTELLECTUAL BEAUTY

The awful shadow of some unseen Power
  Floats though unseen amongst us—visiting
  This various world with as inconstant wing

As summer winds that creep from flower to flower—
Like moonbeams that behind some piny mountain shower,
 It visits with inconstant glance
 Each human heart and countenance;
Like hues and harmonies of evening—
 Like clouds in starlight widely spread—
 Like memory of music fled—   10
 Like aught that for its grace may be
Dear, and yet dearer for its mystery.

Spirit of Beauty, that dost consecrate
 With thine own hues all thou dost shine upon
 Of human thought or form—where art thou gone?
Why dost thou pass away and leave our state,
This dim vast vale of tears, vacant and desolate?
 Ask why the sunlight not forever
 Weaves rainbows o'er yon mountain river,
Why aught should fail and fade that once is shown, 20
 Why fear and dream and death and birth
 Cast on the daylight of this earth
 Such gloom—why man has such a scope
For love and hate, despondency and hope?

No voice from some sublimer world hath ever
 To sage or poet these responses given—
 Therefore the names of Daemon, Ghost, and Heaven,
Remain the records of their vain endeavor,
Frail spells—whose uttered charm might not avail to
  sever,
 From all we hear and all we see,   30
 Doubt, chance, and mutability.
Thy light alone—like mist o'er mountains driven,
 Or music by the night wind sent,
 Through strings of some still instrument,
 Or moonlight on a midnight stream,
Gives grace and truth to life's unquiet dream.

Love, Hope, and Self-Esteem, like clouds depart
  And come, for some uncertain moments lent,
  Man were immortal, and omnipotent,
Didst thou, unknown and awful as thou art,   40
Keep with thy glorious train firm state within his heart.
    Thou messenger of sympathies,
    That wax and wane in lovers' eyes—
Thou—that to human thought art nourishment,
    Like darkness to a dying flame!
    Depart not as thy shadow came,
    Depart not—lest the grave should be,
Like life and fear, a dark reality.

While yet a boy I sought for ghosts, and sped
  Through many a listening chamber, cave and ruin,   50
  And starlight wood, with fearful steps pursuing
Hopes of high talk with the departed dead.
I called on poisonous names with which our youth is fed;
    I was not heard—I saw them not—
    When musing deeply on the lot
Of life, at the sweet time when winds are wooing
    All vital things that wake to bring
    News of birds and blossoming—
    Sudden, thy shadow fell on me;
I shrieked, and clasped my hands in ecstasy!   60

I vowed that I would dedicate my powers
  To thee and thine—have I not kept the vow?
  With beating heart and streaming eyes, even now
I call the phantoms of a thousand hours
Each from his voiceless grave; they have in visioned
        bowers
    Of studious zeal or love's delight
    Outwatched with me the envious night—
They know that never joy illumed my brow
    Unlinked with hope that thou wouldst free

   This world from its dark slavery,   70
    That thou—O awful Loveliness,
Wouldst give whate'er these words cannot express.

The day becomes more solemn and serene
   When noon is past—there is a harmony
   In autumn, and a luster in its sky,
Which through the summer is not heard or seen,
As if it could not be, as if it had not been!
    Thus let thy power, which like the truth
    Of nature on my passive youth
Descended, to my onward life supply   80
    Its calm—to one who worships thee,
    And every form containing thee,
    Whom, Spirit fair, thy spells did bind
To fear himself, and love all human kind.

                    1817

OZYMANDIAS

I met a traveler from an antique land
Who said: Two vast and trunkless legs of stone
Stand in the desert. Near them, on the sand,
Half sunk, a shattered visage lies, whose frown,
And wrinkled lip, and sneer of cold command,
Tell that its sculptor well those passions read
Which yet survive, stamped on these lifeless things,
The hand that mocked them and the heart that fed.
And on the pedestal these words appear:
"My name is Ozymandias, king of kings;   10
Look on my works, ye Mighty, and despair!"
Nothing beside remains. Round the decay
Of that colossal wreck, boundless and bare
The lone and level sands stretch far away.

                    1818

THE CLOUD

I bring fresh showers for the thirsting flowers,
    From the seas and the streams;
I bear light shade for the leaves when laid
    In their noonday dreams.
From my wings are shaken the dews that waken
    The sweet buds every one,
When rocked to rest on their mother's breast,
    As she dances about the sun.
I wield the flail of the lashing hail,
    And whiten the green plains under,   10
And then again I dissolve it in rain,
    And laugh as I pass in thunder.

I sift the snow on the mountains below,
    And their great pines groan aghast;
And all the night 'tis my pillow white,
    While I sleep in the arms of the blast.
Sublime on the towers of my skyey bowers,
    Lightning my pilot sits;
In a cavern under is fettered the thunder;
    It struggles and howls at fits.   20
Over earth and ocean, with gentle motion,
    This pilot is guiding me,
Lured by the love of the genii that move
    In the depths of the purple sea;
Over the rills, and the crags, and the hills,
    Over the lakes and the plains,
Wherever he dream, under mountain or stream,
    The Spirit he loves remains;
And I all the while bask in heaven's blue smile,
    Whilst he is dissolving in rains.   30

The sanguine sunrise, with his meteor eyes,
    And his burning plumes outspread,

Leaps on the back of my sailing rack,
    When the morning star shines dead,
As on the jag of a mountain crag,
    Which an earthquake rocks and swings,
An eagle alit one moment may sit
    In the light of its golden wings.
And when sunset may breathe, from the lit sea beneath,
    Its ardors of rest and of love,   40
And the crimson pall of eve may fall
    From the depth of heaven above,
With wings folded I rest, on mine airy nest,
    As still as a brooding dove.

That orbéd maiden, with white fire laden,
    Whom mortals call the moon,
Glides glimmering o'er my fleece-like floor,
    By the midnight breezes strewn;
And wherever the beat of her unseen feet,
    Which only the angels hear,   50
May have broken the woof of my tent's thin roof,
    The stars peep behind her and peer;
And I laugh to see them whirl and flee,
    Like a swarm of golden bees,
When I widen the rent in my wind-built tent,
    Till the calm rivers, lakes, and seas,
Like strips of the sky fallen through me on high,
    Are each paved with the moon and these.

I bind the sun's throne with a burning zone,
    And the moon's with a girdle of pearl;   60
The volcanoes are dim, and the stars reel and swim,
    When the whirlwinds my banner unfurl.
From cape to cape, with a bridge-like shape,
    Over a torrent sea,
Sunbeam-proof, I hang like a roof,
    The mountains its columns be.

The triumphal arch through which I march
    With hurricane, fire, and snow,
When the powers of the air are chained to my chair,
    Is the million-coloured bow;   70
The sphere-fire above its soft colours wove,
    While the moist earth was laughing below.

I am the daughter of earth and water,
    And the nursling of the sky;
I pass through the pores of the ocean and shores;
    I change, but I cannot die.
For after the rain when, with never a stain,
    The pavilion of heaven is bare,
And the winds and sunbeams with their convex gleams
    Build up the blue dome of air,   80
I silently laugh at my own cenotaph,
    And out of the caverns of rain,
Like a child from the womb, like a ghost from the tomb,
    I arise and unbuild it again.

        1820

TO A SKY-LARK

    Hail to thee, blithe spirit!
      Bird thou never wert,
    That from heaven, or near it,
      Pourest thy full heart
In profuse strains of unpremeditated art.

    Higher still and higher
      From the earth thou springest
    Like a cloud of fire;
      The blue deep thou wingest,
And singing still dost soar, and soaring ever singest. 10

In the golden lightning
   Of the sunken sun,
O'er which clouds are bright'ning,
   Thou dost float and run;
Like an unbodied joy whose race is just begun.

The pale purple even
   Melts around thy flight;
Like a star of heaven
   In the broad daylight
Thou art unseen, but yet I hear thy shrill delight,   20

Keen as are the arrows
   Of that silver sphere,
Whose intense lamp narrows
   In the white dawn clear,
Until we hardly see, we feel that it is there.

All the earth and air
   With thy voice is loud,
As, when night is bare,
   From one lonely cloud   29
The moon rains out her beams, and heaven is overflowed.

What thou art we know not;
   What is most like thee?
From rainbow clouds there flow not
   Drops so bright to see
As from thy presence showers a rain of melody.

 Like a poet hidden
   In the light of thought,
Singing hymns unbidden,
   Till the world is wrought
To sympathy with hopes and fears it heeded not;   40

Like a high-born maiden
    In a palace tower,
Soothing her love-laden
    Soul in secret hour
With music sweet as love, which overflows her bower;

Like a glowworm golden
    In a dell of dew,
Scattering unbeholden
    Its aërial hue   49
Among the flowers and grass which screen it from the view;

Like a rose embowered
    In its own green leaves,
By warm winds deflowered,
    Till the scent it gives
Makes faint with too much sweet those heavy-wingéd
        thieves.

Sound of vernal showers
    On the twinkling grass,
Rain-awakened flowers,
    All that ever was
Joyous, and clear, and fresh, thy music doth surpass.   60

Teach us, sprite or bird,
    What sweet thoughts are thine;
I have never heard
    Praise of love or wine
That panted forth a flood of rapture so divine:

Chorus Hymeneal,
    Or triumphal chaunt,
Matched with thine, would be all
    But an empty vaunt,
A thing wherein we feel there is some hidden want.   70

What objects are the fountains
　　Of thy happy strain?
What fields, or waves, or mountains?
　　What shapes of sky or plain?
What love of thine own kind? what ignorance of pain?

With thy clear keen joyance
　　Languor cannot be—
Shadow of annoyance
　　Never came near thee:　ᶫ
Thou lovest—but ne'er knew love's sad satiety.　　　　80

Waking or asleep,
　　Thou of death must deem
Things more true and deep
　　Than we mortals dream,
Or how could thy notes flow in such a crystal stream?

We look before and after
　　And pine for what is not;
Our sincerest laughter
　　With some pain is fraught;
Our sweetest songs are those that tell of saddest thought. 90

Yet if we could scorn
　　Hate, and pride, and fear;
If we were things born
　　Not to shed a tear,
I know not how thy joy we ever should come near.

Better than all measures
　　Of delightful sound—
Better than all treasures
　　That in books are found—
Thy skill to poet were, thou scorner of the ground!　　100

> Teach me half the gladness
>   That thy brain must know,
> Such harmonious madness
>   From my lips would flow,
> The world should listen then—as I am listening now.

1820

ODE TO THE WEST WIND

I

O wild West Wind, thou breath of Autumn's being,
Thou, from whose unseen presence the leaves dead
Are driven, like ghosts from an enchanter fleeing,

Yellow, and black, and pale, and hectic red,
Pestilence-stricken multitudes; O thou,
Who chariotest to their dark wintry bed

The wingéd seeds, where they lie cold and low,
Each like a corpse within its grave, until
Thine azure sister of the Spring shall blow

Her clarion o'er the dreaming earth, and fill   10
(Driving sweet buds like flocks to feed in air)
With living hues and odours plain and hill—

Wild Spirit, which art moving everywhere;
Destroyer and preserver—hear, oh, hear!

II

Thou on whose stream, 'mid the steep sky's commotion,
Loose clouds like earth's decaying leaves are shed,
Shook from the tangled boughs of heaven and ocean,

Angels of rain and lightning—there are spread
On the blue surface of thine airy surge,
Like the bright hair uplifted from the head   20

Of some fierce Maenad, even from the dim verge
Of the horizon to the zenith's height
The locks of the approaching storm. Thou dirge

Of the dying year, to which this closing night
Will be the dome of a vast sepulcher,
Vaulted with all thy congregated might

Of vapors, from whose solid atmosphere
Black rain, and fire, and hail will burst—oh, hear!

III

Thou who didst waken from his summer dreams
The blue Mediterranean, where he lay,   30
Lulled by the coil of his crystalline streams,

Beside a pumice isle in Baiae's bay,
And saw in sleep old palaces and towers
Quivering within the wave's intenser day,

All overgrown with azure moss and flowers
So sweet the sense faints picturing them! Thou
For whose path the Atlantic's level powers

Cleave themselves into chasms, while far below
The sea-blooms and the oozy woods which wear
The sapless foliage of the ocean, know   40

Thy voice, and suddenly grow gray with fear,
And tremble and despoil themselves—oh, hear!

IV

If I were a dead leaf thou mightest bear;
If I were a swift cloud to fly with thee;
A wave to pant beneath thy power, and share

The impulse of thy strength, only less free
Than thou, O uncontrollable! If even
I were as in my boyhood, and could be

The comrade of thy wanderings over heaven,
As then, when to outstrip thy skyey speed   50
Scarce seemed a vision; I would ne'er have striven

As thus with thee in prayer in my sore need.
Oh! lift me as a wave, a leaf, a cloud!
I fall upon the thorns of life! I bleed!

A heavy weight of hours has chained and bowed
One too like thee: tameless, and swift, and proud.

V

Make me thy lyre, even as the forest is;
What if my leaves are falling like its own!
The tumult of thy mighty harmonies

Will take from both a deep, autumnal tone,   60
Sweet though in sadness. Be thou, spirit fierce,   .
My spirit! Be thou me, impetuous one!

Drive my dead thoughts over the universe
Like withered leaves to quicken a new birth!
And, by the incantation of this verse,

Scatter, as from an unextinguished hearth
Ashes and sparks, my words among mankind!
Be through my lips to unawakened earth

The trumpet of a prophecy! O Wind,
If Winter comes, can Spring be far behind?

1820

ADONAIS

I weep for Adonais—he is dead!
Oh, weep for Adonais! though our tears
Thaw not the frost which binds so dear a head!
And thou, sad Hour, selected from all years
To mourn our loss, rouse thy obscure compeers,
And teach them thine own sorrow! Say: "With me
Died Adonais; till the Future dares
Forget the Past, his fate and fame shall be
An echo and a light unto eternity."

Where wert thou, mighty Mother, when he lay,   10
When thy son lay, pierced by the shaft which flies
In darkness? Where was lorn Urania
When Adonais died? With veiléd eyes,
'Mid listening Echoes, in her Paradise
She sate, while one, with soft enamored breath,
Rekindled all the fading melodies,
With which, like flowers that mock the corse beneath,
He had adorned and hid the coming bulk of death.

Oh, weep for Adonais—he is dead!
Wake, melancholy Mother, wake and weep!   20
Yet wherefore? Quench within their burning bed
Thy fiery tears, and let thy loud heart keep,
Like his, a mute and uncomplaining sleep;
For he is gone, where all things wise and fair
Descend—oh, dream not that the amorous Deep
Will yet restore him to the vital air;
Death feeds on his mute voice, and laughs at our despair.

Most musical of mourners, weep again!
Lament anew, Urania!—He died—
Who was the Sire of an immortal strain,   30
Blind, old, and lonely, when his country's pride,

The priest, the slave, and the liberticide,
Trampled and mocked with many a loathèd rite
Of lust and blood; he went, unterrified,
Into the gulf of death; but his clear Sprite
Yet reigns o'er earth—the third among the sons of light.

Most musical of mourners, weep anew!
Not all to that bright station dared to climb;
And happier they their happiness who knew,
Whose tapers yet burn through that night of time   40
In which suns perished; others more sublime,
Struck by the envious wrath of man or God,
Have sunk, extinct in their refulgent prime;
And some yet live, treading the thorny road,
Which leads, through toil and hate, to Fame's serene abode.

But now, thy youngest, dearest one has perished,
The nursling of thy widowhood, who grew,
Like a pale flower by some sad maiden cherished,
And fed with true-love tears, instead of dew;
Most musical of mourners, weep anew!   50
Thy extreme hope, the loveliest and the last,
The bloom, whose petals, nipped before they blew,
Died on the promise of the fruit, is waste;
The broken lily lies—the storm is overpast.

To that high Capital, where kingly Death
Keeps his pale court in beauty and decay,
He came; and bought, with price of purest breath,
A grave among the eternal.—Come away!
Haste, while the vault of blue Italian day
Is yet his fitting charnel-roof! while still   60
He lies, as if in dewy sleep he lay;
Awake him not! surely he takes his fill
Of deep and liquid rest, forgetful of all ill.

He will awake no more, oh, never more!—
Within the twilight chamber spreads apace

The shadow of white Death, and at the door
Invisible Corruption waits to trace
His extreme way to her dim dwelling-place;
The eternal Hunger sits, but pity and awe
Soothe her pale rage, nor dares she to deface   70
So fair a prey, till darkness and the law
Of change shall o'er his sleep the mortal curtain draw.

Oh, weep for Adonais!—The quick Dreams,
The passion-wingéd Ministers of thought,
Who were his flocks, whom near the living streams
Of his young spirit he fed, and whom he taught
The love which was its music, wander not—
Wander no more, from kindling brain to brain,
But droop there, whence they sprung; and mourn their lot
Round the cold heart, where, after their sweet pain, 80
They ne'er will gather strength, or find a home again.

And one with trembling hands clasps his cold head,
And fans him with her moonlight wings, and cries:
"Our love, our hope, our sorrow, is not dead;
See, on the silken fringe of his faint eyes,
Like dew upon a sleeping flower, there lies
A tear some Dream has loosened from his brain."
Lost Angel of a ruined Paradise!
She knew not 'twas her own; as with no stain
She faded, like a cloud which had outwept its rain.   90

One from a lucid urn of starry dew
Washed his light limbs as if embalming them;
Another clipped her profuse locks, and threw
The wreath upon him, like an anadem,
Which frozen tears instead of pearls begem;
Another in her willful grief would break
Her bow and wingéd reeds, as if to stem
A greater loss with one which was more weak;
And dull the barbéd fire against his frozen cheek.

Another Splendor on his mouth alit,   100
That mouth, whence it was wont to draw the breath
Which gave it strength to pierce the guarded wit,
And pass into the panting heart beneath
With lightning and with music; the damp death
Quenched its caress upon his icy lips;
And, as a dying meteor stains a wreath
Of moonlight vapor, which the cold night clips,
It flushed through his pale limbs, and passed to its eclipse.

And others came—Desires and Adorations,
Wingéd Persuasions and veiled Destinies,   110
Splendors, and Glooms, and glimmering Incarnations
Of hopes and fears, and twilight Phantasies;
And Sorrow, with her family of Sighs,
And Pleasure, blind with tears, led by the gleam
Of her own dying smile instead of eyes,
Came in slow pomp—the moving pomp might seem
Like pageantry of mist on an autumnal stream.

All he had loved, and moulded into thought
From shape, and hue, and odour, and sweet sound,
Lamented Adonais. Morning sought   120
Her eastern watchtower, and her hair unbound,
Wet with the tears which should adorn the ground,
Dimmed the aërial eyes that kindle day;
Afar the melancholy thunder moaned,
Pale Ocean in unquiet slumber lay,
And the wild winds flew round, sobbing in their dismay.

Lost Echo sits amid the voiceless mountains,
And feeds her grief with his remembered lay,
And will no more reply to winds or fountains,
Or amorous birds perched on the young green spray,
Or herdsman's horn, or bell at closing day;   131
Since she can mimic not his lips, more dear

Than those for whose disdain she pined away
Into a shadow of all sounds—a drear
Murmur, between their songs, is all the woodmen hear.

Grief made the young Spring wild, and she threw down
Her kindling buds, as if she Autumn were,
Or they dead leaves; since her delight is flown,
For whom should she have waked the sullen year?
To Phoebus was not Hyacinth so dear   140
Nor to himself Narcissus, as to both
Thou, Adonais. Wan they stand and sear
Amid the faint companions of their youth,
With dew all turned to tears; odour, to sighing ruth.

Thy spirit's sister, the lorn nightingale,
Mourns not her mate with such melodious pain;
Not so the eagle, who like thee could scale
Heaven, and could nourish in the sun's domain
Her mighty youth with morning, doth complain,
Soaring and screaming round her empty nest,   150
As Albion wails for thee. The curse of Cain
Light on his head who pierced thy innocent breast,
And scared the angel soul that was its earthly guest!

Ah, woe is me! Winter is come and gone,
But grief returns with the revolving year;
The airs and streams renew their joyous tone;
The ants, the bees, the swallows reappear;
Fresh leaves and flowers deck the dead Seasons' bier;
The amorous birds now pair in every brake,
And build their mossy homes in field and brere;   160
And the green lizard, and the golden snake,
Like unimprisoned flames, out of their trance awake.

Through wood and stream and field and hill and ocean
A quickening life from the earth's heart has burst,
As it has ever done, with change and motion

From the great morning of the world when first
God dawned on Chaos; in its stream immersed
The lamps of heaven flash with a softer light;
All baser things pant with life's sacred thirst,
Diffuse themselves, and spend in love's delight   170
The beauty and the joy of their renewéd might.

The leprous corpse, touched by this spirit tender
Exhales itself in flowers of gentle breath;
Like incarnations of the stars, when splendor
Is changed to fragrance, they illumine death
And mock the merry worm that wakes beneath;
Naught we know, dies. Shall that alone which knows
Be as a sword consumed before the sheath
By sightless lightning?—th' intense atom glows
A moment, then is quenched in a most cold repose.   180

Alas! that all we loved of him should be,
But for our grief, as if it had not been,
And grief itself be mortal! Woe is me!
Whence are we, and why are we? Of what scene
The actors or spectators? Great and mean
Meet massed in death, who lends what life must borrow.
As long as skies are blue, and fields are green,
Evening must usher night, night urge the morrow,
Month follow month with woe, and year wake year to
     sorrow.

He will awake no more, oh, never more!   190
"Wake thou," cried Misery, "childless Mother, rise
Out of thy sleep, and slake, in thy heart's core,
A wound more fierce than his with tears and sighs."
And all the Dreams that watched Urania's eyes,
And all the Echoes whom their sister's song
Had held in holy silence, cried: "Arise!"
Swift as a Thought by the snake Memory stung,
From her ambrosial rest the fading Splendor sprung.

She rose like an autumnal Night, that springs
Out of the East, and follows wild and drear 200
The golden Day, which, on eternal wings,
Even as a ghost abandoning a bier,
Had left the earth a corpse. Sorrow and fear
So struck, so roused, so rapt Urania;
So saddened round her like an atmosphere
Of stormy mist; so swept her on her way
Even to the mournful place where Adonais lay.

Out of her secret Paradise she sped,
Through camps and cities rough with stone, and steel,
And human hearts, which to her aëry tread 210
Yielding not, wounded the invisible
Palms of her tender feet where'er they fell;
And barbéd tongues, and thoughts more sharp than they,
Rent the soft Form they never could repel,
Whose sacred blood, like the young tears of May,
Paved with eternal flowers that undeserving way.

In the death chamber for a moment Death,
Shamed by the presence of that living Might,
Blushed to annihilation, and the breath
Revisited those lips, and life's pale light 220
Flashed through those limbs, so late her dear delight.
"Leave me not wild and drear and comfortless,
As silent lightning leaves the starless night!
Leave me not!" cried Urania. Her distress
Roused Death; Death rose and smiled, and met her vain
    caress.

"Stay yet awhile! speak to me once again;
Kiss me, so long but as a kiss may live;
And in my heartless breast and burning brain
That word, that kiss shall all thoughts else survive,
With food of saddest memory kept alive, 230
Now thou art dead, as if it were a part

Of thee, my Adonais! I would give
All that I am to be as thou now art!
But I am chained to Time, and cannot thence depart!

"O gentle child, beautiful as thou wert,
Why didst thou leave the trodden paths of men
Too soon, and with weak hands though mighty heart
Dare the unpastured dragon in his den?
Defenseless as thou wert, oh, where was then
Wisdom the mirrored shield, or scorn the spear?   240
Or hadst thou waited the full cycle, when
Thy spirit should have filled its crescent sphere,
The monsters of life's waste had fled from thee like deer.

"The herded wolves, bold only to pursue;
The obscene ravens, clamorous o'er the dead;
The vultures to the conqueror's banner true,
Who feed where Desolation first has fed,
And whose wings rain contagion—how they fled,
When like Apollo, from his golden bow,
The Pythian of the age one arrow sped   250
And smiled!—The spoilers tempt no second blow;
They fawn on the proud feet that spurn them lying low.

"The sun comes forth, and many reptiles spawn;
He sets, and each ephemeral insect then
Is gathered into death without a dawn,
And the immortal stars awake again;
So is it in the world of living men:
A godlike mind soars forth, in its delight
Making earth bare and veiling heaven, and when
It sinks, the swarms that dimmed or shared its light
Leave to its kindred lamps the spirit's awful night."   261

Thus ceased she; and the mountain shepherds came,
Their garlands sear, their magic mantles rent;
The Pilgrim of Eternity, whose fame

Over his living head like heaven is bent,
An early but enduring monument,
Came, veiling all the lightnings of his song
In sorrow; from her wilds Ierne sent
The sweetest lyrist of her saddest wrong,
And love taught grief to fall like music from his tongue.

Midst others of less note, came one frail Form,   271
A phantom among men, companionless
As the last cloud of an expiring storm
Whose thunder is its knell; he, as I guess,
Had gazed on Nature's naked loveliness,
Actaeon-like, and now he fled astray
With feeble steps o'er the world's wilderness,
And his own thoughts, along that rugged way,
Pursued, like raging hounds, their father and their prey.

A pardlike Spirit beautiful and swift—   280
A Love in desolation masked—a Power
Girt round with weaknesses—it can scarce uplift
The weight of the superincumbent hour;
It is a dying lamp, a falling shower,
A breaking billow—even whilst we speak
Is it not broken? On the withering flower
The killing sun smiles brightly; on a cheek
The life can burn in blood, even while the heart may break.

His head was bound with pansies overblown,
And faded violets, white, and pied, and blue;   290
And a light spear topped with a cypress cone,
Round whose rude shaft dark ivy tresses grew
Yet dripping with the forest's noonday dew,
Vibrated, as the ever-beating heart
Shook the weak hand that grasped it; of that crew
He came the last, neglected and apart;
A herd-abandoned deer, struck by the hunter's dart.

All stood aloof, and at his partial moan
Smiled through their tears; well knew that gentle band
Who in another's fate now wept his own;   300
As, in the accents of an unknown land,
He sung new sorrow; sad Urania scanned
The Stranger's mien, and murmured, "Who art thou?"
He answered not, but with a sudden hand
Made bare his branded and ensanguined brow,
Which was like Cain's or Christ's—Oh! that it should be so!

What softer voice is hushed over the dead?
Athwart what brow is that dark mantle thrown?
What form leans sadly o'er the white deathbed,
In mockery of monumental stone,   310
The heavy heart heaving without a moan?
If it be He, who, gentlest of the wise,
Taught, soothed, loved, honoured the departed one,
Let me not vex with inharmonious sighs
The silence of that heart's accepted sacrifice.

Our Adonais has drunk poison—oh!
What deaf and viprous murderer could crown
Life's early cup with such a draft of woe?
The nameless worm would now itself disown.
It felt, yet could escape the magic tone   320
Whose prelude held all envy, hate, and wrong,
But what was howling in one breast alone,
Silent with expectation of the song,
Whose master's hand is cold, whose silver lyre unstrung.

Live thou, whose infamy is not thy fame!
Live! fear no heavier chastisement from me,
Thou noteless blot on a remembered name!
But be thyself, and know thyself to be!
And ever at thy season be thou free
To spill the venom when thy fangs o'erflow.   330

Remorse and self-contempt shall cling to thee;
Hot shame shall burn upon thy secret brow,
And like a beaten hound tremble thou shalt—as now.

Nor let us weep that our delight is fled
Far from these carrion kites that scream below;
He wakes or sleeps with the enduring dead;
Thou canst not soar where he is sitting now.—
Dust to the dust! but the pure spirit shall flow
Back to the burning fountain whence it came,
A portion of the Eternal, which must glow   340
Through time and change, unquenchably the same,
Whilst thy cold embers choke the sordid hearth of shame.

Peace, peace! he is not dead, he doth not sleep—
He hath awakened from the dream of life—
'Tis we who, lost in stormy visions, keep
With phantoms an unprofitable strife,
And in mad trance strike with our spirit's knife
Invulnerable nothings.—*We* decay
Like corpses in a charnel; fear and grief
Convulse us and consume us day by day,   350
And cold hopes swarm like worms within our living clay.

He has outsoared the shadow of our night;
Envy and calumny and hate and pain,
And that unrest which men miscall delight,
Can touch him not and torture not again;
From the contagion of the world's slow stain
He is secure, and now can never mourn
A heart grown cold, a head grown gray in vain;
Nor, when the spirit's self has ceased to burn,
With sparkless ashes load an unlamented urn.   360

He lives, he wakes—'tis Death is dead, not he;
Mourn not for Adonais.—Thou young Dawn,

Turn all thy dew to splendor, for from thee
The spirit thou lamentest is not gone;
Ye caverns and ye forests, cease to moan!
Cease, ye faint flowers and fountains, and thou Air,
Which like a mourning veil thy scarf hadst thrown
O'er the abandoned earth, now leave it bare
Even to the joyous stars which smile on its despair!

He is made one with Nature; there is heard   370
His voice in all her music, from the moan
Of thunder, to the song of night's sweet bird;
He is a presence to be felt and known
In darkness and in light, from herb and stone,
Spreading itself where'er that Power may move
Which has withdrawn his being to its own;
Which wields the world with never-wearied love,
Sustains it from beneath, and kindles it above.

He is a portion of the loveliness
Which once he made more lovely; he doth bear   380
His part, while the one Spirit's plastic stress
Sweeps through the dull, dense world, compelling there
All new successions to the forms they wear;
Torturing th' unwilling dross that checks its flight
To its own likeness, as each mass may bear;
And bursting in its beauty and its might
From trees and beasts and men into the heaven's light.

The splendors of the firmament of time
May be eclipsed, but are extinguished not;
Like stars to their appointed height they climb   390
And death is a low mist which cannot blot
The brightness it may veil. When lofty thought
Lifts a young heart above its mortal lair,
And love and life contend in it for what
Shall be its earthly doom, the dead live there
And move like winds of light on dark and stormy air.

The inheritors of unfulfilled renown
Rose from their thrones, built beyond mortal thought,
Far in the Unapparent. Chatterton
Rose pale; his solemn agony had not   400
Yet faded from him. Sidney, as he fought
And as he fell and as he lived and loved,
Sublimely mild, a Spirit without spot,
Arose. And Lucan, by his death approved—
Oblivion, as they rose, shrank like a thing reproved.

And many more, whose names on earth are dark
But whose transmitted effluence cannot die
So long as fire outlives the parent spark,
Rose, robed in dazzling immortality.
"Thou art become as one of us," they cry,   410
"It was for thee yon kingless sphere has long
Swung blind in unascended majesty,
Silent alone amid an Heaven of Song.
Assume thy wingéd throne, thou Vesper of our throng!"

Who mourns for Adonais? oh, come forth,
Fond wretch! and know thyself and him aright.
Clasp with thy panting soul the pendulous Earth;
As from a center, dart thy spirit's light
Beyond all worlds, until its spacious might
Satiate the void circumference. Then shrink   420
Even to a point within our day and night;
And keep thy heart light, lest it make thee sink,
When hope has kindled hope, and lured thee to the brink.

Or go to Rome, which is the sepulcher,
Oh, not of him, but of our joy; 'tis naught
That ages, empires, and religions there
Lie buried in the ravage they have wrought;
For such as he can lend—they borrow not
Glory from those who made the world their prey;

And he is gathered to the kings of thought   430
Who waged contention with their time's decay,
And of the past are all that cannot pass away.

Go thou to Rome—at once the Paradise,
The grave, the city, and the wilderness;
And where its wrecks like shattered mountains rise,
And flowering weeds and fragrant copses dress
The bones of Desolation's nakedness,
Pass, till the Spirit of the spot shall lead
Thy footsteps to a slope of green access
Where, like an infant's smile, over the dead,   440
A light of laughing flowers along the grass is spread.

And gray walls moulder round, on which dull Time
Feeds, like slow fire upon a hoary brand;
And one keen pyramid with wedge sublime,
Pavilioning the dust of him who planned
This refuge for his memory, doth stand
Like flame transformed to marble; and beneath,
A field is spread, on which a newer band
Have pitched in Heaven's smile their camp of death,
Welcoming him we lose with scarce extinguished breath.

Here pause. These graves are all too young as yet   451
To have outgrown the sorrow which consigned
Its charge to each; and if the seal is set,
Here, on one fountain of a mourning mind,
Break it not thou! too surely shalt thou find
Thine own well full, if thou returnest home,
Of tears and gall. From the world's bitter wind
Seek shelter in the shadow of the tomb.
What Adonais is, why fear we to become?

The One remains, the many change and pass;   460
Heaven's light forever shines, earth's shadows fly;
Life, like a dome of many-coloured glass,

Stains the white radiance of Eternity,
Until Death tramples it to fragments.—Die,
If thou wouldst be with that which thou dost seek!
Follow where all is fled!—Rome's azure sky,
Flowers, ruins, statues, music, words, are weak
The glory they transfuse with fitting truth to speak.

Why linger, why turn back, why shrink, my Heart?
Thy hopes are gone before; from all things here   470
They have departed; thou shouldst now depart!
A light is past from the revolving year,
And man, and woman; and what still is dear
Attracts to crush, repels to make thee wither.
The soft sky smiles—the low wind whispers near;
'Tis Adonais calls! oh, hasten thither,
No more let Life divide what Death can join together.

That Light whose smile kindles the universe,
That Beauty in which all things work and move,
That Benediction which the eclipsing Curse   480
Of birth can quench not, that sustaining Love
Which, through the web of being blindly wove
By man and beast and earth and air and sea,
Burns bright or dim, as each are mirrors of
The fire for which all thirst, now beams on me,
Consuming the last clouds of cold mortality.

The breath whose might I have invoked in song
Descends on me; my spirit's bark is driven,
Far from the shore, far from the trembling throng
Whose sails were never to the tempest given;   490
The massy earth and spheréd skies are riven!
I am borne darkly, fearfully, afar;
Whilst burning through the inmost veil of heaven,
The soul of Adonais, like a star,
Beacons from the abode where the Eternal are.

1821

THE INDIAN SERENADE

I arise from dreams of thee
In the first sweet sleep of night,
When the winds are breathing low,
And the stars are shining bright;
I arise from dreams of thee,
And a spirit in my feet
Hath led me—who knows how!
To thy chamber window, Sweet!

The wandering airs they faint
On the dark, the silent stream—   10
And the Champak odours fail
Like sweet thoughts in a dream;
The nightingale's complaint,
It dies upon her heart—
As I must on thine,
O! beloved as thou art!

Oh, lift me from the grass!
I die! I faint! I fail!
Let thy love in kisses rain
On my lips and eyelids pale.   20
My cheek is cold and white, alas!
My heart beats loud and fast—
Oh, press it to thine own again,
Where it will break at last!

1822

HELLAS

CHORUS

The world's great age begins anew,
   The golden years return,
The earth doth like a snake renew
   Her winter weeds outworn;

Heaven smiles, and faiths and empires gleam,
Like wrecks of a dissolving dream.

A brighter Hellas rears its mountains
   From waves serener far;
A new Peneus rolls his fountains
   Against the morning-star.   10
Where fairer Tempes bloom, there sleep
Young Cyclads on a sunnier deep.

A loftier Argo cleaves the main,
   Fraught with a later prize;
Another Orpheus sings again,
   And loves, and weeps, and dies.
A new Ulysses leaves once more
Calypso for his native shore.

Oh, write no more the tale of Troy,
   If earth Death's scroll must be!   20
Nor mix with Laian rage the joy
   Which dawns upon the free;
Although a subtler Sphinx renew
Riddles of death Thebes never knew.

Another Athens shall arise,
   And to remoter time
Bequeath, like sunset to the skies,
   The splendour of its prime;
And leave, if naught so bright may live,
All earth can take or Heaven can give.   30

Saturn and Love their long repose
   Shall burst, more bright and good
Than all who fell, than One who rose,
   Than many unsubdued;
Not gold, not blood, their altar dowers,
But votive tears and symbol flowers.

O cease! must hate and death return?
 Cease! must men kill and die?
Cease! drain not to its dregs the urn
 Of bitter prophecy.   40
The world is weary of the past,
O might it die or rest at last!

                                    1822

TO NIGHT

Swiftly walk over the western wave,
 Spirit of Night!
Out of the misty eastern cave—
Where, all the long and lone daylight,
Thou wovest dreams of joy and fear
Which make thee terrible and dear—
 Swift be thy flight!

Wrap thy form in a mantle gray,
 Star-inwrought!
Blind with thine hair the eyes of Day;   10
Kiss her until she be wearied out.
Then wander o'er city and sea and land,
Touching all with thine opiate wand—
 Come, long-sought!

When I arose and saw the dawn,
 I sighed for thee;
When light rode high, and the dew was gone,
And noon lay heavy on flower and tree,
And the weary Day turned to her rest,
Lingering like an unloved guest,   20
 I sighed for thee.

Thy brother Death came, and cried,
 "Wouldst thou me?"
Thy sweet child Sleep, the filmy-eyed,
Murmured like a noontide bee,

"Shall I nestle near thy side?
Wouldst thou me?"—And I replied,
   "No, not thee!"

Death will come when thou art dead,
      Soon, too soon—   30
Sleep will come when thou art fled.
Of neither would I ask the boon
I ask of thee, beloved Night—
Swift be thine approaching flight,
      Come soon, soon!

                                   1824

A LAMENT

O world! O life! O time!
On whose last steps I climb,
   Trembling at that where I had stood before;
When will return the glory of your prime?
      No more—oh, nevermore!

Out of the day and night
A joy has taken flight;
   Fresh spring, and summer, and winter hoar,
Move my faint heart with grief, but with delight
      No more—oh, nevermore!   10
                                   1824

TO ———

Music, when soft voices die,
Vibrates in the memory—
Odours, when sweet violets sicken,
Live within the sense they quicken,

Rose leaves, when the rose is dead,
Are heaped for the beloved's bed;
And so thy thoughts, when thou art gone,
Love itself shall slumber on.

1824

LINES

When the lamp is shattered,
The light in the dust lies dead—
  When the cloud is scattered,
The rainbow's glory is shed.
  When the lute is broken,
Sweet tones are remembered not;
  When the lips have spoken,
Loved accents are soon forgot.

  As music and splendour
Survive not the lamp and the lute,   10
  The heart's echoes render
No song when the spirit is mute—
  No song but sad dirges,
Like the wind through a ruined cell,
  Or the mournful surges
That ring the dead seaman's knell.

  When hearts have once mingled,
Love first leaves the well-built nest—
  The weak one is singled
To endure what it once possessed.   20
  O Love! who bewailest
The frailty of all things here,
  Why choose you the frailest
For your cradle, your home, and your bier?

  Its passions will rock thee
As the storms rock the ravens on high;
  Bright reason will mock thee,

Like the sun from a wintry sky.
    From thy nest every rafter
Will rot, and thine eagle home   30
    Leave thee naked to laughter,
When leaves fall and cold winds come.

                                        1824

JOHN KEATS (1795–1821)

ON FIRST LOOKING INTO
CHAPMAN'S HOMER

Much have I traveled in the realms of gold,
And many goodly states and kingdoms seen;
    Round many western islands have I been
Which bards in fealty to Apollo hold.
Oft of one wide expanse had I been told
    That deep-browed Homer ruled as his demesne;
    Yet did I never breathe its pure serene
Till I heard Chapman speak out loud and bold.
Then felt I like some watcher of the skies
When a new planet swims into his ken;   10
Or like stout Cortez, when with eagle eyes
    He stared at the Pacific—and all his men
Looked at each other with a wild surmise—
    Silent, upon a peak in Darien.

                                        1817

ON THE GRASSHOPPER AND CRICKET

The poetry of earth is never dead:
    When all the birds are faint with the hot sun,
    And hide in cooling trees, a voice will run
From hedge to hedge about the new-mown mead;

That is the Grasshopper's—he takes the lead
  In summer luxury,—he has never done
  With his delights, for when tired out with fun,
He rests at ease beneath some pleasant weed.
The poetry of earth is ceasing never:
  On a lone winter evening, when the frost   10
    Has wrought a silence, from the stove there shrills
The Cricket's song, in warmth increasing ever,
  And seems to one in drowsiness half lost,
    The Grasshopper's among some grassy hills.

1817

TO ONE WHO HAS BEEN LONG IN CITY PENT

To one who has been long in city pent,
  'Tis very sweet to look into the fair
  And open face of heaven,—to breathe a prayer
Full in the smile of the blue firmament.
Who is more happy, when, with heart's content,
  Fatigued he sinks into some pleasant lair
  Of wavy grass, and reads a debonair
And gentle tale of love and languishment?
Returning home at evening, with an ear
  Catching the notes of Philomel,—an eye   10
Watching the sailing cloudlet's bright career,
  He mourns that day so soon has glided by:
E'en like the passage of an angel's tear
  That falls through the clear ether silently.

1817

LA BELLE DAME SANS MERCI

"O what can ail thee, knight-at-arms,
  Alone and palely loitering?
The sedge has wither'd from the lake,
  And no birds sing.

"O what can ail thee, knight-at-arms!
    So haggard and so woe-begone?
The squirrel's granary is full,
    And the harvest's done.

"I see a lily on thy brow
    With anguish moist and fever-dew,   10
And on thy cheeks a fading rose
    Fast withereth too."

"I met a lady in the meads,
    Full beautiful—a faëry's child,
Her hair was long, her foot was light,
    And her eyes were wild.

"I made a garland for her head,
    And bracelets too, and fragrant zone;
She look'd at me as she did love,
    And made sweet moan.   20

"I set her on my pacing steed
    And nothing else saw all day long,
For sidelong would she bend, and sing
    A faëry's song.

"She found me roots of relish sweet,
    And honey wild and manna-dew,
And sure in language strange she said—
    'I love thee true.'

"She took me to her elfin grot,
    And there she wept and sigh'd full sore;   30
And there I shut her wild, wild eyes
    With kisses four.

"And there she lulléd me asleep,
    And there I dream'd—Ah! woe betide!
The latest dream I ever dream'd
    On the cold hill's side.

"I saw pale kings and princes too,
   Pale warriors, death-pale were they all:
They cried—'La Belle Dame sans Merci
   Hath thee in thrall!'   40

"I saw their starved lips in the gloam
   With horrid warning gapéd wide,
And I awoke and found me here
   On the cold hill's side.

"And this is why I sojourn here
   Alone and palely loitering,
Though the sedge is wither'd from the lake,
   And no birds sing."

   1820

LINES ON THE MERMAID TAVERN

Souls of Poets dead and gone,
What Elysium have ye known,
Happy field or mossy cavern,
Choicer than the Mermaid Tavern?
Have ye tippled drink more fine
Than mine host's Canary wine?
Or are fruits of Paradise
Sweeter than those dainty pies
Of venison? O generous food!
Dressed as though bold Robin Hood   10
Would, with his maid Marian,
Sup and bowse from horn and can.

   I have heard that on a day
Mine host's signboard flew away,
Nobody knew whither, till
An astrologer's old quill
To a sheepskin gave the story—
Said he saw you in your glory,

Underneath a new old sign
Sipping beverage divine,   20
And pledging with contented smack
The Mermaid in the Zodiac.

Souls of Poets dead and gone,
What Elysium have ye known,
Happy field or mossy cavern,
Choicer than the Mermaid Tavern?

1820

TO AUTUMN

Season of mist and mellow fruitfulness,
    Close bosom-friend of the maturing sun;
Conspiring with him how to load and bless
    With fruit the vines that round the thatch-eves run;
To bend with apples the mossed cottage-trees,
    And fill all fruit with ripeness to the core;
        To swell the gourd, and plump the hazel shells
With a sweet kernel; to set budding more,
    And still more, later flowers for the bees,
    Until they think warm days will never cease,   10
        For summer has o'er-brimmed their clammy cells.

Who hath not seen thee oft amid thy store?
    Sometimes whoever seeks abroad may find
Thee sitting careless on a granary floor,
    Thy hair soft-lifted by the winnowing wind;
Or on a half-reaped furrow sound asleep,
    Drowsed with the fume of poppies, while thy hook
        Spares the next swath and all its twinéd flowers;
And sometimes like a gleaner thou dost keep
    Steady thy laden head across a brook;   20
    Or by a cider-press, with patient look,
        Thou watchest the last oozings hours by hours.

Where are the songs of spring? Aye, where are they?
    Think not of them, thou hast thy music too—
While barréd clouds bloom the soft-dying day,
    And touch the stubble-plains with rosy hue;
Then in a wailful choir the small gnats mourn
      Among the river sallows, borne aloft
        Or sinking as the light wind lives or dies;
And full-grown lambs loud bleat from hilly bourn;   30
      Hedge-crickets sing; and now with treble soft
      The redbreast whistles from a garden-croft;
        And gathering swallows twitter in the skies.

                                    1820

ODE ON MELANCHOLY

No, no, go not to Lethe, neither twist
    Wolf's-bane, tight-rooted, for its poisonous wine;
Nor suffer thy pale forehead to be kissed
    By nightshade, ruby grape of Proserpine;
Make not your rosary of yew-berries,
      Nor let the beetle, nor the death-moth be
        Your mournful Psyche, nor the downy owl
A partner in your sorrow's mysteries;
      For shade to shade will come too drowsily,
        And drown the wakeful anguish of the soul.   10

But when the melancholy fit shall fall
    Sudden from heaven like a weeping cloud,
That fosters the droop-headed flowers all,
    And hides the green hills in an April shroud,
Then glut thy sorrow on a morning rose,
      Or on the rainbow of the salt sand-wave,
        Or on the wealth of globéd peonies.
Or if thy mistress some rich anger shows,
      Emprison her soft hand, and let her rave,
        And feed deep, deep upon her peerless eyes.   20

She dwells with Beauty—Beauty that must die;
　And Joy, whose hand is ever at his lips,
Bidding adieu; and aching Pleasure nigh,
　Turning to poison while the bee mouth sips.
Aye, in the very temple of Delight
　Veiled Melancholy has her sovran shrine,
　　Though seen of none save him whose strenuous tongue
Can burst Joy's grape against his palate fine.
　His soul shall taste the sadness of her might,
　And be among her cloudy trophies hung.   30
                                              1820

ODE ON A GRECIAN URN

Thou still unravished bride of quietness,
　Thou foster-child of silence and slow time,
Silvan historian, who canst thus express
　A flowery tale more sweetly than our rhyme:
What leaf-fringed legend haunts about thy shape
　Of deities or mortals, or of both,
　　In Tempe or the dales of Arcady?
What men or gods are these? What maidens loath?
What mad pursuit? What struggle to escape?   9
　　What pipes and timbrels? What wild ecstasy?

Heard melodies are sweet, but those unheard
　Are sweeter; therefore, ye soft pipes, play on;
Not to the sensual ear, but, more endeared,
　Pipe to the spirit ditties of no tone;
Fair youth, beneath the trees, thou canst not leave
　Thy song, nor ever can those trees be bare;
　Bold lover, never, never canst thou kiss
Though winning near the goal—yet, do not grieve;
　She cannot fade, though thou hast not thy bliss,
　　Forever wilt thou love, and she be fair!   20

Ah, happy, happy boughs! that cannot shed
  Your leaves, nor ever bid the Spring adieu;
And, happy melodist, unwearied,
  Forever piping songs forever new;
More happy love! more happy, happy love!
  Forever warm and still to be enjoyed,
    Forever panting, and forever young,
All breathing human passion far above,
  That leaves a heart high-sorrowful and cloyed,
    A burning forehead, and a parching tongue.   30

Who are these coming to the sacrifice?
  To what green altar, O mysterious priest,
Lead'st thou that heifer lowing at the skies,
  And all her silken flanks with garlands dressed?
What little town by river or sea shore,
  Or mountain-built with peaceful citadel,
    Is emptied of this folk, this pious morn?
And, little town, thy streets for evermore
  Will silent be; and not a soul to tell
    Why thou art desolate, can e'er return.   40

O Attic shape! Fair attitude! with brede
  Of marble men and maidens overwrought,
With forest branches and the trodden weed;
  Thou, silent form, dost tease us out of thought
As doth eternity. Cold Pastoral!
  When old age shall this generation waste,
    Thou shalt remain, in midst of other woe
Than ours, a friend to man, to whom thou say'st,
  "Beauty is truth, truth beauty"—that is all
    Ye know on earth, and all ye need to know.

                                      1820

ODE TO A NIGHTINGALE

My heart aches, and a drowsy numbness pains
  My sense, as though of hemlock I had drunk,
Or emptied some dull opiate to the drains
  One minute past, and Lethe-wards had sunk.
'Tis not through envy of thy happy lot,
  But being too happy in thine happiness—
    That thou, light wingéd Dryad of the trees,
      In some melodious plot
  Of beechen green, and shadows numberless,
    Singest of summer in full-throated ease.   10

Oh, for a draught of vintage that hath been
  Cooled a long age in the deep-delved earth,
Tasting of Flora and the country green,
  Dance, and Provençal song, and sunburnt mirth!
Oh, for a beaker full of the warm South,
  Full of the true, the blushful Hippocrene,
    With beaded bubbles winking at the brim,
      And purple-stainéd mouth;
  That I might drink, and leave the world unseen,
    And with thee fade away into the forest dim—   20

Fade far away, dissolve, and quite forget
  What thou among the leaves hast never known,
The weariness, the fever, and the fret
  Here, where men sit and hear each other groan;
Where palsy shakes a few, sad, last gray hairs,
  Where youth grows pale, and specter-thin, and dies;
    Where but to think is to be full of sorrow
      And leaden-eyed despairs,
  Where Beauty cannot keep her lustrous eyes,
    Or new Love pine at them beyond tomorrow.   30

Away! away! for I will fly to thee,
  Not charioted by Bacchus and his pards,

But on the viewless wings of Poesy,
  Though the dull brain perplexes and retards:
Already with thee! tender is the night,
  And haply the Queen-Moon is on her throne,
    Clustered around by all her starry Fays;
      But here there is no light,
  Save what from heaven is with the breezes blown   39
    Through verdurous glooms and winding, mossy ways.

I cannot see what flowers are at my feet,
  Nor what soft incense hangs upon the boughs,
But, in embalméd darkness, guess each sweet
  Wherewith the seasonable month endows
The grass, the thicket, and the fruit-tree wild;
  White hawthorn, and the pastoral eglantine;
    Fast fading violets covered up in leaves;
      And mid-May's eldest child,
  The coming musk-rose, full of dewy wine,
    The murmurous haunt of flies on summer eves.   50

Darkling I listen; and, for many a time
  I have been half in love with easeful Death,
Called him soft names in many a muséd rime,
  To take into the air my quiet breath;
Now more than ever seems it rich to die,
  To cease upon the midnight with no pain,
    While thou art pouring forth thy soul abroad
      In such an ecstasy!
  Still wouldst thou sing, and I have ears in vain—
    To thy high requiem become a sod.   60

Thou wast not born for death, immortal Bird!
  No hungry generations tread thee down;
The voice I hear this passing night was heard
  In ancient days by emperor and clown:

Perhaps the self-same song that found a path
  Through the sad heart of Ruth, when, sick for home,
    She stood in tears amid the alien corn;
      The same that ofttimes hath
  Charmed magic casements, opening on the foam
    Of perilous seas, in faëry lands forlorn.   70

Forlorn! the very word is like a bell
  To toll me back from thee to my sole self!
Adieu! the fancy cannot cheat so well
  As she is famed to do, deceiving elf.
Adieu! adieu! thy plaintive anthem fades
  Past the near meadows, over the still stream,
    Up the hillside; and now 'tis buried deep
      In the next valley-glades:
  Was it a vision, or a waking dream?
    Fled is that music—do I wake or sleep?

                          1820

THE EVE OF ST. AGNES

St. Agnes' Eve—ah, bitter chill it was!
The owl, for all his feathers, was a-cold;
The hare limped trembling through the frozen grass,
And silent was the flock in woolly fold.
Numb were the Beadsman's fingers, while he told
His rosary, and while his frosted breath,
Like pious incense from a censer old,
Seemed taking flight for heaven, without a death,
Past the sweet Virgin's picture, while his prayer he saith.

His prayer he saith, this patient, holy man;   10
Then takes his lamp, and riseth from his knees,
And back returneth, meager, barefoot, wan,
Along the chapel aisle by slow degrees.
The sculptured dead, on each side, seem to freeze,

Imprisoned in black, purgatorial rails.
Knights, ladies, praying in dumb orat'ries,
He passeth by; and his weak spirit fails
To think how they may ache in icy hoods and mails.

Northward he turneth through a little door,
And scarce three steps, ere Music's golden tongue   2c
Flattered to tears this aged man and poor;
But no—already had his deathbell rung;
The joys of all his life were said and sung;
His was harsh penance on St. Agnes' Eve.
Another way he went, and soon among
Rough ashes sat he for his soul's reprieve,
And all night kept awake, for sinner's sake to grieve.

That ancient Beadsman heard the prelude soft;
And so it chanced, for many a door was wide,
From hurry to and fro. Soon, up aloft,   30
The silver, snarling trumpets 'gan to chide;
The level chambers, ready with their pride,
Were glowing to receive a thousand guests;
The carvéd angels, ever eager-eyed,
Stared, where upon their heads the cornice rests,
With hair blown back, and wings put crosswise on their
      breasts.

At length burst in the argent revelry,
With plume, tiara, and all rich array,
Numerous as shadows haunting faërily
The brain, new-stuffed, in youth, with triumphs gay   40
Of old romance. These let us wish away,
And turn, sole-thoughted, to one Lady there,
Whose heart had brooded, all that wintry day,
On love, and winged St. Agnes' saintly care,
As she had heard old dames full many times declare.

They told her how, upon St. Agnes' Eve,
Young virgins might have visions of delight,
And soft adorings from their loves receive
Upon the honeyed middle of the night,
if ceremonies due they did aright;   50
As, supperless to bed they must retire,
And couch supine their beauties, lily white;
Nor look behind, nor sideways, but require
Of Heaven with upward eyes for all that they desire.

Full of this whim was thoughtful Madeline.
The music, yearning like a god in pain,
She scarcely heard; her maiden eyes divine,
Fixed on the floor, saw many a sweeping train
Pass by—she heeded not at all. In vain
Came many a tiptoe, amorous cavalier,   60
And back retired; not cooled by high disdain,
But she saw not—her heart was otherwhere—
She sighed for Agnes' dreams, the sweetest of the year.

She danced along with vague, regardless eyes;
Anxious her lips, her breathing quick and short.
The hallowed hour was near at hand; she sighs
Amid the timbrels and the thronged resort
Of whisperers in anger, or in sport;
Mid looks of love, defiance, hate, and scorn,
Hoodwinked with faëry fancy; all amort,   70
Save to St. Agnes and her lambs unshorn,
And all the bliss to be before tomorrow morn.

So, purposing each moment to retire,
She lingered still. Meantime, across the moors,
Had come young Porphyro, with heart on fire
For Madeline. Beside the portal doors,
Buttressed from moonlight, stands he, and implores

All saints to give him sight of Madeline,
But for one moment in the tedious hours,
That he might gaze and worship all unseen;　　　80
Perchance speak, kneel, touch, kiss—in sooth such things
　　　have been.

He ventures in; let no buzzed whisper tell;
All eyes be muffled, or a hundred swords
Will storm his heart, Love's fev'rous citadel.
For him those chambers held barbarian hordes,
Hyena foemen, and hot-blooded lords,
Whose very dogs would execrations howl
Against his lineage; not one breast affords
Him any mercy, in that mansion foul,
Save one old beldame, weak in body and in soul.　　　90

Ah, happy chance! the aged creature came,
Shuffling along with ivory-headed wand,
To where he stood, hid from the torch's flame,
Behind a broad hall-pillar, far beyond
The sound of merriment and chorus bland.
He startled her; but soon she knew his face,
And grasped his fingers in her palsied hand,
Saying, "Mercy, Porphyro! hie thee from this place;
They are all here tonight, the whole blood-thirsty race!

"Get hence! get hence! there's dwarfish Hildebrand;　100
He had a fever late, and in the fit
He curséd thee and thine, both house and land;
Then there's that old Lord Maurice, not a whit
More tame for his gray hairs—alas me! flit!
Flit like a ghost away." "Ah, Gossip dear,
We're safe enough; here in this arm-chair sit,
And tell me how"—"Good Saints! not here, not here;
Follow me, child, or else these stones will be thy bier."

He followed through a lowly archéd way,
Brushing the cobwebs with his lofty plume;   110
And as she muttered, "Well-a—well-a-day!"
He found him in a little moonlight room,
Pale, latticed, chill, and silent as a tomb.
"Now tell me where is Madeline," said he,
"O tell me, Angela, by the holy loom
Which none but secret sisterhood may see,
When they St. Agnes' wool are weaving piously."

"St. Agnes! Ah! it is St. Agnes' Eve—
Yet men will murder upon holy days;
Thou must hold water in a witch's sieve,   120
And be liege-lord of all the elves and fays,
To venture so; it fills me with amaze
To see thee, Porphyro!—St. Agnes' Eve!
God's help! my lady fair the conjuror plays
This very night; good angels her deceive!
But let me laugh awhile, I've mickle time to grieve."

Feebly she laugheth in the languid moon,
While Porphyro upon her face doth look,
Like puzzled urchin on an aged crone
Who keepeth closed a wond'rous riddle-book,   130
As spectacled she sits in chimney nook.
But soon his eyes grew brilliant, when she told
His lady's purpose; and he scarce could brook
Tears, at the thought of those enchantments cold,
And Madeline asleep in lap of legends old.

Sudden a thought came like a full-blown rose,
Flushing his brow, and in his painéd heart
Made purple riot; then doth he propose
A stratagem that makes the beldame start.
"A cruel man and impious thou art;   140

Sweet lady, let her pray, and sleep, and dream
Alone with her good angels, far apart
From wicked men like thee. Go, go!—I deem
Thou canst not surely be the same that thou didst seem."

"I will not harm her, by all saints I swear,"
Quoth Porphyro. "O may I ne'er find grace
When my weak voice shall whisper its last prayer,
If one of her soft ringlets I displace,
Or look with ruffian passion in her face.
Good Angela, believe me by these tears,　　　　150
Or I will, even in a moment's space,
Awake, with horrid shout, my foemen's ears,
And beard them, though they be more fanged than wolves
　　　and bears."

"Ah! why wilt thou affright a feeble soul?
A poor, weak, palsy-stricken, churchyard thing,
Whose passing-bell may ere the midnight toll;
Whose prayers for thee, each morn and evening,
Were never missed." Thus plaining, doth she bring
A gentler speech from burning Porphyro;
So woeful, and of such deep sorrowing,　　　　160
That Angela gives promise she will do
Whatever he shall wish, betide her weal or woe—

Which was, to lead him, in close secrecy,
Even to Madeline's chamber, and there hide
Him in a closet, of such privacy
That he might see her beauty unespied,
And win perhaps that night a peerless bride,
While legioned fairies paced the coverlet,
And pale enchantment held her sleepy-eyed.
Never on such a night have lovers met,　　　　170
Since Merlin paid his Demon all the monstrous debt.

"It shall be as thou wishest," said the Dame.
"All cates and dainties shall be storéd there
Quickly on this feast-night; by the tambour frame
Her own lute thou wilt see; no time to spare,
For I am slow and feeble, and scarce dare
On such a catering trust my dizzy head.
Wait here, my child, with patience; kneel in prayer
The while. Ah! thou must needs the lady wed,
Or may I never leave my grave among the dead." 180

So saying, she hobbled off with busy fear.
The lover's endless minutes slowly passed;
The Dame returned, and whispered in his ear
To follow her; with aged eyes aghast
From fright of dim espial. Safe at last,
Through many a dusky gallery, they gain
The maiden's chamber, silken, hushed, and chaste,
Where Porphyro took covert, pleased amain.
His poor guide hurried back with agues in her brain.

Her falt'ring hand upon the balustrade, 190
Old Angela was feeling for the stair,
When Madeline, St. Agnes' charméd maid,
Rose, like a missioned spirit, unaware.
With silver taper's light, and pious care,
She turned, and down the aged gossip led
To a safe, level matting. Now prepare,
Young Porphyro, for gazing on that bed;
She comes, she comes again, like ring-dove frayed and fled.

Out went the taper as she hurried in;
Its little smoke, in pallid moonshine, died. 200
She closed the door, she panted, all akin
To spirits of the air, and visions wide;
No uttered syllable, or, woe betide!
But to her heart, her heart was voluble,

Paining with eloquence her balmy side,
As though a tongueless nightingale should swell
Her throat in vain, and die, heart-stifled, in her deil.

A casement high and triple-arched there was,
All garlanded with carven imageries
Of fruits, and flowers, and bunches of knotgrass,   210
And diamonded with panes of quaint device,
Innumerable of stains and splendid dyes,
As are the tiger-moth's deep-damasked wings;
And in the midst, 'mong thousand heraldries,
And twilight saints, and dim emblazonings,
A shielded scutcheon blushed with blood of queens and
        kings.

Full on this casement shone the wintry moon,
And threw warm gules on Madeline's fair breast,
As down she knelt for Heaven's grace and boon;
Rose-bloom fell on her hands, together pressed,   220
And on her silver cross soft amethyst,
And on her hair a glory, like a saint;
She seemed a splendid angel, newly dressed,
Save wings, for Heaven—Porphyro grew faint—
She knelt, so pure a thing, so free from mortal taint.

Anon his heart revives; her vespers done,
Of all its wreathéd pearls her hair she frees,
Unclasps her warméd jewels one by one,
Loosens her fragrant bodice; by degrees
Her rich attire creeps rustling to her knees.   230
Half-hidden, like a mermaid in seaweed,
Pensive awhile she dreams awake, and sees,
In fancy, fair St. Agnes in her bed,
But dares not look behind, or all the charm is fled.

Soon, trembling in her soft and chilly nest,
In sort of wakeful swoon, perplexed she lay,

Until the poppied warmth of sleep oppressed
Her soothéd limbs, and soul fatigued away;
Flown, like a thought, until the morrow-day,
Blissfully havened both from joy and pain,   240
Clasped like a missal where swart Paynims pray,
Blinded alike from sunshine and from rain,
As though a rose should shut, and be a bud again.

Stolen to this paradise, and so entranced,
Porphyro gazed upon her empty dress,
And listened to her breathing, if it chanced
To wake into a slumberous tenderness;
Which when he heard, that minute did he bless,
And breathed himself; then from the closet crept,
Noiseless as fear in a wide wilderness,   250
And over the hushéd carpet, silent, stepped,
And 'tween the curtains peeped, where, lo!—how fast she
    slept.

Then by the bedside, where the faded moon
Made a dim, silver twilight, soft he set
A table, and, half anguished, threw thereon
A cloth of woven crimson, gold, and jet.
O for some drowsy Morphean amulet!
The boisterous, midnight, festive clarion,
The kettledrum, and far-heard clarionet,
Affray his ears, though but in dying tone—   260
The hall door shuts again, and all the noise is gone.

And still she slept an azure-lidded sleep,
In blanchéd linen, smooth, and lavendered,
While he from forth the closet brought a heap
Of candied apple, quince, and plum, and gourd,
With jellies soother than the creamy curd,
And lucent sirups, tinct with cinnamon,
Manna and dates, in argosy transferred

From Fez, and spicéd dainties, every one,
From silken Samarcand to cedared Lebanon.   270

These delicates he heaped with glowing hand
On golden dishes and in baskets bright
Of wreathéd silver; sumptuous they stand
In the retiréd quiet of the night,
Filling the chilly room with perfume light.
"And now, my love, my seraph fair, awake!
Thou art my heaven, and I thine eremite.
Open thine eyes, for meek St. Agnes' sake,
Or I shall drowse beside thee, so my soul doth ache."

Thus whispering, his warm, unnervéd arm   280
Sank in her pillow. Shaded was her dream
By the dusk curtains—'twas a midnight charm
Impossible to melt as icéd stream.
The lustrous salvers in the moonlight gleam;
Broad golden fringe upon the carpet lies;
It seemed he never, never could redeem
From such a steadfast spell his lady's eyes;
So mused awhile, entoiled in wooféd phantasies.

Awakening up, he took her hollow lute—
Tumultuous—and, in chords that tenderest be,   290
He played an ancient ditty, long since mute,
In Provence called "La belle dame sans mercy";
Close to her ear touching the melody—
Wherewith disturbed, she uttered a soft moan.
He ceased—she panted quick—and suddenly
Her blue affrayéd eyes wide open shone;
Upon his knees he sank, pale as smooth-sculptured stone.

Her eyes were open, but she still beheld,
Now wide awake, the vision of her sleep;
There was a painful change, that nigh expelled   300

The blisses of her dream so pure and deep;
At which fair Madeline began to weep,
And moan forth witless words with many a sigh,
While still her gaze on Porphyro would keep,
Who knelt, with joinéd hands and piteous eye,
Fearing to move or speak, she looked so dreamingly.

"Ah, Porphyro!" said she, "but even now
Thy voice was at sweet tremble in mine ear,
Made tunable with every sweetest vow;
And those sad eyes were spiritual and clear.   310
How changed thou art! how pallid, chill, and drear!
Give me that voice again, my Porphyro,
Those looks immortal, those complainings dear!
Oh, leave me not in this eternal woe,
For if thou diest, my Love, I know not where to go."

Beyond a mortal man impassioned far
At these voluptuous accents, he arose,
Ethereal, flushed, and like a throbbing star
Seen mid the sapphire heaven's deep repose;
Into her dream he melted, as the rose   320
Blendeth its odour with the violet—
Solution sweet; meantime the frost-wind blows
Like Love's alarum, pattering the sharp sleet
Against the windowpanes; St. Agnes' moon hath set.

'Tis dark; quick pattereth the flaw-blown sleet.
"This is no dream, my bride, my Madeline!"
'Tis dark; the icéd gusts still rave and beat.
"No dream, alas! alas! and woe is mine!
Porphyro will leave me here to fade and pine.
Cruel! what traitor could thee hither bring?   330
I curse not, for my heart is lost in thine,
Though thou forsakest a deceivéd thing,
A dove forlorn and lost with sick, unprunéd wing."

"My Madeline! sweet dreamer! lovely bride!
Say, may I be for aye thy vassal blest?
Thy beauty's shield, heart-shaped and vermeil dyed?
Ah, silver shrine, here will I take my rest
After so many hours of toil and quest,
A famished pilgrim, saved by miracle.
Though I have found, I will not rob thy nest   340
Saving of thy sweet self; if thou think'st well
To trust, fair Madeline, to no rude infidel.

"Hark! 'tis an elfin storm from faëry land,
Of haggard seeming, but a boon indeed;
Arise—arise! the morning is at hand—
The bloated wassailers will never heed.
Let us away, my love, with happy speed;
There are no ears to hear, or eyes to see—
Drowned all in Rhenish and the sleepy mead.
Awake! arise! my love, and fearless be,   350
For o'er the southern moors I have a home for thee."

She hurried at his words, beset with fears,
For there were sleeping dragons all around,
At glaring watch, perhaps, with ready spears;
Down the wide stairs a darkling way they found;
In all the house was heard no human sound.
A chain-drooped lamp was flickering by each door;
The arras, rich with horseman, hawk, and hound,
Fluttered in the besieging wind's uproar;
And the long carpets rose along the gusty floor.   360

They glide, like phantoms, into the wide hall;
Like phantoms to the iron porch they glide,
Where lay the Porter, in uneasy sprawl,
With a huge, empty flagon by his side.
The wakeful bloodhound rose, and shook his hide,

But his sagacious eye an inmate owns.
By one, and one, the bolts full easy slide;
The chains lie silent on the footworn stones;
The key turns, and the door upon its hinges groans.

And they are gone; aye, ages long ago   370
These lovers fled away into the storm.
That night the Baron dreamt of many a woe,
And all his warrior-guests, with shade and form
Of witch, and demon, and large coffin-worm,
Were long be-nightmared. Angela the old
Died palsy-twitched, with meager face deform;
The Beadsman, after thousand aves told,
For aye unsought-for slept among his ashes cold.

1820

WHEN I HAVE FEARS THAT I
MAY CEASE TO BE

When I have fears that I may cease to be
Before my pen has gleaned my teeming brain,
Before high-pilèd books, in charact'ry,
Hold like rich garners the full-ripened grain;
When I behold, upon the night's starred face,
Huge cloudy symbols of a high romance,
And think that I may never live to trace
Their shadows, with the magic hand of chance;
And when I feel, fair creature of an hour,
That I shall never look upon thee more,   10
Never have relish in the faëry power
Of unreflecting love—then on the shore
  Of the wide world I stand alone, and think,
  Till love and fame to nothingness do sink.

1848

BRIGHT STAR! WOULD I WERE
STEADFAST AS THOU ART

Bright star! would I were steadfast as thou art—
Not in lone splendour hung aloft the night,
And watching, with eternal lids apart,
Like Nature's patient sleepless Eremite,
The moving waters at their priestlike task
Of pure ablution round earth's human shores,
Or gazing on the new soft-fallen mask
Of snow upon the mountains and the moors—
No—yet still steadfast, still unchangeable,
Pillowed upon my fair love's ripening breast,   10
To feel forever its soft fall and swell,
Awake forever in a sweet unrest,
Still, still to hear her tender-taken breath,
And so live ever—or else swoon to death.

1848

ELIZABETH BARRETT
BROWNING (1806–1861)

SONNETS FROM THE PORTUGUESE

I

I thought once how Theocritus had sung
Of the sweet years, the dear and wished-for years,
Who each one in a gracious hand appears
To bear a gift for mortals, old or young.
And, as I mused it in his antique tongue,
I saw, in gradual vision through my tears,
The sweet, sad years, the melancholy years,
Those of my own life, who by turns had flung
A shadow across me. Straightway I was 'ware,
So weeping, how a mystic Shape did move   10

Behind me, and drew me backward by the hair;
And a voice said in mastery, while I strove—
"Guess now who holds thee?"—"Death," I said.   But,
    there,
The silver answer rang—"Not Death, but Love."

XIV

If thou must love me, let it be for nought
Except for love's sake only. Do not say
"I love her for her smile—her look—her way
Of speaking gently,—for a trick of thought
That falls in well with mine, and certes brought
A sense of pleasant ease on such a day"—
For these things in themselves, Belovéd, may
Be changed, or change for thee,—and love, so wrought,
May be unwrought so. Neither love me for
Thine own dear pity's wiping my cheeks dry,—   10
A creature might forget to weep, who bore
Thy comfort long, and lose thy love thereby!

XLIII

How do I love thee? Let me count the ways.
I love thee to the depth and breadth and height
My soul can reach, when feeling out of sight
For the ends of Being and ideal Grace.
I love thee to the level of every day's
Most quiet need, by sun and candlelight.
I love thee freely, as men strive for Right;
I love thee purely, as they turn from Praise.
I love thee with the passion put to use
In my old griefs, and with my childhood's faith.   10
I love thee with a love I seemed to lose
With my lost saints—I love thee with the breath,
Smiles, tears, of all my life!—and, if God choose,
I shall but love thee better after death.

                                                1847

ALFRED, LORD TENNYSON
(1809–1892)

THE LADY OF SHALOTT
Part I

On either side the river lie
Long fields of barley and of rye,
That clothe the wold and meet the sky;
And through the field the road runs by
　　To many-towered Camelot;
And up and down the people go,
Gazing where the lilies blow
Round an island there below,
　　The island of Shalott.

Willows whiten, aspens quiver,　　　　　　　10
Little breezes dusk and shiver
Through the wave that runs forever
By the island in the river
　　Flowing down to Camelot.
Four gray walls, and four gray towers,
Overlook a space of flowers,
And the silent isle imbowers
　　The Lady of Shalott.

By the margin, willow-veiled,
Slide the heavy barges trailed　　　　　　　20
By slow horses; and unhailed
The shallop flitteth silken-sailed
　　Skimming down to Camelot.
But who hath seen her wave her hand?
Or at the casement seen her stand?
Or is she known in all the land,
　　The Lady of Shalott?

Only reapers, reaping early
In among the bearded barley,
Hear a song that echoes cheerly   30
From the river winding clearly,
   Down to towered Camelot;
And by the moon the reaper weary,
Piling sheaves in uplands airy,
Listening, whispers "'Tis the fairy
   Lady of Shalott."

Part II

There she weaves by night and day
A magic web with colors gay.
She has heard a whisper say
A curse is on her if she stay   40
   To look down to Camelot.
She knows not what the curse may be,
And so she weaveth steadily,
And little other care hath she,
   The Lady of Shalott.

And moving through a mirror clear
That hangs before her all the year,
Shadows of the world appear.
There she sees the highway near
   Winding down to Camelot;   50
There the river eddy whirls,
And there the surly village-churls,
And the red cloaks of market girls,
   Pass onward from Shalott.

Sometimes a troop of damsels glad,
An abbot on an ambling pad,
Sometimes a curly shepherd-lad,
Or long-haired page in crimson clad,
   Goes by to towered Camelot.

And sometimes through the mirror blue   60
The knights come riding two and two.
She hath no loyal knight and true,
   The Lady of Shalott.

But in her web she still delights
To weave the mirror's magic sights,
For often through the silent nights
A funeral, with plumes and lights
   And music, went to Camelot.
Or when the moon was overhead,
Came two young lovers lately wed;   70
"I am half sick of shadows," said
   The Lady of Shalott.

Part III

A bow-shot from her bower-eaves,
He rode between the barley-sheaves,
The sun came dazzling through the leaves,
And flamed upon the brazen greaves
   Of bold Sir Lancelot.
A red-cross knight forever kneeled
To a lady in his shield,
That sparkled on the yellow field,   80
   Beside remote Shalott.

The gemmy bridle glittered free,
Like to some branch of stars we see
Hung in the golden Galaxy.
The bridle bells rang merrily
   As he rode down to Camelot.
And from his blazoned baldric slung
A mighty silver bugle hung,
And as he rode his armor rung,
   Beside remote Shalott.   90

All in the blue unclouded weather,
Thick-jeweled shone the saddle-leather;
The helmet and the helmet-feather
Burned like one burning flame together,
   As he rode down to Camelot;
As often through the purple night,
Below the starry clusters bright,
Some bearded meteor, trailing light,
   Moves over still Shalott.

His broad clear brow in sunlight glowed;   100
On burnished hooves his war-horse trode;
From underneath his helmet flowed
His coal-black curls as on he rode,
   As he rode down to Camelot.
From the bank and from the river
He flashed into the crystal mirror,
"Tirra lirra," by the river
   Sang Sir Lancelot.

She left the web, she left the loom,
She made three paces through the room,   110
She saw the water-lily bloom,
She saw the helmet and the plume,
   She looked down to Camelot.
Out flew the web and floated wide;
The mirror cracked from side to side;
"The curse is come upon me," cried
   The Lady of Shalott.

Part IV

In the stormy east-wind straining,
The pale yellow woods were waning,
The broad stream in his banks complaining,   120
Heavily the low sky raining
   Over towered Camelot;

Down she came and found a boat
Beneath a willow left afloat,
And round about the prow she wrote
    The Lady of Shalott.

And down the river's dim expanse
Like some bold seer in a trance,
Seeing all his own mischance—
With a glassy countenance   130
    Did she look to Camelot.
And at the closing of the day
She loosed the chain, and down she lay;
The broad stream bore her far away,
    The Lady of Shalott.

Lying, robed in snowy white
That loosely flew to left and right—
The leaves upon her falling light—
Through the noises of the night
    She floated down to Camelot;   140
And as the boat-head wound along
The willowy hills and fields among,
They heard her singing her last song,
    The Lady of Shalott.

Heard a carol, mournful, holy,
Chanted loudly, chanted lowly,
Till her blood was frozen slowly,
And her eyes were darkened wholly,
    Turned to towered Camelot.
For ere she reached upon the tide   150
The first house by the water side,
Singing in her song she died,
    The Lady of Shalott.

Under tower and balcony,
By garden-wall and gallery,

A gleaming shape she floated by,
Dead-pale between the houses high,
   Silent into Camelot.
Out upon the wharfs they came,
Knight and burgher, lord and dame,   160
And round the prow they read her name,
   The Lady of Shalott.

Who is this? and what is here?
And in the lighted palace near
Died the sound of royal cheer;
And they crossed themselves for fear,
   All the knights at Camelot.
But Lancelot mused a little space;
He said, "She has a lovely face;
God in his mercy lend her grace,   170
   The Lady of Shalott."

               1833, 1842

THE LOTOS-EATERS

"Courage!" he said, and pointed toward the land,
"This mounting wave will roll us shoreward soon."
In the afternoon they came unto a land
In which it seeméd always afternoon.
All round the coast the languid air did swoon,
Breathing like one that hath a weary dream.
Full-faced above the valley stood the moon;
And, like a downward smoke, the slender stream
Along the cliff to fall and pause and fall did seem.

A land of streams! some, like a downward smoke,   10
Slow-dropping veils of thinnest lawn, did go;
And some through wavering lights and shadows broke,

Rolling a slumbrous sheet of foam below.
They saw the gleaming river seaward flow
From the inner land; far off, three mountain-tops,
Three silent pinnacles of aged snow,
Stood sunset-flushed; and, dewed with showery drops,
Up-clomb the shadowy pine above the woven copse.

The charméd sunset lingered low adown
In the red west; through mountain clefts the dale   20
Was seen far inland, and the yellow down
Bordered with palm, and many a winding vale
And meadow, set with slender galingale;
A land where all things always seemed the same!
And round about the keel with faces pale,
Dark faces pale against that rosy flame,
The mild-eyed melancholy Lotos-eaters came.

Branches they bore of that enchanted stem,
Laden with flower and fruit, whereof they gave
To each, but whoso did receive of them   30
And taste, to him the gushing of the wave
Far, far away did seem to mourn and rave
On alien shores; and if his fellow spake,
His voice was thin, as voices from the grave;
And deep-asleep he seemed, yet all awake,
And music in his ears his beating heart did make.

They sat them down upon the yellow sand,
Between the sun and moon upon the shore;
And sweet it was to dream of fatherland,
Of child, and wife and slave; but evermore   40
Most weary seemed the sea, weary the oar,
Weary the wandering fields of barren foam.
Then someone said, "We will return no more";
And all at once they sang, "Our island home
Is far beyond the wave; we will no longer roam."

CHORIC SONG

I

There is sweet music here that softer falls
Than petals from blown roses on the grass,
Or night-dews on still waters between walls
Of shadowy granite, in a gleaming pass;
Music that gentlier on the spirit lies,   50
Than tired eyelids upon tired eyes;
Music that brings sweet sleep down from the blissful skies.
Here are cool mosses deep,
And through the moss the ivies creep,
And in the stream the long-leaved flowers weep,
And from the craggy ledge the poppy hangs in sleep.

II

Why are we weighed upon with heaviness,
And utterly consumed with sharp distress,
While all things else have rest from weariness?
All things have rest; why should we toil alone,   60
We only toil, who are the first of things,
And make perpetual moan,
Still from one sorrow to another thrown;
Nor ever fold our wings,
And cease from wanderings,
Nor steep our brows in slumber's holy balm;
Nor harken what the inner spirit sings,
"There is no joy but calm!"—
Why should we only toil, the roof and crown of things?

III

Lo! in the middle of the wood,   70
The folded leaf is wooed from out the bud
With winds upon the branch, and there
Grows green and broad, and takes no care,
Sun-steeped at noon, and in the moon
Nightly dew-fed; and turning yellow

Falls, and floats adown the air.
Lo! sweetened with the summer light,
The full-juiced apple, waxing over-mellow,
Drops in a silent autumn night.
All its allotted length of days   80
The flower ripens in its place,
Ripens and fades, and falls, and hath no toil,
Fast-rooted in the fruitful soil.

IV

Hateful is the dark-blue sky,
Vaulted o'er the dark-blue sea.
Death is the end of life; ah, why
Should life all labour be?
Let us alone. Time driveth onward fast,
And in a little while our lips are dumb.
Let us alone. What is it that will last?   90
All things are taken from us, and become
Portions and parcels of the dreadful past.
Let us alone. What pleasure can we have
To war with evil? Is there any peace
In ever climbing up the climbing wave?
All things have rest, and ripen toward the grave
In silence—ripen, fall, and cease.
Give us long rest or death, dark death, or dreamful ease.

V

How sweet it were, hearing the downward stream,
With half-shut eyes ever to seem   100
Falling asleep in a half-dream!
To dream and dream, like yonder amber light,
Which will not leave the myrrh-bush on the height;
To hear each other's whispered speech;
Eating the Lotos day by day,
To watch the crisping ripples on the beach,
And tender curving lines of creamy spray;

To lend our hearts and spirits wholly
To the influence of mild-minded melancholy;
To muse and brood and live again in memory,   110
With those old faces of our infancy
Heaped over with a mound of grass,
Two handfuls of white dust, shut in an urn of brass!

VI

Dear is the memory of our wedded lives,
And dear the last embraces of our wives
And their warm tears; but all hath suffered change;
For surely now our household hearths are cold;
Our sons inherit us; our looks are strange;
And we should come like ghosts to trouble joy.
Or else the island princes over-bold   120
Have eat our substance, and the minstrel sings
Before them of the ten years' war in Troy,
And our great deeds, as half-forgotten things.
Is there confusion in the little isle?
Let what is broken so remain.
The gods are hard to reconcile;
'Tis hard to settle order once again.
There *is* confusion worse than death,
Trouble on trouble, pain on pain,
Long labor unto aged breath,   130
Sore task to hearts worn out by many wars
And eyes grown dim with gazing on the pilot-stars.

VII

But, propped on beds of amaranth and moly,
How sweet—while warm airs lull us, blowing lowly—
With half-dropped eyelid still,
Beneath a heaven dark and holy,
To watch the long bright river drawing slowly
His waters from the purple hill—
To hear the dewy echoes calling

From cave to cave through the thick-twined vine—   140
To watch the emerald-coloured water falling
Through many a woven acanthus-wreath divine!
Only to hear and see the far-off sparkling brine.
Only to hear were sweet, stretched out beneath the
    pine.

VIII

The Lotos blooms below the barren peak,
The Lotos blows by every winding creek;
All day the wind breathes low with mellower tone;
Through every hollow cave and alley lone
Round and round the spicy downs the yellow Lotos-dust
    is blown.
We have had enough of action, and of motion we,   150
Rolled to starboard, rolled to larboard, when the surge
    was seething free,
Where the wallowing monster spouted his foam-fountains
    in the sea.
Let us swear an oath, and keep it with an equal mind,
In the hollow Lotos-land to live and lie reclined
On the hills like gods together, careless of mankind.
For they lie beside their nectar, and the bolts are hurled
Far below them in the valleys, and the clouds are lightly
    curled
Round their golden houses, girdled with the gleaming
    world;
Where they smile in secret, looking over wasted lands,
Blight and famine, plague and earthquake, roaring deeps
    and fiery sands,   160
Clanging fights, and flaming towns, and sinking ships,
    and praying hands.
But they smile, they find a music centered in a doleful
    song
Steaming up, a lamentation and an ancient tale of wrong,
Like a tale of little meaning though the words are strong;

Chanted from an ill-used race of men that cleave the
    soil,
Sow the seed, and reap the harvest with enduring toil,
Storing yearly little dues of wheat, and wine and oil;
Till they perish and they suffer—some, 'tis whispered—
    down in hell
Suffer endless anguish, others in Elysian valleys dwell,
Resting weary limbs at last on beds of asphodel.   170
Surely, surely, slumber is more sweet than toil, the shore
Than labour in the deep mid-ocean, wind and wave and oar;
Oh, rest ye, brother mariners, we will not wander more.

1833, 1842

MORTE D'ARTHUR

So all day long the noise of battle roll'd
Among the mountains by the winter sea,
Until King Arthur's table, man by man,
Had fallen in Lyonnesse about their lord,
King Arthur; then, because his wound was deep,
The bold Sir Bedivere uplifted him,
Sir Bedivere, the last of all his knights,
And bore him to a chapel nigh the field,
A broken chancel with a broken cross,
That stood on a dark strait of barren land.   10
On one side lay the ocean, and on one
Lay a great water, and the moon was full.
    Then spake King Arthur to Sir Bedivere:
"The sequel of to-day unsolders all
The goodliest fellowship of famous knights
Whereof this world holds record. Such a sleep
They sleep—the men I loved. I think that we
Shall never more, at any future time,
Delight our souls with talk of knightly deeds,
Walking about the gardens and the halls   20
Of Camelot, as in the days that were.

I perish by this people which I made,—
Tho' Merlin sware that I should come again
To rule once more—but let what will be, be,
I am so deeply smitten thro' the helm
That without help I cannot last till morn.
Thou therefore take my brand Excalibur,
Which was my pride; for thou rememberest how
In those old days, one summer noon, an arm
Rose up from out the bosom of the lake,   30
Clothed in white samite, mystic, wonderful,
Holding the sword—and how I row'd across
And took it, and have worn it, like a king;
And, wheresoever I am sung or told
In aftertime, this also shall be known.
But now delay not; take Excalibur,
And fling him far into the middle mere;
Watch what thou seest, and lightly bring me word."
    To him replied the bold Sir Bedivere:
"It is not meet, Sir King, to leave thee thus,   40
Aidless, alone, and smitten thro' the helm.
A little thing may harm a wounded man.
Yet I thy hest will all perform at full,
Watch what I see, and lightly bring thee word."
    So saying, from the ruin'd shrine he stept
And in the moon athwart the place of tombs,
Where lay the mighty bones of ancient men,
Old knights, and over them the sea-wind sang
Shrill, chill, with flakes of foam. He, stepping down
By zigzag paths and juts of pointed rock,   50
Came on the shining levels of the lake.
    There drew he forth the brand Excalibur,
And o'er him, drawing it, the winter moon,
Brightening the skirts of a long cloud, ran forth
And sparkled keen with frost against the hilt;
For all the haft twinkled with diamond sparks,
Myriads of topaz-lights, and jacinth-work

Of subtlest jewelry. He gazed so long
That both his eyes were dazzled, as he stood,
This way and that dividing the swift mind,   60
In act to throw; but at the last it seem'd
Better to leave Excalibur conceal'd
There in the many-knotted water-flags,
That whistled stiff and dry about the marge.
So strode he back slow to the wounded king.
    Then spake King Arthur to Sir Bedivere:
"Hast thou perform'd my mission which I gave?
What is it thou hast seen, or what hast heard?"
    And answer made the bold Sir Bedivere:
"I heard the ripple washing in the reeds,   70
And the wild water lapping on the crag."
    To whom replied King Arthur, faint and pale:
"Thou hast betray'd thy nature and thy name,
Not rendering true answer, as beseem'd
Thy fealty, nor like a noble knight;
For surer sign had follow'd, either hand,
Or voice, or else a motion of the mere.
This is a shameful thing for men to lie.
Yet now, I charge thee, quickly go again
As thou art lief and dear, and do the thing   80
I bade thee, watch, and lightly bring me word."
    Then went Sir Bedivere the second time
Across the ridge, and paced beside the mere,
Counting the dewy pebbles, fix'd in thought;
But when he saw the wonder of the hilt,
How curiously and strangely chased, he smote
His palms together, and he cried aloud:
    "And if indeed I cast the brand away,
Surely a precious thing, one worthy note,
Should thus be lost forever from the earth,   90
Which might have pleased the eyes of many men.
What good should follow this, if this were done?
What harm, undone? deep harm to disobey,

Seeing obedience is the bond of rule.
Were it well to obey then, if a king demand
An act unprofitable, against himself?
The king is sick, and knows not what he does.
What record, or what relic of my lord
Should be to aftertime, but empty breath
And rumours of a doubt? but were this kept,   100
Stored in some treasure-house of mighty kings,
Some one might show it at a joust of arms,
Saying, 'King Arthur's sword, Excalibur,
Wrought by the lonely maiden of the lake;
Nine years she wrought it, sitting in the deeps
Upon the hidden bases of the hills.'
So might some old man speak in the aftertime
To all the people, winning reverence;
But now much honour and much fame were lost."

So spake he, clouded with his own conceit,   110
And hid Excalibur the second time,
And so strode back slow to the wounded king.

Then spoke King Arthur, breathing heavily:
"What is it thou hast seen, or what hast heard?"

And answer made the bold Sir Bedivere:
"I heard the water lapping on the crag,
And the long ripple washing in the reeds."

To whom replied King Arthur, much in wrath:
"Ah, miserable and unkind, untrue,
Unknightly, traitor-hearted! Woe is me!   120
Authority forgets a dying king,
Laid widow'd of the power in his eye
That bow'd the will. I see thee what thou art,
For thou, the latest-left of all my knights,
In whom should meet the offices of all,
Thou wouldst betray me for the precious hilt;
Either from lust of gold, or like a girl
Valuing the giddy pleasure of the eyes.
Yet, for a man may fail in duty twice,

And the third time may prosper, get thee hence;   130
But, if thou spare to fling Excalibur,
I will arise and slay thee with my hands."
    Then quickly rose Sir Bedivere, and ran,
And, leaping down the ridges lightly, plunged
Among the bulrush-beds, and clutch'd the sword,
And strongly wheel'd and threw it. The great brand
Made lightnings in the splendor of the moon,
And flashing round and round, and whirl'd in an arch
Shot like a streamer of the northern morn,
Seen where the moving isles of winter shock   140
By night, with noises of the northern sea.
So flash'd and fell the brand Excalibur;
But ere he dipt the surface, rose an arm
Cloth'd in white samite, mystic, wonderful,
And caught him by the hilt, and brandish'd him
Three times, and drew him under in the mere.
And lightly went the other to the king.
    Then spoke King Arthur, drawing thicker breath:
"Now see I by thine eyes that this is done.
Speak out; what is it thou hast heard, or seen?"   150
    And answer made the bold Sir Bedivere:
"Sir King, I closed mine eyelids, lest the gems
Should blind my purpose, for I never saw,
Nor shall see, here or elsewhere, till I die,
Not tho' I live three lives of mortal men,
So great a miracle as yonder hilt.
Then with both hands I flung him, wheeling him;
But when I look'd again, behold an arm,
Clothed in white samite, mystic, wonderful,
That caught him by the hilt, and brandish'd him   160
Three times, and drew him under in the mere."
    And answer made King Arthur, breathing hard:
"My end draws nigh; 'tis time that I were gone.
Make broad thy shoulders to receive my weight,
And bear me to the margin; yet I fear

My wound hath taken cold, and I shall die."
    So saying, from the pavement he half rose,
Slowly, with pain, reclining on his arm,
And looking wistfully with wide blue eyes
As in a picture. Him Sir Bedivere   170
Remorsefully regarded thro' his tears,
And would have spoken, but he found not words,
Then took with care, and kneeling on one knee,
O'er both his shoulders drew the languid hands,
And rising bore him thro' the place of tombs.
    But, as he walk'd, King Arthur panted hard,
Like one that feels a nightmare on his bed
When all the house is mute. So sigh'd the king,
Muttering and murmuring at his ear, "Quick, quick!
I fear it is too late, and I shall die."   180
But the other swiftly strode from ridge to ridge,
Clothed with his breath, and looking, as he walk'd,
Larger than human on the frozen hills.
He heard the deep behind him, and a cry
Before. His own thought drove him like a goad.
Dry clash'd his harness in the icy caves
And barren chasms, and all to left and right
The bare black cliff clang'd round him, as he based
His feet on juts of slippery crag that rang
Sharp-smitten with the dint of armed heels—   190
And on a sudden, lo! the level lake,
And the long glories of the winter moon.
    Then saw they how there hove a dusky barge,
Dark as a funeral scarf from stem to stern,
Beneath them; and descending they were ware
That all the decks were dense with stately forms
Black-stoled, black-hooded, like a dream—by these
Three queens with crowns of gold—and from them rose
A cry that shiver'd to the tingling stars,
And, as it were one voice, an agony   200
Of lamentation, like a wind that shrills

All night in a waste land, where no one comes,
Or hath come, since the making of the world.
　Then murmur'd Arthur, "Place me in the barge,"
And to the barge they came. There those three queens
Put forth their hands, and took the king, and wept.
But she that rose the tallest of them all
And fairest laid his head upon her lap
And loosed the shatter'd casque, and chafed his hands,
And call'd him by his name, complaining loud,   210
And dropping bitter tears against his brow
Striped with dark blood; for all his face was white
And colourless, and like the wither'd moon
Smote by the fresh beam of the springing east;
And all his greaves and cuisses dash'd with drops
Of onset; and the light and lustrous curls—
That made his forehead like a rising sun
High from the dais-throne—were parch'd with dust;
Or, clotted into points and hanging loose,
Mix'd with the knightly growth that fringed his lips. 220
So like a shatter'd column lay the king;
Not like that Arthur who, with lance in rest,
From spur to plume a star of tournament,
Shot thro' the lists of Camelot, and charged
Before the eyes of ladies and of kings.
　Then loudly cried the bold Sir Bedivere:
"Ah! my Lord Arthur, whither shall I go?
Where shall I hide my forehead and my eyes?
For now I see the true old times are dead,
When every morning brought a noble chance,   230
And every chance brought out a noble knight.
Such times have been not since the light that led
The holy Elders with the gift of myrrh.
But now the whole ROUND TABLE is dissolved
Which was an image of the mighty world;
And I, the last, go forth companionless,
And the days darken round me, and the years,

Among new men, strange faces, other minds."
  And slowly answer'd Arthur from the barge:
"The old order changeth, yielding place to new,   240
And God fulfills himself in many ways,
Lest one good custom should corrupt the world.
Comfort thyself; what comfort is in me?
I have lived my life, and that which I have done
May He within himself make pure! but thou,
If thou shouldst never see my face again,
Pray for my soul. More things are wrought by prayer
Than this world dreams of. Wherefore, let thy voice
Rise like a fountain for me night and day.
For what are men better than sheep or goats   250
That nourish a blind life within the brain,
If, knowing God, they lift not hands of prayer
Both for themselves and those who call them friend?
For so the whole round earth is every way
Bound by gold chains about the feet of God.
But now farewell. I am going a long way
With these thou seest—if indeed I go—
For all my mind is clouded with a doubt—
To the island-valley of Avilion;
Where falls not hail, or rain, or any snow,   260
Nor ever wind blows loudly, but it lies
Deep-meadow'd, happy, fair with orchard lawns
And bowery hollows crown'd with summer sea,
Where I will heal me of my grievous wound."
  So said he, and the barge with oar and sail
Moved from the brink, like some full-breasted swan
That, fluting a wild carol ere her death,
Ruffles her pure cold plume, and takes the flood
With swarthy webs. Long stood Sir Bedivere
Revolving many memories, till the hull   270
Look'd one black dot against the verge of dawn,
And on the mere the wailing died away.

                  1842

ULYSSES

It little profits that an idle king,
By this still hearth, among these barren crags,
Matched with an aged wife, I mete and dole
Unequal laws unto a savage race,
That hoard, and sleep, and feed, and know not me.
I cannot rest from travel. I will drink
Life to the lees. All times I have enjoyed
Greatly, have suffered greatly, both with those
That loved me, and alone; on shore, and when
Through scudding drifts the rainy Hyades   10
Vexed the dim sea. I am become a name;
For always roaming with a hungry heart
Much have I seen and known; cities of men,
And manners, climates, councils, governments,
Myself not least, but honoured of them all,—
And drunk delight of battle with my peers,
Far on the ringing plains of windy Troy.
I am a part of all that I have met;
Yet all experience is an arch where-through
Gleams that untravelled world whose margin fades   20
Forever and forever when I move.
How dull it is to pause, to make an end,
To rust unburnished, not to shine in use!
As though to breathe were life! Life piled on life
Were all too little, and of one to me
Little remains; but every hour is saved
From that eternal silence, something more,
A bringer of new things; and vile it were
For some three suns to store and hoard myself,
And this gray spirit yearning in desire   30
To follow knowledge like a sinking star,
Beyond the utmost bound of human thought.

    This is my son, mine own Telemachus,
To whom I leave the sceptre and the isle—

Well-loved of me, discerning to fulfil
This labour, by slow prudence to make mild
A rugged people, and through soft degrees
Subdue them to the useful and the good.
Most blameless is he, centred in the sphere
Of common duties, decent not to fail   40
In offices of tenderness, and pay
Meet adoration to my household gods,
When I am gone. He works his work, I mine.
   There lies the port; the vessel puffs her sail;
There gloom the dark, broad seas. My mariners,
Souls that have toiled, and wrought, and thought with
    me,—
That ever with a frolic welcome took
The thunder and the sunshine, and opposed
Free hearts, free foreheads—you and I are old;
Old age hath yet his honour and his toil;   50
Death closes all. But something ere the end,
Some work of noble note, may yet be done,
Not unbecoming men that strove with gods.
The lights begin to twinkle from the rocks;
The long day wanes; the slow moon climbs; the deep
Moans round with many voices. Come, my friends,
'Tis not too late to seek a newer world.
Push off, and sitting well in order smite
The sounding furrows; for my purpose holds
To sail beyond the sunset, and the baths   60
Of all the western stars, until I die.
It may be that the gulfs will wash us down.
It may be we shall touch the Happy Isles,
And see the great Achilles, whom we knew.
Though much is taken, much abides; and though
We are not now that strength which in old days
Moved earth and heaven, that which we are, we
    are;
  One equal temper of heroic hearts,

Made weak by time and fate, but strong in will
To strive, to seek, to find, and not to yield.

1842

AS THROUGH THE LAND AT EVE WE WENT

As through the land at eve we went,
  And plucked the ripened ears,
We fell out, my wife and I,
Oh, we fell out, I know not why,
  And kissed again with tears.
And blessings on the falling out
  That all the more endears,
When we fall out with those we love
  And kiss again with tears!
For when we came where lies the child   10
  We lost in other years,
There above the little grave,
Oh, there above the little grave,
  We kissed again with tears.

1850

THE SPLENDOUR FALLS ON CASTLE WALLS

The splendour falls on castle walls
  And snowy summits old in story;
The long light shakes across the lakes,
  And the wild cataract leaps in glory.
Blow, bugle, blow, set the wild echoes flying,
Blow, bugle; answer, echoes, dying, dying, dying.

Oh, hark, oh, hear! how thin and clear,
  And thinner, clearer, farther going!
Oh, sweet and far from cliff and scar
  The horns of Elfland faintly blowing!   10

Blow, let us hear the purple glens replying,
Blow, bugle; answer, echoes, dying, dying, dying.

O love, they die in yon rich sky,
    They faint on hill or field or river;
Our echoes roll from soul to soul,
    And grow forever and forever.
Blow, bugle, blow, set the wild echoes flying,
And answer, echoes, answer, dying, dying, dying.

1850

TEARS, IDLE TEARS

Tears, idle tears, I know not what they mean,
Tears from the depth of some divine despair
Rise in the heart, and gather to the eyes,
In looking on the happy autumn-fields,
And thinking of the days that are no more.

Fresh as the first beam glittering on a sail,
That brings our friends up from the underworld,
Sad as the last which reddens over one
That sinks with all we love below the verge;
So sad, so fresh, the days that are no more.   10

Ah, sad and strange as in dark summer dawns
The earliest pipe of half-awakened birds
To dying ears, when unto dying eyes
The casement slowly grows a glimmering square;
So sad, so strange, the days that are no more.

Dear as remembered kisses after death,
And sweet as those by hopeless fancy feigned
On lips that are for others; deep as love,
Deep as first love, and wild with all regret;
O Death in Life, the days that are no more.

1847

ASK ME NO MORE

Ask me no more. The moon may draw the sea;
  The cloud may stoop from heaven and take the shape,
  With fold to fold, of mountain or of cape;
But O too fond, when have I answered thee?
      Ask me no more.

Ask me no more. What answer should I give?
  I love not hollow cheek or faded eye;
  Yet, O my friend, I will not have thee die!
Ask me no more, lest I should bid thee live;
      Ask me no more.   10

Ask me no more. Thy fate and mine are sealed;
  I strove against the stream and all in vain;
  Let the great river take me to the main.
No more, dear love, for at a touch I yield;
      Ask me no more.

                    1850

NOW SLEEPS THE CRIMSON PETAL

  Now sleeps the crimson petal, now the white;
Nor waves the cypress in the palace walk;
Nor winks the gold fin in the porphyry font.
The firefly wakens. Waken thou with me.

  Now droops the milk-white peacock like a ghost,
And like a ghost she glimmers on to me.

  Now lies the Earth all Danaë to the stars,
And all thy heart lies open unto me.

  Now slides the silent meteor on, and leaves
A shining furrow, as thy thoughts in me.   10

Now folds the lily all her sweetness up,
And slips into the bosom of the lake;
So fold thyself, my dearest, thou, and slip
Into my bosom and be lost in me.

1847

From IN MEMORIAM A. H. H.

OBIIT MDCCCXXXIII

PROEM

Strong Son of God, immortal Love,
    Whom we, that have not seen thy face,
    By faith, and faith alone, embrace,
Believing where we cannot prove;

Thine are these orbs of light and shade;
    Thou madest life in man and brute;
    Thou madest death; and lo, thy foot
Is on the skull which thou hast made.

Thou wilt not leave us in the dust:
    Thou madest man, he knows not why,   10
    He thinks he was not made to die;
And thou hast made him; thou art just.

Thou seemest human and divine,
    The highest, holiest manhood, thou.
    Our wills are ours, we know not how;
Our wills are ours, to make them thine.

Our little systems have their day;
    They have their day and cease to be;
    They are but broken lights of thee,
And thou, O Lord, are more than they.   20

We have but faith; we cannot know,
　　For knowledge is of things we see;
　　And yet we trust it comes from thee,
A beam in darkness; let it grow.

Let knowledge grow from more to more,
　　But more of reverence in us dwell;
　　That mind and soul, according well,
May make one music as before,

But vaster. We are fools and slight;
　　We mock thee when we do not fear.   30
　　But help thy foolish ones to bear;
Help thy vain worlds to bear thy light.

Forgive what seemed my sin in me,
　　What seemed my worth since I began;
　　For merit lives from man to man,
And not from man, O Lord, to thee.

Forgive my grief for one removed,
　　Thy creature, whom I found so fair.
　　I trust he lives in thee, and there
I find him worthier to be loved.   40

Forgive these wild and wandering cries,
　　Confusions of a wasted youth;
　　Forgive them where they fail in truth,
And in thy wisdom make me wise.

I

I held it truth, with him who sings
　　To one clear harp in divers tones,
　　That men may rise on stepping-stones
Of their dead selves to higher things.

But who shall so forecast the years
　　And find in loss a gain to match?
　　Or reach a hand through time to catch
The far-off interest of tears?

Let Love clasp Grief lest both be drowned;
　　Let darkness keep her raven gloss.　　　　　10
　　Ah, sweeter to be drunk with loss,
To dance with Death, to beat the ground,

Than that the victor Hours should scorn
　　The long result of love, and boast,
　　"Behold the man that loved and lost,
But all he was is overworn."

VII

Dark house, by which once more I stand
　　Here in the long unlovely street,
　　Doors, where my heart was used to beat
So quickly, waiting for a hand,

A hand that can be clasp'd no more—
　　Behold me, for I cannot sleep,
　　And like a guilty thing I creep
At earliest morning to the door.

He is not here; but far away
　　The noise of life begins again,　　　　　10
　　And ghastly thro' the drizzling rain
On the bald street breaks the blank day.

IX

Fair ship, that from the Italian shore
　　Sailest the placid ocean-plains
　　With my lost Arthur's loved remains,
Spread thy full wings, and waft him o'er.

So draw him home to those that mourn
   In vain; a favourable speed
   Ruffle thy mirrored mast, and lead
Through prosperous floods his holy urn.

All night no ruder air perplex
   Thy sliding keel, till Phosphor, bright   10
   As our pure love, through early light
Shall glimmer on the dewy decks.

Sphere all your lights around, above;
   Sleep, gentle heavens, before the prow;
   Sleep, gentle winds, as he sleeps now,
My friend, the brother of my love;

My Arthur, whom I shall not see
   Till all my widowed race be run;
   Dear as the mother to the son,
More than my brothers are to me.   20

XI

Calm is the morn without a sound,
   Calm as to suit a calmer grief,
   And only through the faded leaf
The chestnut pattering to the ground;

Calm and deep peace on this high wold,
   And on these dews that drench the furze,
   And all the silvery gossamers
That twinkle into green and gold;

Calm and still light on yon great plain
   That sweeps with all its autumn bowers,   10
   And crowded farms and lessening towers,
To mingle with the bounding main.

Calm and deep peace in this wide air,
　These leaves that redden to the fall;
　And in my heart, if calm at all,
If any calm, a calm despair.

Calm on the seas, and silver sleep,
　And waves that sway themselves in rest,
　And dead calm in that noble breast
Which heaves but with the heaving deep.　20

XXVII

I envy not in any moods
　The captive void of noble rage,
　The linnet born within the cage,
That never knew the summer woods;

I envy not the beast that takes
　His license in the field of time,
　Unfetter'd by the sense of crime,
To whom a conscience never wakes;

Nor, what may count itself as blest,
　The heart that never plighted troth　10
　But stagnates in the weeds of sloth;
Nor any want-begotten rest.

I hold it true, whate'er befall;
　I feel it, when I sorrow most;
　'Tis better to have loved and lost
Than never to have loved at all.

LIII

O yet we trust that somehow good
　Will be the final goal of ill,
　To pangs of nature, sins of will,
Defects of doubt, and taints of blood;

That nothing walks with aimless feet;
  That not one life shall be destroyed,
  Or cast as rubbish to the void,
When God hath made the pile complete;

That not a worm is cloven in vain;
  That not a moth with vain desire   10
  Is shriveled in a fruitless fire,
Or but subserves another's gain.

Behold, we know not anything;
  I can but trust that good shall fall
  At last—far off—at last, to all,
And every winter change to spring.

So runs my dream. But what am I?
  An infant crying in the night;
  An infant crying for the light;
And with no language but a cry.   20

LV

"So careful of the type?" but no.
  From scarpéd cliff and quarried stone
  She cries, "A thousand types are gone.
I care for nothing, all shall go.

"Thou makest thine appeal to me;
  I bring to life, I bring to death;
  The spirit does but mean the breath.
I know no more." And he, shall he,

Man, her last work, who seemed so fair,
  Such splendid purpose in his eyes,   10
  Who rolled the psalm to wintry skies,
Who built him fanes of fruitless prayer,

Who trusted God was love indeed
   And love Creation's final law—
   Though Nature, red in tooth and claw
With ravine, shrieked against his creed—

Who loved, who suffered countless ills,
   Who battled for the True, the Just,
   Be blown about the desert dust,
Or sealed within the iron hills?   20

No more? A monster then, a dream,
   A discord. Dragons of the prime,
   That tare each other in their slime,
Were mellow music matched with him.

O life as futile, then, as frail!
   O for thy voice to soothe and bless!
   What hope of answer, or redress?
Behind the veil, behind the veil.

XCV

You say, but with no touch of scorn,
   Sweet-hearted, you, whose light-blue eyes
   Are tender over drowning flies,
You tell me, doubt is Devil-born.

I know not: one indeed I knew
   In many a subtle question versed,
   Who touch'd a jarring lyre at first,
But ever strove to make it true;

Perplext in faith, but pure in deeds,
   At last he beat his music out.   10
   There lives more faith in honest doubt,
Believe me, than in half the creeds.

He fought his doubts and gather'd strength,
 He would not make his judgment blind,
 He faced the specters of the mind
And laid them; thus he came at length

To find a stronger faith his own,
 And Power was with him in the night,
 Which makes the darkness and the light,
And dwells not in the light alone,   20

But in the darkness and the cloud,
 As over Sinai's peaks of old,
 While Israel made their gods of gold,
Altho' the trumpet blew so loud.

CV

Ring out, wild bells, to the wild sky,
 The flying cloud, the frosty light;
 The year is dying in the night;
Ring out, wild bells, and let him die.

Ring out the old, ring in the new,
 Ring, happy bells, across the snow;
 The year is going, let him go;
Ring out the false, ring in the true.

Ring out the grief that saps the mind,
 For those that here we see no more;   10
 Ring out the feud of rich and poor;
Ring in redress to all mankind.

Ring out a slowly dying cause,
 And ancient forms of party strife;
 Ring in the nobler modes of life,
With sweeter manners, purer laws.

Ring out the want, the care, the sin,
  The faithless coldness of the times;
  Ring out, ring out my mournful rimes,
But ring the fuller minstrel in.   20

Ring out false pride in place and blood,
  The civic slander and the spite;
  Ring in the love of truth and right;
Ring in the common love of good.

Ring out old shapes of foul disease;
  Ring out the narrowing lust of gold;
  Ring out the thousand wars of old,
Ring in the thousand years of peace.

Ring in the valiant man and free,
  The larger heart, the kindlier hand;   30
  Ring out the darkness of the land.
Ring in the Christ that is to be.

CXXIX

Thy voice is on the rolling air;
  I hear thee where the waters run;
  Thou standest in the rising sun,
And in the setting thou art fair.

What art thou then? I cannot guess;
  But tho' I seem in star and flower
  To feel thee some diffusive power,
I do not therefore love thee less.

My love involves the love before;
  My love is vaster passion now;   10
  Tho' mix'd with God and Nature thou,
I seem to love thee more and more.

Far off thou art, but ever nigh;
  I have thee still, and I rejoice;
  I prosper, circled with thy voice;
I shall not lose thee tho' I die.

CXXXI

O living will that shalt endure
  When all that seems shall suffer shock,
  Rise in the spiritual rock,
Flow thro' our deeds and make them pure,

That we may lift from out of dust
  A voice as unto him that hears,
  A cry above the conquer'd years
To one that with us works, and trust,

With faith that comes of self-control,
  The truths that never can be proved   10
  Until we close with all we loved,
And all we flow from, soul in soul.

         .   .   .   .

Again the feast, the speech, the glee,
  The shade of passing thought, the wealth
  Of words and wit, the double health,
The crowning cup, the three-times-three,

And last the dance;—till I retire.
  Dumb is that tower which spake so loud,
  And high in heaven the streaming cloud,
And on the downs a rising fire: 120

And rise, O moon, from yonder down
  Till over down and over dale
  All night the shining vapor sail
And pass the silent-lighted town,

The white-faced halls, the glancing rills,
   And catch at every mountain head,
   And o'er the friths that branch and spread
Their sleeping silver thro' the hills;

And touch with shade the bridal doors,
   With tender gloom the roof, the wall;   130
   And breaking let the splendor fall
To spangle all the happy shores

By which they rest, and ocean sounds,
   And, star and system rolling past,
   A soul shall draw from out the vast
And strike his being into bounds,

And, moved thro' life of lower phase,
   Result in man, be born and think,
   And act and love, a closer link
Betwixt us and the crowning race   140

Of those that, eye to eye, shall look
   On knowledge; under whose command
   Is Earth and Earth's, and in their hand
Is Nature like an open book;

No longer half-akin to brute,
   For all we thought and loved and did,
   And hoped, and suffer'd, is but seed
Of what in them is flower and fruit;

Whereof the man that with me trod
   This planet was a noble type   150
   Appearing ere the times were ripe,
That friend of mine who lives in God,

That God, which ever lives and loves,
One God, one law, one element,
And one far-off divine event,
To which the whole creation moves.

1850

THE EAGLE

FRAGMENT

He clasps the crag with crooked hands;
Close to the sun in lonely lands,
Ring'd with the azure world, he stands.

The wrinkled sea beneath him crawls;
He watches from his mountain walls,
And like a thunderbolt he falls.

1851

ODE ON THE DEATH OF THE DUKE OF WELLINGTON

Bury the Great Duke
  With an empire's lamentation;
Let us bury the Great Duke
  To the noise of the mourning of a mighty nation;
Mourning when their leaders fall,
Warriors carry the warrior's pall,
And sorrow darkens hamlet and hall.

Where shall we lay the man whom we deplore?
Here, in streaming London's central roar.
Let the sound of those he wrought for,   10
And the feet of those he fought for,
Echo round his bones for evermore.

Lead out the pageant; sad and slow,
As fits an universal woe,
Let the long, long procession go,
And let the sorrowing crowd about it grow,
And let the mournful martial music blow;
The last great Englishman is low.

Mourn, for to us he seems the last,
Remembering all his greatness in the past.　　　20
No more in soldier fashion will he greet
With lifted hand the gazer in the street.
O friends, our chief state-oracle is mute!
Mourn for the man of long-enduring blood,
The statesman-warrior, moderate, resolute,
Whole in himself, a common good.
Mourn for the man of amplest influence,
Yet clearest of ambitious crime,
Our greatest yet with least pretense,
Great in council and great in war.　　　30
Foremost captain of his time,
Rich in saving common-sense,
And, as the greatest only are,
In his simplicity sublime.
O good gray head which all men knew,
O voice from which their omens all men drew,
O iron nerve to true occasion true,
O fallen at length that tower of strength
Which stood four-square to all the winds that blew!
Such was he whom we deplore.　　　40
The long self-sacrifice of life is o'er.
The great World-victor's victor will be seen no more.

All is over and done.
Render thanks to the Giver,
England, for thy son.
Let the bell be tolled.

Render thanks to the Giver,
And render him to the mould.
Under the cross of gold
That shines over city and river, 50
There he shall rest forever
Among the wise and the bold.
Let the bell be tolled,
And a reverent people behold
The towering car, the sable steeds.
Bright let it be with its blazoned deeds,
Dark in its funeral fold.
Let the bell be tolled,
And a deeper knell in the heart be knolled;
And the sound of the sorrowing anthem rolled 60
Through the dome of the golden cross;
And the volleying cannon thunder his loss;
He knew their voices of old.
For many a time in many a clime
His captain's-ear has heard them boom,
Bellowing victory, bellowing doom.
When he with those deep voices wrought
Guarding realms and kings from shame,
With those deep voices our dead captain taught
The tyrant, and asserts his claim 70
In that dread sound to the great name
Which he has worn so pure of blame,
In praise and in dispraise the same,
A man of well-attempered frame.
O civic muse, to such a name,
To such a name for ages long,
To such a name,
Preserve a broad approach of fame,
And ever-echoing avenues of song!

"Who is he that cometh, like an honoured guest, 80
With banner and with music, with soldier and with priest,

With a nation weeping, and breaking on my rest?"—
Mighty Seaman, this is he
Was great by land as thou by sea.
Thine island loves thee well, thou famous man,
The greatest sailor since our world began.
Now, to the roll of muffled drums,
To thee the greatest soldier comes;
For this is he
Was great by land as thou by sea.   90
His foes were thine; he kept us free;
Oh, give him welcome, this is he
Worthy of our gorgeous rites,
And worthy to be laid by thee;
For this is England's greatest son,
He that gained a hundred fights,
Nor ever lost an English gun;
This is he that far away
Against the myriads of Assaye
Clashed with his fiery few and won;   100
And underneath another sun,
Warring on a later day,
Round affrighted Lisbon drew
The treble works, the vast designs
Of his labored rampart-lines,
Where he greatly stood at bay,
Whence he issued forth anew,
And ever great and greater grew,
Beating from the wasted vines
Back to France her banded swarms,   110
Back to France with countless blows,
Till o'er the hills her eagles flew
Beyond the Pyrenean pines,
Followed up in valley and glen
With blare of bugle, clamour of men,
Roll of cannon and clash of arms,
And England pouring on her foes,

Such a war had such a close.
Again their ravening eagle rose
In anger, wheeled on Europe-shadowing wings,   120
And barking for the thrones of kings;
Till one that sought but Duty's iron crown
On that loud Sabbath shook the spoiler down;
A day of onsets of despair!
Dashed on every rocky square,
Their surging charges foamed themselves away;
Last, the Prussian trumpet blew;
Through the long-tormented air
Heaven flashed a sudden jubilant ray,
And down we swept and charged and overthrew. 130
So great a soldier taught us there
What long-enduring hearts could do
In that world-earthquake, Waterloo!
Mighty Seaman, tender and true,
And pure as he from taint of craven guile,
O savior of the silver-coasted isle,
O shaker of the Baltic and the Nile,
If aught of things that here befall
Touch a spirit among things divine,
If love of country move thee there at all,   140
Be glad, because his bones are laid by thine!
And through the centuries let a people's voice
In full acclaim,
A people's voice,
The proof and echo of all human fame,
A people's voice, when they rejoice
At civic revel and pomp and game,
Attest their great commander's claim
With honour, honour, honour, honour to him,
Eternal honour to his name.   150

A people's voice! we are a people yet.
Though all men else their nobler dreams forget,

Confused by brainless mobs and lawless Powers,
Thank Him who isled us here, and roughly set
His Briton in blown seas and storming showers,
We have a voice with which to pay the debt
Of boundless love and reverence and regret
To those great men who fought, and kept it ours.
And keep it ours, O God, from brute control!
O statesmen, guard us, guard the eye, the soul   160
Of Europe, keep our noble England whole,
And save the one true seed of freedom sown
Betwixt a people and their ancient throne,
That sober freedom out of which there springs
Our loyal passion for our temperate kings!
For, saving that, ye help to save mankind
Till public wrong be crumbled into dust,
And drill the raw world for the march of mind,
Till crowds at length be sane and crowns be just.
But wink no more in slothful overtrust.   170
Remember him who led your hosts;
He bade you guard the sacred coasts.
Your cannons moulder on the seaward wall;
His voice is silent in your council-hall
Forever; and whatever tempests lour
Forever silent; even if they broke
In thunder, silent; yet remember all
He spoke among you, and the Man who spoke;
Who never sold the truth to serve the hour,
Nor paltered with Eternal God for power;   180
Who let the turbid streams of rumour flow
Through either babbling world of high and low;
Whose life was work, whose language rife
With rugged maxims hewn from life;
Who never spoke against a foe;
Whose eighty winters freeze with one rebuke
All great self-seekers trampling on the right.
Truth-teller was our England's Alfred named;

Truth-lover was our English Duke!
Whatever record leap to light   190
He never shall be shamed.

Lo! the leader in these glorious wars
Now to glorious burial slowly borne,
Followed by the brave of other lands,
He, on whom from both her open hands
Lavish Honour showered all her stars,
And affluent Fortune emptied all her horn.
Yea, let all good things await
Him who cares not to be great
But as he saves or serves the state.   200
Not once or twice in our rough island-story
The path of duty was the way to glory.
He that walks it, only thirsting
For the right, and learns to deaden
Love of self, before his journey closes,
He shall find the stubborn thistle bursting
Into glossy purples, which out-redden
All voluptuous garden-roses.
Not once or twice in our fair island-story
The path of duty was the way to glory.   210
He, that ever following her commands,
On with toil of heart and knees and hands,
Through the long gorge to the far light has won
His path upward, and prevailed,
Shall find the toppling crags of Duty scaled
Are close upon the shining table lands
To which our God himself is moon and sun.
Such was he; his work is done.
But while the races of mankind endure
Let his great example stand   220
Colossal, seen of every land,
And keep the soldier firm, the statesman pure;
Till in all lands and through all human story

The path of duty be the way to glory.
And let the land whose hearths he saved from shame
For many and many an age proclaim
At civic revel and pomp and game,
And when the long-illumined cities flame,
Their ever-loyal iron leader's fame,
With honour, honour, honour, honour to him,   230
Eternal honour to his name.

Peace, his triumph will be sung
By some yet unmoulded tongue
Far on in summers that we shall not see.
Peace, it is a day of pain
For one about whose patriarchal knee
Late the little children clung.
O peace, it is a day of pain
For one upon whose hand and heart and brain
Once the weight and fate of Europe hung.   240
Ours the pain, be his the gain!
More than is of man's degree
Must be with us, watching here
At this, our great solemnity.
Whom we see not we revere;
We revere, and we refrain
From talk of battles loud and vain,
And brawling memories all too free
For such a wise humility
As befits a solemn fane.   250
We revere, and while we hear
The tides of Music's golden sea
Setting toward eternity,
Uplifted high in heart and hope are we,
Until we doubt not that for one so true
There must be other nobler work to do
Than when he fought at Waterloo,
And victor he must ever be.

For though the Giant Ages heave the hill
And break the shore, and evermore   260
Make and break, and work their will,
Though world on world in myriad myriads roll
Round us, each with different powers,
And other forms of life than ours,
What know we greater than the soul?
On God and Godlike men we build our trust.
Hush, the Dead March wails in the people's ears;
The dark crowd moves, and there are sobs and tears;
The black earth yawns; the mortal disappears;
Ashes to ashes, dust to dust;   270
He is gone who seemed so great.—
Gone, but nothing can bereave him
Of the force he made his own
Being here, and we believe him
Something far advanced in state,
And that he wears a truer crown
Than any wreath that man can weave him.
Speak no more of his renown,
Lay your earthly fancies down,
And in the vast cathedral leave him,   280
God accept him, Christ receive him!

                                          1852

IDYLLS OF THE KING

DEDICATION

These to His Memory—since he held them dear,
Perchance as finding there unconsciously
Some image of himself—I dedicate,
I dedicate, I consecrate with tears—
These Idylls.

            And indeed he seems to me
Scarce other than my king's ideal knight,

"Who reverenced his conscience as his king;
Whose glory was, redressing human wrong;
Who spake no slander, no, nor listen'd to it;
Who loved one only and who clave to her—"   10
Her—over all whose realms to their last isle,
Commingled with the gloom of imminent war,
The shadow of his loss drew like eclipse,
Darkening the world. We have lost him; he is gone.
We know him now; all narrow jealousies
Are silent, and we see him as he moved,
How modest, kindly, all-accomplish'd, wise,
With what sublime repression of himself,
And in what limits, and how tenderly;
Not swaying to this faction or to that;   20
Not making his high place the lawless perch
Of wing'd ambitions, nor a vantage-ground
For pleasure; but thro' all this tract of years
Wearing the white flower of a blameless life,
Before a thousand peering littlenesses,
In that fierce light which beats upon a throne
And blackens every blot; for where is he
Who dares foreshadow for an only son
A lovelier life, a more unstain'd, than his?
Or how should England dreaming of *his* sons   30
Hope more for these than some inheritance
Of such a life, a heart, a mind as thine,
Thou noble Father of her Kings to be,
Laborious for her people and her poor—
Voice in the rich dawn of an ampler day—
Far-sighted summoner of War and Waste
To fruitful strifes and rivalries of peace—
Sweet nature gilded by the gracious gleam
Of letters, dear to Science, dear to Art,
Dear to thy land and ours, a Prince indeed,   40
Beyond all titles, and a household name,
Hereafter, thro' all times, Albert the Good.

Break not, O woman's-heart, but still endure;
Break not, for thou art royal, but endure,
Remembering all the beauty of that star
Which shone so close beside thee that ye made
One light together, but has past and leaves
The Crown a lonely splendour.

                May all love,
His love, unseen but felt, o'ershadow thee,
The love of all thy sons encompass thee,   50
The love of all thy daughters cherish thee,
The love of all thy people comfort thee,
Till God's love set thee at his side again!

                      1862

MILTON

ALCAICS

O mighty-mouthed inventor of harmonies,
O skilled to sing of Time or Eternity,
  God-gifted organ-voice of England,
    Milton, a name to resound for ages:
Whose Titan angels, Gabriel, Abdiel,
Starred from Jehovah's gorgeous armories,
  Tower, as the deep-domed empyrean
    Rings to the roar of an angel onset!
Me rather all that bowery loneliness,
The brooks of Eden mazily murmuring,   10
  And bloom profuse and cedar arches
    Charm, as a wanderer out in ocean,
Where some refulgent sunset of India
Streams o'er a rich ambrosial ocean isle,
  And crimson-hued the stately palm-woods
    Whisper in odourous heights of even.

                    1863

FLOWER IN THE CRANNIED WALL

Flower in the crannied wall,
I pluck you out of the crannies,
I hold you here, root and all, in my hand,
Little flower—but *if* I could understand
What you are, root and all, and all in all,
I should know what God and man is.

1869

THE REVENGE

A BALLAD OF THE FLEET

I

At Flores in the Azores Sir Richard Grenville lay,
And a pinnace, like a fluttered bird, came flying from far
    away:
"Spanish ships of war at sea! we have sighted fifty-three!"
Then sware Lord Thomas Howard: "'Fore God I am no
    coward;
But I cannot meet them here, for my ships are out of gear,
And the half my men are sick. I must fly, but follow quick,
We are six ships of the line; can we fight with fifty-three?"

II

Then spake Sir Richard Grenville: "I know you are no
    coward;
You fly them for a moment to fight with them again.
But I've ninety men and more that are lying sick ashore. 10
I should count myself the coward if I left them, my Lord
    Howard,
To these Inquisition dogs and the devildoms of Spain."

III

So Lord Howard passed away with five ships of war that
    day,
Till he melted like a cloud in the silent summer heaven;

But Sir Richard bore in hand all his sick men from the land
Very carefully and slow,
Men of Bideford in Devon,
And we laid them on the ballast down below;
For we brought them all aboard,
And they blest him in their pain, that they were not left
    to Spain, 20
To the thumbscrew and the stake, for the glory of the
    Lord.

IV

He had only 'a hundred seamen to work the ship and to
    fight,
And he sailed away from Flores till the Spaniard came in
    sight,
With his huge sea-castles heaving upon the weather bow.
"Shall we fight or shall we fly?
Good Sir Richard, tell us now,
For to fight is but to die!
There'll be little of us left by the time this sun be set."
And Sir Richard said again: "We be all good English
    men.
Let us bang these dogs of Seville, the children of the devil,
For I never turned my back upon Don or devil yet." 31

V

Sir Richard spoke and he laughed, and we roared a hurrah,
    and so
The little Revenge ran on sheer into the heart of the
    foe,
With her hundred fighters on deck, and her ninety sick
    below;
For half of their fleet to the right and half to the left were
    seen,
And the little Revenge ran on through the long sea-lane
    between.

VI

Thousands of their soldiers looked down from their decks
and laughed,
Thousands of their seamen made mock at the mad little
craft
Running on and on, till delayed
By their mountain-like San Philip that, of fifteen hundred
tons,   40
And up-shadowing high above us with her yawning tiers
of guns,
Took the breath from our sails, and we stayed.

VII

And while now the great San Philip hung above us like a
cloud
Whence the thunderbolt will fall
Long and loud,
Four galleons drew away
From the Spanish fleet that day,
And two upon the larboard and two upon the starboard
lay,
And the battle-thunder broke from them all.

VIII

But anon the great San Philip, she bethought herself and
went,   50
Having that within her womb that had left her ill con-
tent;
And the rest they came aboard us, and they fought us
hand to hand,
For a dozen times they came with their pikes and mus-
queteers,
And a dozen times we shook 'em off as a dog that shakes
his ears
When he leaps from the water to the land.

IX

And the sun went down, and the stars came out far over
    the summer sea,
But never a moment ceased the fight of the one and the
    fifty-three.
Ship after ship, the whole night long, their high-built
    galleons came,
Ship after ship, the whole night long, with her battle-
    thunder and flame;
Ship after ship, the whole night long, drew back with her
    dead and her shame.   60
For some were sunk and many were shattered and so
    could fight us no more—
God of battles, was ever a battle like this in the world
    before?

X

For he said, "Fight on! fight on!"
Though his vessel was all but a wreck;
And it chanced that, when half of the short summer night
    was gone,
With a grisly wound to be drest he had left the deck,
But a bullet struck him that was dressing it suddenly dead,
And himself he was wounded again in the side and the
    head,
And he said, "Fight on! fight on!"

XI

And the night went down, and the sun smiled out far
    over the summer sea,   70
And the Spanish fleet with broken sides lay round us all
    in a ring;
But they dared not touch us again, for they feared that
    we still could sting,
So they watched what the end would be.
And we had not fought them in vain,

But in perilous plight were we,
Seeing forty of our poor hundred were slain,
And half of the rest of us maimed for life
In the crash of the cannonades and the desperate strife;
And the sick men down in the hold were most of them
    stark and cold,
And the pikes were all broken or bent, and the powder
    was all of it spent;   80
And the masts and the rigging were lying over the side;
But Sir Richard cried in his English pride:
"We have fought such a fight for a day and a night
As may never be fought again!
We have won great glory, my men!
And a day less or more
At sea or ashore,
We die—does it matter when?
Sink me the ship, Master Gunner—sink her, split her in
    twain!
Fall into the hands of God, not into the hands of Spain!" 90

XII

And the gunner said, "Ay, ay," but the seamen made
    reply:
"We have children, we have wives,
And the Lord hath spared our lives.
We will make the Spaniard promise, if we yield, to let us go;
We shall live to fight again and to strike another blow."
And the lion there lay dying, and they yielded to the foe.

XIII

And the stately Spanish men to their flagship bore him
    then,
Where they laid him by the mast, old Sir Richard caught
    at last,
And they praised him to his face with their courtly foreign
    grace;
But he rose upon their decks, and he cried: 100

"I have fought for Queen and Faith like a valiant man
  and true;
I have only done my duty as a man is bound to do.
With a joyful spirit I Sir Richard Grenville die!"
And he fell upon their decks, and he died.

XIV

And they stared at the dead that had been so valiant and
  true,
And had holden the power and glory of Spain so cheap
That he dared her with one little ship and his English few;
Was he devil or man? He was devil for aught they knew,
But they sank his body with honour down into the deep,
And they manned the Revenge with a swarthier alien
  crew,   110
And away she sailed with her loss and longed for her own;
When a wind from the lands they had ruined awoke from
  sleep,
And the water began to heave and the weather to moan,
And or ever that evening ended a great gale blew,
And a wave like the wave that is raised by an earthquake
  grew,
Till it smote on their hulls and their sails and their masts
  and their flags,
And the whole sea plunged and fell on the shot shattered
  navy of Spain,
And the little Revenge herself went down by the island
  crags
To be lost evermore in the main.

1878

TO VIRGIL

Roman Virgil, thou that singest Ilion's lofty temples robed
  in fire,
Ilion falling, Rome arising, wars, and filial faith, and Dido's
  pyre;

Landscape-lover, lord of language more than he that sang
    the "Works and Days,"
All the chosen coin of fancy flashing out from many a
    golden phrase;

Thou that singest wheat and woodland, tilth and vine-
    yard, hive and horse and herd;
All the charm of all the Muses often flowering in a lonely
    word;

Poet of the happy Tityrus piping underneath his beechen
    bowers;
Poet of the poet-satyr whom the laughing shepherd bound
    with flowers;

Chanter of the Pollio, glorying in the blissful years again
    to be,
Summers of the snakeless meadow, unlaborious earth and
    oarless sea;   10

Thou that seest Universal Nature moved by Universal
    Mind;
Thou majestic in thy sadness at the doubtful doom of
    human kind;

Light among the vanished ages; star that gildest yet this
    phantom shore;
Golden branch amid the shadows, kings and realms that
    pass to rise no more;

Now thy Forum roars no longer, fallen every purple
    Caesar's dome—
Though thine ocean-roll of rhythm sound forever of Im-
    perial Rome—

Now the Rome of slaves hath perished, and the Rome of
    freemen holds her place,
I, from out the northern island sundered once from all
    the human race,

I salute thee, Mantovano, I that loved thee since my day
    began,
Wielder of the stateliest measure ever moulded by the lips
    of man.

1882

MERLIN AND THE GLEAM

I

O young Mariner,
You from the haven
Under the sea-cliff,
You that are watching
The gray Magician
With eyes of wonder,
I am Merlin,
And *I* am dying,
I am Merlin
Who follow the Gleam.   10

II

Mighty the Wizard
Who found me at sunrise
Sleeping, and woke me
And learn'd me Magic!
Great the Master,
And sweet the Magic,
When over the valley,
In early summers,
Over the mountain,
On human faces,   20
And all around me,
Moving to melody,
Floated the Gleam.

III

Once at the croak of a Raven who crost it,
    A barbarous people,
    Blind to the magic
    And deaf to the melody,
    Snarl'd at and cursed me.
    A demon vext me,
    The light retreated,   30
    The landskip darken'd,
    The melody deaden'd,
    The Master whisper'd,
    "Follow the Gleam."

IV

    Then to the melody,
    Over a wilderness
    Gliding, and glancing at
    Elf of the woodland,
    Gnome of the cavern,
    Griffin and Giant,   40
    And dancing of Fairies
    In desolate hollows,
    And wraiths of the mountain,
    And rolling of dragons
    By warble of water,
    Or cataract music
    Of falling torrents,
    Flitted the Gleam.

V

    Down from the mountain
    And over the level,   50
    And streaming and shining on
    Silent river,
    Silvery willow,

Pasture and plowland,
Innocent maidens,
Garrulous children,
Homestead and harvest,
Reaper and gleaner,
And rough-ruddy faces
Of lowly labour,   60
Slided the Gleam—

VI

Then, with a melody
Stronger and statelier,
Led me at length
To the city and palace
Of Arthur the King;
Touch'd at the golden
Cross of the churches,
Flash'd on the tournament,
Flicker'd and bicker'd   70
From helmet to helmet,
And last on the forehead
Of Arthur the blameless
Rested the Gleam.

VII

Clouds and darkness
Closed upon Camelot;
Arthur had vanish'd
I knew not whither,
The king who loved me,
And cannot die;   80
For out of the darkness
Silent and slowly
The Gleam, that had waned to a wintry glimmer
On icy fallow
And faded forest,

Drew to the valley
Named of the shadow,
And slowly brightening
Out of the glimmer,
And slowly moving again to a melody   90
Yearningly tender,
Fell on the shadow,
No longer a shadow,
But clothed with the Gleam.

VIII

And broader and brighter
The Gleam flying onward,
Wed to the melody,
Sang thro' the world;
And slower and fainter,
Old and weary,   100
But eager to follow,
I saw, whenever
In passing it glanced upon
Hamlet or city,
That under the Crosses
The dead man's garden,
The mortal hillock,
Would break into blossom;
And so to the land's
Last limit I came—
And can no longer,   110
But die rejoicing,
For thro' the Magic
Of Him the Mighty,
Who taught me in childhood,
There on the border
Of boundless Ocean,
And all but in Heaven
Hovers the Gleam.

IX

Not of the sunlight,
Not of the moonlight,   120
Not of the starlight!
O young Mariner,
Down to the haven,
Call your companions,
Launch your vessel
And crowd your canvas,
And, ere it vanishes
Over the margin,
After it, follow it,
Follow the Gleam.

1889

CROSSING THE BAR

Sunset and evening star,
  And one clear call for me!
And may there be no moaning of the bar,
  When I put out to sea,

But such a tide as moving seems asleep,
  Too full for sound and foam,
When that which drew from out the boundless deep
  Turns again home.

Twilight and evening bell,
  And after that the dark!   10
And may there be no sadness of farewell,
  When I embark;

For though from out our bourne of Time and Place
  The flood may bear me far,
I hope to see my Pilot face to face
  When I have crossed the bar.

1889

ROBERT BROWNING (1812–1889)

MY LAST DUCHESS

That's my last Duchess painted on the wall,
Looking as if she were alive. I call
That piece a wonder, now. Fra Pandolf's hands
Worked busily a day, and there she stands.
Will 't please you sit and look at her? I said
"Fra Pandolf" by design, for never read
Strangers like you that pictured countenance,
The depth and passion of its earnest glance,
But to myself they turned—since none puts by
The curtain I have drawn for you, but I—   10
And seemed as they would ask me, if they durst,
How such a glance came there; so, not the first
Are you to turn and ask thus. Sir, 'twas not
Her husband's presence only called that spot
Of joy into the Duchess' cheek. Perhaps
Fra Pandolf chanced to say, "Her mantle laps
Over my lady's wrist too much," or "Paint
Must never hope to reproduce the faint
Half-flush that dies along her throat"; such stuff
Was courtesy, she thought, and cause enough   20
For calling up that spot of joy. She had
A heart—how shall I say?—too soon made glad,
Too easily impressed; she liked whate'er
She looked on, and her looks went everywhere.
Sir, 'twas all one! My favor at her breast,
The dropping of the daylight in the west,
The bough of cherries some officious fool
Broke in the orchard for her, the white mule
She rode with round the terrace—all and each
Would draw from her alike the approving speech,   30
Or blush, at least. She thanked men—good! but thanked
Somehow—I know not how—as if she ranked

My gift of a nine-hundred-years-old name
With anybody's gift. Who'd stoop to blame
This sort of trifling? Even had you skill
In speech—which I have not—to make your will
Quite clear to such an one, and say, "Just this
Or that in you disgusts me; here you miss,
Or there exceed, the mark"—and if she let
Herself be lessoned so, nor plainly set   40
Her wits to yours, forsooth, and made excuse,
—E'en then would be some stooping; and I choose
Never to stoop. Oh, sir, she smiled, no doubt,
Whene'er I passed her; but who passed without
Much the same smile? This grew; I gave commands;
Then all smiles stopped together. There she stands
As if alive. Will 't please you rise? We'll meet
The company below, then. I repeat,
The Count your master's known munificence
Is ample warrant that no just pretense   50
Of mine for dowry will be disallowed;
Though his fair daughter's self, as I avowed
At starting, is my object. Nay, we'll go
Together down, sir. Notice Neptune, though,
Taming a sea-horse, thought a rarity,
Which Claus of Innsbruck cast in bronze for me!

1842

SOLILOQUY OF THE SPANISH CLOISTER

    Gr-r-r—there go, my heart's abhorrence!
      Water your damned flower-pots, do!
    If hate killed men, Brother Lawrence,
      God's blood, would not mine kill you!
    What? your myrtle-bush wants trimming?
      Oh, that rose has prior claims—
    Needs its leaden vase filled brimming?
      Hell dry you up with its flames!

At the meal we sit together:
　　Salve tibi! I must hear　　　　　　　　　10
Wise talk of the kind of weather,
　　Sort of season, time of year:
Not a plenteous cork-crop: scarcely
　　Dare we hope oak-galls, I doubt:
What 's the Latin name for "parsley"?
　　What 's the Greek name for Swine's Snout?

Whew! We 'll have our platter burnished,
　　Laid with care on our own shelf!
With a fire-new spoon we 've furnished,
　　And a goblet for ourself,　　　　　　　　20
Rinsed like something sacrificial
　　Ere 'tis fit to touch our chaps—
Marked with L for our initial!
　　(He-he! There his lily snaps!)

Saint, forsooth! While brown Dolores
　　Squats outside the Convent bank
With Sanchicha, telling stories,
　　Steeping tressès in the tank,
Blue-black, lustrous, thick like horsehairs,
　　—Can't I see his dead eye glow,　　　　30
Bright as 'twere a Barbary corsair's?
　　(That is, if he 'd let it show!)

When he finishes refection,
　　Knife and fork he never lays
Cross-wise, to my recollection,
　　As do I, in Jesu's praise.
I the Trinity illustrate,
　　Drinking watered orange-pulp—
In three sips the Arian frustrate;
　　While he drains his at one gulp.　　　　40

Oh, those melons! If he's able
  We're to have a feast! so nice!
One goes to the Abbot's table,
  All of us get each a slice.
How go on your flowers? None double?
  Not one fruit-sort can you spy?
Strange!—And I, too, at such trouble,
  Keep them close-nipped on the sly!

There's a great text in Galatians,
  Once you trip on it, entails   50
Twenty-nine distinct damnations,
  One sure, if another fails:
If I trip him just a-dying,
  Sure of heaven as sure can be,
Spin him round and send him flying
  Off to hell, a Manichee?

Or, my scrofulous French novel
  On gray paper with blunt type!
Simply glance at it, you grovel
  Hand and foot in Belial's gripe: 60
If I double down its pages
  At the woeful sixteenth print,
When he gathers his greengages,
  Ope a sieve and slip it in't?

Or, there's Satan!—one might venture
  Pledge one's soul to him, yet leave
Such a flaw in the indenture
  As he'd miss till, past retrieve,
Blasted lay that rose-acacia
  We're so proud of! *Hy, Zy, Hine* . . .   70
'St, there's Vespers! *Plena gratiâ,*
  Ave, Virgo! Gr-r-r—you swine!

1842

THE LABORATORY

ANCIEN RÉGIME

Now that I, tying thy glass mask tightly,
May gaze through these faint smokes curling whitely,
As thou pliest thy trade in this devil's smithy—
Which is the poison to poison her, prithee?

He is with her; and they know that I know
Where they are, what they do. They believe my tears flow
While they laugh, laugh at me, at me fled to the drear
Empty church, to pray God in, for them!—I am here.

Grind away, moisten and mash up thy paste,
Pound at thy powder—I am not in haste!   10
Better sit thus, and observe thy strange things,
Than go where men wait me and dance at the King's.

That in the mortar—you call it a gum?
Ah, the brave tree whence such gold oozings come!
And yonder soft phial, the exquisite blue,
Sure to taste sweetly—is that poison too?

Had I but all of them, thee and thy treasures,
What a wild crowd of invisible pleasures!
To carry pure death in an earring, a casket,
A signet, a fan-mount, a filigree-basket!   20

Soon, at the King's, a mere lozenge to give,
And Pauline should have just thirty minutes to live!
But to light a pastille, and Elise, with her head,
And her breast, and her arms, and her hands, should drop
     dead!

Quick—is it finished? The colour's too grim!
Why not soft like the phial's, enticing and dim?
Let it brighten her drink, let her turn it and stir,
And try it and taste, ere she fix and prefer!

What, a drop? She's not little, no minion like me!
That's why she ensnared him; this never will free   30
The soul from those masculine eyes—say, "no!"
To that pulse's magnificent come-and-go.

For only last night, as they whispered, I brought
My own eyes to bear on her so, that I thought
Could I keep them one half minute fixed, she would fall,
Shriveled; she fell not; yet this does it all!

Not that I bid you spare her the pain!
Let death be felt and the proof remain;
Brand, burn up, bite into its grace—
He is sure to remember her dying face!   40

Is it done? Take my mask off; Nay, be not morose;
It kills her, and this prevents seeing it close:
The delicate droplet, my whole fortune's fee—
If it hurts her, beside, can it ever hurt me?

Now, take all my jewels, gorge gold to your fill,
You may kiss me, old man, on my mouth if you will!
But brush this dust off me, lest horror it brings
Ere I know it—next moment I dance at the King's!

                                        1844

THE BISHOP ORDERS HIS TOMB AT
ST. PRAXED'S CHURCH

Rome, 15—

Vanity, saith the preacher, vanity!
Draw round my bed; is Anselm keeping back?
Nephews—sons mine . . . ah God, I know not! Well—
She, men would have to be your mother once,
Old Gandolf envied me, so fair she was!
What's done is done, and she is dead beside,
Dead long ago, and I am Bishop since,

And as she died so must we die ourselves,
And thence ye may perceive the world's a dream.
Life, how and what is it? As here I lie   10
In this state-chamber, dying by degrees,
Hours and long hours in the dead night, I ask,
"Do I live; am I dead?" Peace, peace seems all.
St. Praxed's ever was the church for peace;
And so, about this tomb of mine. I fought
With tooth and nail to save my niche, ye know.
—Old Gandolf cozened me, despite my care;
Shrewd was that snatch from out the corner south
He graced his carrion with, God curse the same!
Yet still my niche is not so cramped but thence   20
One sees the pulpit o' the epistle-side,
And somewhat of the choir, those silent seats,
And up into the aëry dome where live
The angels, and a sunbeam's sure to lurk.
And I shall fill my slab of basalt there,
And 'neath my tabernacle take my rest,
With those nine columns round me, two and two,
The odd one at my feet where Anselm stands,
Peach-blossom marble all, the rare, the ripe,
As fresh-poured red wine of a mighty pulse.   30
—Old Gandolf with his paltry onion-stone,
Put me where I may look at him! True peach,
Rosy and flawless; how I earned the prize!
Draw close. That conflagration of my church
—What then? So much was saved if aught were missed!
My sons, ye would not be my death? Go dig
The white-grape vineyard where the oil-press stood,
Drop water gently till the surface sinks,
And if ye find . . . ah God, I know not, I! . . .
Bedded in store of rotten fig-leaves soft,   40
And corded up in a tight olive-frail,
Some lump, ah God, of *lapis lazuli*,
Big as a Jew's head cut off at the nape,

Blue as a vein o'er the Madonna's breast—
Sons, all have I bequeathed you, villas, all,
That brave Frascati villa with its bath—
So, let the blue lump poise between my knees,
Like God the Father's globe on both his hands
Ye worship in the Jesu Church so gay,
For Gandolf shall not choose but see and burst!   50
Swift as a weaver's shuttle fleet our years;
Man goeth to the grave, and where is he?
Did I say basalt for my slab, sons? Black—
'Twas ever antique-black I meant! How else
Shall ye contrast my frieze to come beneath?
The bas-relief in bronze ye promised me,
Those Pans and Nymphs ye wot of, and perchance
Some tripod, thyrsus, with a vase or so,
The Savior at his sermon on the mount,
St. Praxed in a glory, and one Pan   60
Ready to twitch the Nymph's last garment off,
And Moses with the tables . . . but I know
Ye mark me not! What do they whisper thee,
Child of my bowels, Anselm? Ah, ye hope
To revel down my villas while I gasp
Bricked o'er with beggar's mouldy travertine
Which Gandolf from his tomb-top chuckles at!
Nay, boys, ye love me—all of jasper, then!
'Tis jasper ye stand pledged to, lest I grieve
My bath must needs be left behind, alas!   70
One block, pure green as a pistachio-nut,
There's plenty jasper somewhere in the world—
And have I not St. Praxed's ear to pray
Horses for ye, and brown Greek manuscripts,
And mistresses with great smooth marbly limbs?
—That's if ye carve my epitaph aright,
Choice Latin, picked phrase, Tully's every word,
No gaudy ware like Gandolf's second line—
Tully, my masters? Ulpian serves his need!

And then how I shall lie through centuries,   80
And hear the blessed mutter of the Mass,
And see God made and eaten all day long,
And feel the steady candle-flame, and taste
Good strong, thick, stupefying incense-smoke!
For as I lie here, hours of the dead night,
Dying in state and by such slow degrees,
I fold my arms as if they clasped a crook,
And stretch my feet forth straight as stone can point,
And let the bedclothes for a mort-cloth drop
Into great laps and folds of sculptor's-work.   90
And as yon tapers dwindle, and strange thoughts
Grow, with a certain humming in my ears,
About the life before I lived this life,
And this life too, popes, cardinals, and priests,
St. Praxed at his sermon on the mount,
Your tall pale mother with her talking eyes,
And new-found agate urns as fresh as day,
And marble's language, Latin pure, discreet,
—Aha, ELUCESCEBAT quoth our friend?
No Tully, said I, Ulpian at the best!   100
Evil and brief hath been my pilgrimage.
All *lapis*, all, sons! Else I give the Pope
My villas. Will ye ever eat my heart?
Ever your eyes were as a lizard's quick;
They glitter like your mother's for my soul,
Or ye would heighten my impoverished frieze,
Piece out its starved design, and fill my vase
With grapes, and add a vizor and a Term,
And to the tripod ye would tie a lynx
That in his struggle throws the thyrsus down,   110
To comfort me on my entablature
Whereon I am to lie till I must ask
"Do I live, am I dead?" There, leave me, there!
For ye have stabbed me with ingratitude
To death—ye wish it—God, ye wish it! Stone—

Gritstone, a-crumble! Clammy squares which sweat
As if the corpse they keep were oozing through—
And no more *lapis* to delight the world!
Well, go! I bless ye. Fewer tapers there,
But in a row. And, going, turn your backs   120
—Aye, like departing altar-ministrants,
And leave me in my church, the church for peace,
That I may watch at leisure if he leers—
Old Gandolf—at me, from his onion-stone,
As still he envied me, so fair she was!

                                        1845

THE LOST LEADER

Just for a handful of silver he left us,
    Just for a riband to stick in his coat—
Found the one gift of which fortune bereft us,
    Lost all the others she lets us devote;
They, with the gold to give, doled him out silver,
    So much was theirs who so little allowed.
How all our copper had gone for his service!
    Rags—were they purple, his heart had been proud!
We that had loved him so, followed him, honoured him,
    Lived in his mild and magnificent eye,   10
Learned his great language, caught his clear accents,
    Made him our pattern to live and to die!
Shakespeare was of us, Milton was for us,
    Burns, Shelley, were with us—they watch from their
        graves!
He alone breaks from the van and the freemen
    —He alone sinks to the rear and the slaves!
We shall march prospering—not through his presence;
    Songs may inspirit us—not from his lyre;
Deeds will be done—while he boasts his quiescence,
    Still bidding crouch whom the rest bade aspire.   20
Blot out his name, then, record one lost soul more,

One task more declined, one more footpath untrod,
One more devils'-triumph and sorrow for angels,
    One wrong more to man, one more insult to God!
Life's night begins; let him never come back to us!
    There would be doubt, hesitation, and pain,
Forced praise on our part—the glimmer of twilight,
    Never glad confident morning again!
Best fight on well, for we taught him—strike gallantly,
    Menace our heart ere we master his own;   30
Then let him receive the new knowledge and wait us,
    Pardoned in heaven, the first by the throne!

                                                      1845

HOME-THOUGHTS, FROM ABROAD

Oh, to be in England
Now that April's there,
And whoever wakes in England
Sees, some morning, unaware,
That the lowest boughs and the brushwood sheaf
Round the elm-tree bole are in tiny leaf,
While the chaffinch sings on the orchard bough
In England—now!

And after April, when May follows,
And the whitethroat builds, and all the swallows!   10
Hark, where my blossomed pear-tree in the hedge
Leans to the field and scatters on the clover
Blossoms and dewdrops—at the bent spray's edge—
That's the wise thrush; he sings each song twice over,
Lest you should think he never could recapture
The first fine careless rapture!
And though the fields look rough with hoary dew,
All will be gay when noontide wakes anew
The buttercups, the little children's dower
—Far brighter than this gaudy melon-flower.

                                                      1845

HOME–THOUGHTS, FROM THE SEA

Nobly, nobly Cape Saint Vincent to the northwest died
    away;
Sunset ran, one glorious blood-red, reeking into Cadiz Bay;
Bluish 'mid the burning water, full in face Trafalgar lay;
In the dimmest northeast distance dawned Gibraltar
    grand and gray;
"Here and here did England help me; how can I help
    England?"—say,
Whoso turns as I, this evening, turn to God to praise and
    pray,
While Jove's planet rises yonder, silent over Africa.

1845

MEMORABILIA

Ah, did you once see Shelley plain,
    And did he stop and speak to you,
And did you speak to him again?
    How strange it seems and new!

But you were living before that,
    And also you are living after;
And the memory I started at—
    My starting moves your laughter!

I crossed a moor, with a name of its own
    And a certain use in the world no doubt,   10
Yet a hand's-breath of it shines alone
    'Mid the blank miles round about;

For there I picked up on the heather
    And there I put inside my breast
A moulted feather, an eagle-feather!
    Well, I forget the rest.

1855

THE LAST RIDE TOGETHER

I said—Then, dearest, since 'tis so,
Since now at length my fate I know,
Since nothing all my love avails,
Since all my life seemed meant for, fails,
   Since this was written and needs must be—
My whole heart rises up to bless
Your name in pride and thankfulness!
Take back the hope you gave,—I claim
Only a memory of the same,
—And this beside, if you will not blame,   10
   Your leave for one more last ride with me.

My mistress bent that brow of hers;
Those deep dark eyes where pride demurs
When pity would be softening through,
Fixed me a breathing-while or two
   With life or death in the balance: right!
The blood replenished me again;
My last thought was at least not vain:
I and my mistress, side by side
Shall be together, breathe and ride,   20
So, one day more am I deified.
   Who knows but the world may end to-night?

Hush! if you saw some western cloud
All billowy-bosomed, over-bowed
By many benedictions—sun's
And moon's and evening-star's at once—
   And so, you, looking and loving best,
Conscious grew, your passion drew
Cloud, sunset, moonrise, star-shine too,
Down on you, near and yet more near,   30
Till flesh must fade for heaven was here!—
Thus leant she and lingered—joy and fear!
   Thus lay she a moment on my breast.

Then we began to ride. My soul
Smoothed itself out, a long-cramped scroll
Freshening and fluttering in the wind.
Past hopes already lay behind.
    What need to strive with a life awry?
Had I said that, had I done this,
So might I gain, so might I miss.   40
Might she have loved me? just as well
She might have hated, who can tell!
Where had I been now if the worst befell?
    And here we are riding, she and I.

Fail I alone, in words and deeds?
Why, all men strive, and who succeeds?
We rode; it seemed my spirit flew,
Saw other regions, cities new,
    As the world rushed by on either side.
I thought,—All labour, yet no less   50
Bear up beneath their unsuccess.
Look at the end of work, contrast
The petty done, the undone vast,
This present of theirs with the hopeful past!
    I hoped she would love me; here we ride.

What hand and brain went ever paired?
What heart alike conceived and dared?
What act proved all its thought had been?
What will but felt the fleshly screen?
    We ride and I see her bosom heave.   60
There's many a crown for who can reach.
Ten lines, a statesman's life in each!
The flag stuck on a heap of bones,
A soldier's doing! what atones?
They scratch his name on the Abbey-stones.
    My riding is better, by their leave.

What does it all mean, poet? Well,
Your brains beat into rhythm, you tell
What we felt only; you expressed
You hold things beautiful the best,   70
   And place them in rhyme so, side by side.
'Tis something, nay 'tis much: but then,
Have you yourself what's best for men?
Are you—poor, sick, old ere your time—
Nearer one whit your own sublime
Than we who never have turned a rhyme?
   Sing, riding's a joy! For me, I ride.

And you, great sculptor—so, you gave
A score of years to Art, her slave,
And that's your Venus, whence we turn   80
To yonder girl that fords the burn!
   You acquiesce, and shall I repine?
What, man of music, you grown gray
With notes and nothing else to say,
Is this your sole praise from a friend,
"Greatly his opera's strains intend,
But in music we know how fashions end!"
   I gave my youth; but we ride, in fine.

Who knows what's fit for us? Had fate
Proposed bliss here should sublimate   90
My being—had I signed the bond—
Still one must lead some life beyond,
   Have a bliss to die with, dim-descried.
This foot once planted on the goal,
This glory-garland round my soul,
Could I descry such? Try and test!
I sink back shuddering from the quest.
Earth being so good, would heaven seem best?
   Now, heaven and she are beyond this ride.

And yet—she has not spoke so long!　　　100
What if heaven be that, fair and strong
At life's best, with our eyes upturned
Whither life's flower is first discerned,
　　We, fixed so, ever should so abide?
What if we still ride on, we two,
With life forever old yet new,
Changed not in kind but in degree,
The instant made eternity,—
And heaven just prove that I and she
　　Ride, ride together, forever ride?

1855

"DE GUSTIBUS—"

Your ghost will walk, you lover of trees,
　　(If our loves remain)
　　In an English lane,
By a cornfield-side a-flutter with poppies.
Hark, those two in the hazel coppice—
A boy and a girl, if the good fates please,
　　Making love, say,—
　　The happier they!
Draw yourself up from the light of the moon,
And let them pass, as they will too soon,　　10
　　With the beanflowers' boon,
　　And the blackbird's tune,
　　And May, and June!

What I love best in all the world
Is a castle, precipice-encurled,
In a gash of the wind-grieved Apennine.
Or look for me, old fellow of mine,
(If I get my head from out the mouth
O' the grave, and loose my spirit's bands,
And come again to the land of lands)—　　20
In a sea-side house to the farther South,

Where the baked cicala dies of drouth,
And one sharp tree—'tis a cypress—stands,
By the many hundred years red-rusted,
Rough iron-spiked, ripe fruit-o'ercrusted,
My sentinel to guard the sands
To the water's edge. For, what expands
Before the house, but the great opaque
Blue breadth of sea without a break?
While, in the house, forever crumbles   30
Some fragment of the frescoed walls,
From blisters where a scorpion sprawls.
A girl bare-footed brings, and tumbles
Down on the pavement, green-flesh melons,
And says there's news to-day—the king
Was shot at, touched in the liver-wing,
Goes with his Bourbon arm in a sling:
—She hopes they have not caught the felons.
Italy, my Italy!
Queen Mary's saying serves for me—   40
    (When fortune's malice
    Lost her, Calais)
Open my heart and you will see
Graved inside of it, "Italy."
Such lovers old are I and she:
So it always was, so shall ever be!

                                        1855

LOVE AMONG THE RUINS

Where the quiet-coloured end of evening smiles
          Miles and miles
On the solitary pastures where our sheep
          Half-asleep
Tinkle homeward through the twilight, stray or stop
          As they crop—
Was the site once of a city great and gay,
          (So they say)

Of our country's very capital, its prince
        Ages since   10
Held his court in, gathered councils, wielding far
        Peace or war.

Now,—the country does not even boast a tree,
        As you see,
To distinguish slopes of verdure, certain rills
        From the hills
Intersect and give a name to, (else they run
        Into one)
Where the domed and daring palace shot its spires
        Up like fires   20
O'er the hundred-gated circuit of a wall
        Bounding all,
Made of marble, men might march on nor be pressed,
        Twelve abreast.

And such plenty and perfection, see, of grass
        Never was!
Such a carpet as, this summer-time, o'erspreads
        And embeds
Every vestige of the city, guessed alone,
        Stock or stone—   30
Where a multitude of men breathed joy and woe
        Long ago;
Lust of glory pricked their hearts up, dread of shame
        Struck them tame;
And that glory and that shame alike, the gold
        Bought and sold.

Now,—the single little turret that remains
        On the plains,
By the caper overrooted, by the gourd
        Overscored,   40
While the patching houseleek's head of blossom winks
        Through the chinks—

Marks the basement whence a tower in ancient time
        Sprang sublime,
And a burning ring, all round, the chariots traced
        As they raced,
And the monarch and his minions and his dames
        Viewed the games.

And I know, while thus the quiet-coloured eve
        Smiles to leave   50
To their folding, all our many-tinkling fleece
        In such peace,
And the slopes and rills in undistinguished gray
        Melt away—
That a girl with eager eyes and yellow hair
        Waits me there
In the turret whence the charioteers caught soul
        For the goal,
When the king looked, where she looks now, breathless,
        dumb
        Till I come.   60

But he looked upon the city, every side,
        Far and wide,
All the mountains topped with temples, all the glades'
        Colonnades,
All the causeys, bridges, aqueducts,—and then,
        All the men!
When I do come, she will speak not, she will stand,
        Either hand
On my shoulder, give her eyes the first embrace
        Of my face,   70
Ere we rush, ere we extinguish sight and speech
        Each on each.

In one year they sent a million fighters forth
        South and North,

And they built their gods a brazen pillar high
    As the sky,
Yet reserved a thousand chariots in full force—
    Gold, of course.
Oh heart! oh blood that freezes, blood that burns!
    Earth's returns   80
For whole centuries of folly, noise and sin!
    Shut them in,
With their triumphs and their glories and the rest!
    Love is best.

               1855

FRA LIPPO LIPPI

I am poor brother Lippo, by your leave!
You need not clap your torches to my face.
Zooks, what's to blame? you think you see a monk!
What, 'tis past midnight, and you go the rounds,
And here you catch me at an alley's end
Where sportive ladies leave their doors ajar?
The Carmine's my cloister; hunt it up,
Do—harry out, if you must show your zeal,
Whatever rat, there, haps on his wrong hole,
And nip each softling of a wee white mouse,   10
Weke, weke, that's crept to keep him company!
Aha, you know your betters? Then, you'll take
Your hand away that's fiddling on my throat,
And please to know me likewise. Who am I?
Why, one, sir, who is lodging with a friend
Three streets off—he's a certain . . . how d'ye call?
Master—a . . . Cosimo of the Medici,
In the house that caps the corner. Boh! you were best!
Remember and tell me, the day you're hanged,
How you affected such a gullet's-gripe!   20
But you, sir, it concerns you that your knaves
Pick up a manner nor discredit you.

Zooks, are we pilchards, that they sweep the streets
And count fair prize what comes into their net?
He's Judas to a tittle, that man is!
Just such a face! Why, sir, you make amends.
Lord! I'm not angry! Bid your hang-dogs go
Drink out this quarter-florin to the health
Of the munificent House that harbours me
(And many more beside, lads! more beside!),   30
And all's come square again. I'd like his face—
His, elbowing on his comrade in the door
With the pike and lantern—for the slave that holds
John Baptist's head a-dangle by the hair
With one hand ("Look you, now," as who should say)
And his weapon in the other, yet unwiped!
It's not your chance to have a bit of chalk,
A wood-coal or the like? or you should see!
Yes, I'm the painter, since you style me so.
What, brother Lippo's doings, up and down,   40
You know them and they take you? like enough!
I saw the proper twinkle in your eye—
'Tell you, I liked your looks at very first.
Let's sit and set things straight now, hip to haunch.
Here's spring come, and the nights one makes up bands
To roam the town and sing out carnival,
And I've been three weeks shut within my mew,
A-painting for the great man, saints and saints
And saints again. I could not paint all night—
Ouf! I leaned out of window for fresh air.   50
There came a hurry of feet and little feet,
A sweep of lute-strings, laughs, and whiffs of song—
Flower o' the broom,
Take away love, and our earth is a tomb!
Flower o' the quince,
I let Lisa go, and what good in life since?
Flower o' the thyme—and so on. Round they went.
Scarce had they turned the corner when a titter,

Like the skipping of rabbits by moonlight—three slim
 shapes—
And a face that looked up . . . zooks, sir, flesh and
 blood,   60
That's all I'm made of! Into shreds it went,
Curtain and counterpane and coverlet,
All the bed furniture—a dozen knots,
There was a ladder! Down I let myself,
Hands and feet, scrambling somehow, and so dropped,
And after them. I came up with the fun
Hard by St. Laurence, hail fellow, well met—
Flower o' the rose,
If I've been merry, what matter who knows?
And so as I was stealing back again   70
To get to bed and have a bit of sleep
Ere I rise up tomorrow and go work
On Jerome knocking at his poor old breast
With his great round stone to subdue the flesh,
You snap me of the sudden. Ah, I see!
Though your eye twinkles still, you shake your head—
Mine's shaved—a monk, you say—the sting's in that!
If Master Cosimo announced himself,
Mum's the word naturally; but a monk!
Come, what am I a beast for? tell us, now!   80
I was a baby when my mother died
And father died and left me in the street.
I starved there, God knows how, a year or two
On fig-skins, melon-parings, rinds, and shucks,
Refuse and rubbish. One fine frosty day
My stomach being empty as your hat,
The wind doubled me up and down I went.
Old Aunt Lapaccia trussed me with one hand
(Its fellow was a stinger as I knew),
And so along the wall, over the bridge,   90
By the straight cut to the convent. Six words there,
While I stood munching my first bread that month:

"So, boy, you're minded," quoth the good fat father
Wiping his own mouth—'twas refection-time—
"To quit this very miserable world?
Will you renounce" . . . "the mouthful of bread?"
    thought I;
By no means! Brief, they made a monk of me;
I did renounce the world, its pride and greed,
Palace, farm, villa, shop, and banking-house,
Trash, such as these poor devils of Medici   100
Have given their hearts to—all at eight years old.
Well, sir, I found in time, you may be sure,
'Twas not for nothing—the good bellyful,
The warm serge and the rope that goes all round,
And day-long blessed idleness beside!
"Let's see what the urchin's fit for"—that came next.
Not overmuch their way, I must confess.
Such a to-do! they tried me with their books.
Lord, they'd have taught me Latin in pure waste!
Flower o' the clove,   110
All the Latin I construe is "amo," I love!
But, mind you, when a boy starves in the streets
Eight years together, as my fortune was,
Watching folk's faces to know who will fling
The bit of half-stripped grape-bunch he desires,
And who will curse or kick him for his pains—
Which gentleman processional and fine,
Holding a candle to the Sacrament,
Will wink and let him lift a plate and catch
The droppings of the wax to sell again,   120
Or holla for the Eight and have him whipped—
How say I?—nay, which dog bites, which lets drop
His bone from the heap of offal in the street!
Why, soul and sense of him grow sharp alike,
He learns the look of things, and none the less
For admonitions from the hunger-pinch.
I had a store of such remarks, be sure,

Which, after I found leisure, turned to use:
I drew men's faces on my copybooks,
Scrawled them within the antiphonary's marge,   130
Joined legs and arms to the long music-notes,
Found eyes and nose and chin for A's and B's,
And made a string of pictures of the world
Betwixt the ins and outs of verb and noun,
On the wall, the bench, the door. The monks looked
      black.
"Nay," quoth the Prior, "turn him out, d'ye say?
In no wise. Lose a crow and catch a lark.
What if at last we get our man of parts,
We Carmelites, like those Camaldolese
And Preaching Friars, to do our church up fine   140
And put the front on it that ought to be!"
And hereupon they bade me daub away.
Thank you! my head being crammed, the walls a blank,
Never was such prompt disemburdening.
First, every sort of monk, the black and white,
I drew them, fat and lean; then folks at church,
From good old gossips waiting to confess
Their cribs of barrel-droppings, candle-ends—
To the breathless fellow at the altar-foot,
Fresh from his murder, safe and sitting there   150
With the little children round him in a row
Of admiration, half for his beard and half
For that white anger of his victim's son
Shaking a fist at him with one fierce arm,
Signing himself with the other because of Christ
(Whose sad face on the cross sees only this
After the passion of a thousand years),
Till some poor girl, her apron o'er her head
(Which the intense eyes looked through), came at eve
On tiptoe, said a word, dropped in a loaf,   160
Her pair of earrings, and a bunch of flowers
(The brute took growling), prayed, and then was gone.

I painted all, then cried, "'Tis ask and have—
Choose, for more's ready!"—laid the ladder flat,
And showed my covered bit of cloister-wall.
The monks closed in a circle and praised loud
Till checked, taught what to see and not to see,
Being simple bodies—"That's the very man!
Look at the boy who stoops to pat the dog!
That woman's like the Prior's niece who comes   170
To care about his asthma; it's the life!"
But there my triumph's straw-fire flared and funked—
Their betters took their turn to see and say;
The Prior and the learned pulled a face
And stopped all that in no time. "How? what's here?
Quite from the mark of painting, bless us all!
Faces, arms, legs, and bodies like the true
As much as pea and pea! It's devil's-game!
Your business is not to catch men with show,
With homage to the perishable clay,   180
But lift them over it, ignore it all,
Make them forget there's such a thing as flesh.
Your business is to paint the souls of men—
Man's soul, and it's a fire, smoke . . . no, it's not . . .
It's vapor done up like a newborn babe—
(In that shape when you die it leaves your mouth)
It's . . . well, what matters talking, it's the soul!
Give us no more of body than shows soul.
Here's Giotto, with his Saint a-praising God!
That sets us praising—why not stop with him?   190
Why put all thoughts of praise out of our head
With wonder at lines, colours, and what not?
Paint the soul, never mind the legs and arms!
Rub all out, try at it a second time.
Oh, that white smallish female with the breasts,
She's just my niece . . . Herodias, I would say—
Who went and danced and got men's heads cut off—
Have it all out!" Now, is this sense, I ask?

A fine way to paint soul, by painting body
So ill, the eye can't stop there, must go further   200
And can't fare worse! Thus, yellow does for white
When what you put for yellow 's simply black,
And any sort of meaning looks intense
When all beside itself means and looks naught.
Why can't a painter lift each foot in turn,
Left foot and right foot, go a double step,
Make his flesh liker and his soul more like,
Both in their order? Take the prettiest face,
The Prior's niece . . . patron-saint—is it so pretty
You can't discover if it means hope, fear,   210
Sorrow or joy? Won't beauty go with these?
Suppose I've made her eyes all right and blue,
Can't I take breath and try to add life's flash,
And then add soul and heighten them threefold?
Or say there 's beauty with no soul at all—
(I never saw it—put the case the same—)
If you get simple beauty and nought else,
You get about the best thing God invents—
That 's somewhat. And you 'll find the soul you have
     missed,
Within yourself, when you return Him thanks!   220
"Rub all out!" Well, well, there 's my life, in short,
And so the thing has gone on ever since.
I'm grown a man no doubt, I've broken bounds—
You should not take a fellow eight years old
And make him swear to never kiss the girls—
I'm my own master, paint now as I please—
Having a friend, you see, in the Corner-house!
Lord, it 's fast holding by the rings in front—
Those great rings serve more purposes than just
To plant a flag in, or tie up a horse!   230
And yet the old schooling sticks—the old grave eyes
Are peeping o'er my shoulder as I work,
The heads shake still—"It 's Art's decline, my son!

You're not of the true painters, great and old;
Brother Angelico's the man, you'll find;
Brother Lorenzo stands his single peer.
Fag on at flesh, you'll never make the third!"
Flower o' the pine,
You keep your mistr . . . manners, and I'll stick to mine!
I'm not the third, then; bless us, they must know!   240
Don't you think they're the likeliest to know,
They, with their Latin? So I swallow my rage,
Clench my teeth, suck my lips in tight, and paint
To please them—sometimes do, and sometimes don't,
For, doing most, there's pretty sure to come
A turn—some warm eve finds me at my saints—
A laugh, a cry, the business of the world—
(*Flower o' the peach,*
Death for us all, and his own life for each!)
And my whole soul revolves, the cup runs over,   250
The world and life's too big to pass for a dream,
And I do these wild things in sheer despite,
And play the fooleries you catch me at,
In pure rage! the old mill-horse, out at grass
After hard years, throws up his stiff heels so,
Although the miller does not preach to him
The only good of grass is to make chaff.
What would men have? Do they like grass or no—
May they or mayn't they? all I want's the thing
Settled forever one way. As it is   260
You tell too many lies and hurt yourself.
You don't like what you only like too much,
You do like what, if given you at your word,
You find abundantly detestable.
For me, I think I speak as I was taught—
I always see the Garden and God there
A-making man's wife—and, my lesson learned,
The value and significance of flesh,
I can't unlearn ten minutes afterwards.

You understand me. I'm a beast, I know.   270
But see, now—why, I see as certainly
As that the morning-star's about to shine,
What will hap some day. We've a youngster here
Comes to our convent, studies what I do,
Slouches and stares and lets no atom drop—
His name is Guidi—he'll not mind the monks—
They call him Hulking Tom, he lets them talk—
He picks my practice up—he'll paint apace,
I hope so—though I never live so long,
I know what's sure to follow. You be judge!   280
You speak no Latin more than I, belike—
However, you're my man, you've seen the world
—The beauty and the wonder and the power,
The shapes of things, their colours, lights and shades,
Changes, surprises—and God made it all!
—For what? Do you feel thankful, aye or no,
For this fair town's face, yonder river's line,
The mountain round it, and the sky above,
Much more the figures of man, woman, child,
These are the frame to? What's it all about?   290
To be passed over, despised? or dwelt upon,
Wondered at? oh, this last, of course, you say.
But why not do as well as say—paint these
Just as they are, careless what comes of it?
God's works—paint any one, and count it crime
To let a truth slip. Don't object, "His works
Are here already—nature is complete.
Suppose you reproduce her—(which you can't)
There's no advantage! you must beat her, then."
For, don't you mark? we're made so that we love   300
First when we see them painted, things we have passed
Perhaps a hundred times nor cared to see;
And so they are better, painted—better to us,
Which is the same thing. Art was given for that—
God uses us to help each other so,

Lending our minds out. Have you noticed, now,
Your cullion's hanging face? A bit of chalk,
And trust me but you should, though! how much more,
If I drew higher things with the same truth!
That were to take the Prior's pulpit-place,   310
Interpret God to all of you! Oh, oh,
It makes me mad to see what men shall do
And we in our graves! This world's no blot for us,
Nor blank—it means intensely, and means good;
To find its meaning is my meat and drink.
"Aye, but you don't so instigate to prayer!"
Strikes in the Prior; "when your meaning's plain
It does not say to folks—remember matins—
Or, mind you fast next Friday!" Why, for this
What need of art at all? A skull and bones,   320
Two bits of stick nailed crosswise, or, what's best,
A bell to chime the hour with, does as well.
I painted a St. Laurence six months since
At Prato, splashed the fresco in fine style.
"How looks my painting, now the scaffold's down?"
I ask a brother. "Hugely," he returns—
"Already not one phiz of your three slaves
Who turn the Deacon off his toasted side,
But's scratched and prodded to our heart's content,
The pious people have so eased their own   330
With coming to say prayers there in a rage.
We get on fast to see the bricks beneath.
Expect another job this time next year,
For pity and religion grow i' the crowd—
Your painting serves its purpose!" Hang the fools!

—That is—you'll not mistake an idle word
Spoke in a huff by a poor monk, God wot,
Tasting the air this spicy night which turns
The unaccustomed head like Chianti wine!
Oh, the church knows! don't misreport me, now!   340

It's natural a poor monk out of bounds
Should have his apt word to excuse himself.
And hearken how I plot to make amends.
I have bethought me; I shall paint a piece
. . . There's for you! Give me six months, then go, see
Something in Sant' Ambrogio's! Bless the nuns!
They want a cast o' my office. I shall paint
God in the midst, Madonna and her babe,
Ringed by a bowery, flowery angel-brood,
Lilies and vestments and white faces, sweet   350
As puff on puff of grated orris-root
When ladies crowd to church at midsummer.
And then i' the front, of course a saint or two—
Saint John, because he saves the Florentines,
Saint Ambrose, who puts down in black and white
The convent's friends and gives them a long day,
And Job, I must have him there past mistake,
The man of Uz (and Us without the z,
Painters who need his patience). Well, all these
Secured at their devotions, up shall come   360
Out of a corner when you least expect,
As one by a dark stair into a great light,
Music and talking, who but Lippo! I!—
Mazed, motionless, and moonstruck—I'm the man!
Back I shrink—what is this I see and hear?
I, caught up with my monk's things by mistake,
My old serge gown and rope that goes all round,
I, in this presence, this pure company!
Where's a hole, where's a corner for escape?
Then steps a sweet angelic slip of a thing   370
Forward, puts out a soft palm—"Not so fast!"
—Addresses the celestial presence, "Nay—
He made you and devised you, after all,
Though he's none of you! Could Saint John there draw—
His camel-hair make up a painting-brush?
We come to brother Lippo for all that,

Iste perfecit opus!" So, all smile—
I shuffle sideways with my blushing face
Under the cover of a hundred wings
Thrown like a spread of kirtles when you're gay   380
And play hot cockles, all the doors being shut,
Till, wholly unexpected, in there pops
The hothead husband! Thus I scuttle off
To some safe bench behind, not letting go
The palm of her, the little lily thing
That spoke the good word for me in the nick,
Like the Prior's niece . . . Saint Lucy, I would say.
And so all's saved for me, and for the church
A pretty picture gained. Go, six months hence!
Your hand, sir, and goodby; no lights, no lights!   390
The street's hushed, and I know my own way back—
Don't fear me! There's the gray beginning. Zooks!

                                        1855

ANDREA DEL SARTO

CALLED "THE FAULTLESS PAINTER"

But do not let us quarrel any more,
No, my Lucrezia; bear with me for once.
Sit down and all shall happen as you wish.
You turn your face, but does it bring your heart?
I'll work then for your friend's friend, never fear,
Treat his own subject after his own way,
Fix his own time, accept, too, his own price,
And shut the money into this small hand
When next it takes mine. Will it? tenderly?
Oh, I'll content him—but tomorrow, Love!   10
I often am much wearier than you think,
This evening more than usual, and it seems
As if—forgive now—should you let me sit
Here by the window with your hand in mine
And look a half hour forth on Fiesole,
Both of one mind, as married people use,

Quietly, quietly, the evening through,
I might get up tomorrow to my work
Cheerful and fresh as ever. Let us try.
Tomorrow, how you shall be glad for this!   20
Your soft hand is a woman of itself,
And mine the man's bared breast she curls inside.
Don't count the time lost, neither; you must serve
For each of the five pictures we require—
It saves a model. So! keep looking so—
My serpentining beauty, rounds on rounds!
—How could you ever prick those perfect ears,
Even to put the pearl there! oh, so sweet—
My face, my moon, my everybody's moon,
Which everybody looks on and calls his,   30
And, I suppose, is looked on by in turn,
While she looks—no one's; very dear, no less!
You smile? why, there's my picture ready made.
There's what we painters call our harmony!
A common grayness silvers everything—
All in a twilight, you and I alike
—You, at the point of your first pride in me
(That's gone you know), but I, at every point;
My youth, my hope, my art, being all toned down
To yonder sober pleasant Fiesole.   40
There's the bell clinking from the chapel-top;
That length of convent-wall across the way
Holds the trees safer, huddled more inside;
The last monk leaves the garden; days decrease
And autumn grows, autumn in everything.
Eh? the whole seems to fall into a shape
As if I saw alike my work and self
And all that I was born to be and do,
A twilight-piece. Love, we are in God's hand.
How strange now looks the life he makes us lead;   50
So free we seem, so fettered fast we are!
I feel he laid the fetter; let it lie!

This chamber, for example—turn your head—
All that's behind us! You don't understand
Nor care to understand about my art,
But you can hear at least when people speak;
And that cartoon, the second from the door
—It is the thing, Love! so such things should be—
Behold Madonna! I am bold to say.
I can do with my pencil what I know, 60
What I see, what at bottom of my heart
I wish for, if I ever wish so deep—
Do easily, too—when I say, perfectly,
I do not boast, perhaps. Yourself are judge
Who listened to the Legate's talk last week,
And just as much they used to say in France.
At any rate 'tis easy, all of it!
No sketches first, no studies, that's long past—
I do what many dream of all their lives—
Dream? strive to do, and agonize to do, 70
And fail in doing. I could count twenty such
On twice your fingers, and not leave this town,
Who strive—you don't know how the others strive
To paint a little thing like that you smeared
Carelessly passing with your robes afloat,
Yet do much less, so much less, someone says,
(I know his name, no matter) so much less!
Well, less is more, Lucrezia! I am judged.
There burns a truer light of God in them,
In their vexed, beating, stuffed, and stopped-up brain, 80
Heart, or whate'er else, than goes on to prompt
This low-pulsed forthright craftsman's hand of mine.
Their works drop groundward, but themselves, I know,
Reach many a time a heaven that's shut to me,
Enter and take their place there sure enough,
Though they come back and cannot tell the world.
My works are nearer heaven, but I sit here.
The sudden blood of these men! at a word—

Praise them, it boils, or blame them, it boils, too.
I, painting from myself and to myself,   90
Know what I do, am unmoved by men's blame
Or their praise either. Somebody remarks
Morello's outline there is wrongly traced,
His hue mistaken—what of that? or else,
Rightly traced and well ordered—what of that?
Speak as they please, what does the mountain care?
Ah, but a man's reach should exceed his grasp,
Or what's a heaven for? all is silver-gray
Placid and perfect with my art—the worse!
I know both what I want and what might gain—   100
And yet how profitless to know, to sigh
"Had I been two, another and myself,
Our head would have o'erlooked the world!" No doubt.
Yonder's a work, now, of that famous youth,
The Urbinate who died five years ago.
('Tis copied, George Vasari sent it me.)
Well, I can fancy how he did it all,
Pouring his soul, with kings and popes to see,
Reaching, that Heaven might so replenish him,
Above and through his art—for it gives way;   110
That arm is wrongly put—and there again—
A fault to pardon in the drawing's lines,
Its body, so to speak! its soul is right,
He means right—that a child may understand.
Still, what an arm! and I could alter it.
But all the play, the insight, and the stretch—
Out of me! out of me! And wherefore out?
Had you enjoined them on me, given me soul,
We might have risen to Rafael, I and you.
Nay, Love, you did give all I asked, I think—   120
More than I merit, yes, by many times.
But had you—oh, with the same perfect brow,
And perfect eyes, and more than perfect mouth,
And the low voice my soul hears, as a bird

The fowler's pipe, and follows to the snare—
Had you, with these the same, but brought a mind!
Some women do so. Had the mouth there urged
"God and the glory! never care for gain.
The present by the future, what is that?
Live for fame, side by side with Agnolo!   130
Rafael is waiting. Up to God all three!"
I might have done it for you. So it seems—
Perhaps not. All is as God overrules.
Beside, incentives come from the soul's self;
The rest avail not. Why do I need you?
What wife had Rafael, or has Agnolo?
In this world, who can do a thing, will not—
And who would do it, cannot, I perceive.
Yet the will's somewhat—somewhat, too, the power—
And thus we half-men struggle. At the end,   140
God, I conclude, compensates, punishes.
'Tis safer for me, if the award be strict,
That I am something underrated here,
Poor this long while, despised, to speak the truth.
I dared not, do you know, leave home all day,
For fear of chancing on the Paris lords.
The best is when they pass and look aside;
But they speak sometimes; I must bear it all.
Well may they speak! That Francis, that first time,
And that long festal year at Fontainebleau!   150
I surely then could sometimes leave the ground,
Put on the glory, Rafael's daily wear,
In that humane great monarch's golden look—
One finger in his beard or twisted curl
Over his mouth's good mark that made the smile,
One arm about my shoulder, round my neck,
The jingle of his gold chain in my ear,
I painting proudly with his breath on me,
All his court round him, seeing with his eyes,
Such frank French eyes, and such a fire of souls   160

Profuse, my hand kept plying by those hearts—
And, best of all, this, this, this face beyond,
This in the background, waiting on my work,
To crown the issue with a last reward!
A good time, was it not, my kingly days?
And had you not grown restless—but I know—
'Tis done and past; 'twas right, my instinct said;
Too live the life grew, golden and not gray—
And I'm the weak-eyed bat no sun should tempt
Out of the grange whose four walls make his world. 170
How could it end in any other way?
You called me, and I came home to your heart.
The triumph was—to reach and stay there; since
I reached it ere the triumph, what is lost?
Let my hands frame your face in your hair's gold,
You beautiful Lucrezia that are mine!
"Rafael did this, Andrea painted that—
The Roman's is the better when you pray,
But still the other's Virgin was his wife—"
Men will excuse me. I am glad to judge   180
Both pictures in your presence; clearer grows
My better fortune, I resolve to think.
For, do you know, Lucrezia, as God lives,
Said one day Agnolo, his very self,
To Rafael . . . I have known it all these years . . .
(When the young man was flaming out his thoughts
Upon a palace-wall for Rome to see,
Too lifted up in heart because of it)
"Friend, there's a certain sorry little scrub
Goes up and down our Florence, none cares how,   190
Who, were he set to plan and execute
As you are pricked on by your popes and kings,
Would bring the sweat into that brow of yours!"
To Rafael's!—And indeed the arm is wrong.
I hardly dare—yet, only you to see,
Give the chalk here—quick, thus the line should go!

Ay, but the soul! he's Rafael! rub it out!
Still, all I care for, if he spoke the truth,
(What he? why, who but Michel Agnolo?
Do you forget already words like those?)   200
If really there was such a chance, so lost,
Is, whether you're—not grateful—but more pleased.
Well, let me think so. And you smile indeed!
This hour has been an hour! Another smile?
If you would sit thus by me every night
I should work better, do you comprehend?
I mean that I should earn more, give you more.
See, it is settled dusk now; there's a star,
Morello's gone, the watch-lights show the wall,
The cue-owls speak the name we call them by.   210
Come from the window, Love—come in, at last,
Inside the melancholy little house
We built to be so gay with. God is just.
King Francis may forgive me. Oft at nights
When I look up from painting, eyes tired out,
The walls become illumined, brick from brick
Distinct, instead of mortar, fierce bright gold,
That gold of his I did cement them with!
Let us but love each other. Must you go?
That Cousin here again? he waits outside?   220
Must see you—you, and not with me? Those loans!
More gaming debts to pay? you smiled for that?
Well, let smiles buy me! have you more to spend?
While hand and eye and something of a heart
Are left me, work's my ware, and what's it worth?
I'll pay my fancy. Only let me sit
The gray remainder of the evening out,
Idle, you call it, and muse perfectly
How I could paint were I but back in France,
One picture, just one more—the Virgin's face,   230
Not yours this time! I want you at my side
To hear them—that is, Michel Agnolo—

Judge all I do and tell you of its worth.
Will you? Tomorrow, satisfy your friend.
I take the subjects for his corridor,
Finish the portrait out of hand—there, there,
And throw him in another thing or two
If he demurs; the whole should prove enough
To pay for this same Cousin's freak. Beside,
What's better and what's all I care about,   240
Get you the thirteen scudi for the ruff.
Love, does that please you? Ah, but what does he,
The Cousin, what does he to please you more?

I am grown peaceful as old age tonight.
I regret little, I would change still less.
Since there my past life lies, why alter it?
The very wrong to Francis! it is true
I took his coin, was tempted and complied,
And built this house and sinned, and all is said.
My father and my mother died of want—   250
Well, had I riches of my own? you see
How one gets rich! Let each one bear his lot.
They were born poor, lived poor, and poor they died;
And I have laboured somewhat in my time
And not been paid profusely. Some good son
Paint my two hundred pictures—let him try!
No doubt there's something strikes a balance. Yes,
You loved me quite enough, it seems tonight.
This must suffice me here. What would one have?
In heaven, perhaps, new chances, one more chance—
Four great walls in the New Jerusalem,   261
Meted on each side by the angel's reed,
For Leonard, Rafael, Agnolo, and me
To cover—the three first without a wife,
While I have mine! So—still they overcome
Because there's still Lucrezia—as I choose.

Again the Cousin's whistle! Go, my Love.   1855

A GRAMMARIAN'S FUNERAL

SHORTLY AFTER THE REVIVAL OF LEARNING IN EUROPE

Let us begin and carry up this corpse,
    Singing together.
Leave we the common crofts, the vulgar thorpes
    Each in its tether
Sleeping safe on the bosom of the plain,
    Cared-for till cock-crow;
Look out if yonder be not day again
    Rimming the rock-row!
That's the appropriate country; there, man's thought,
    Rarer, intenser,   10
Self-gathered for an outbreak, as it ought,
    Chafes in the censer.
Leave we the unlettered plain its herd and crop;
    Seek we sepulture
On a tall mountain, citied to the top,
    Crowded with culture!
All the peaks soar, but one the rest excels;
    Clouds overcome it;
No! yonder sparkle is the citadel's
    Circling its summit.   20
Thither our path lies; wind we up the heights;
    Wait ye the warning?
Our low life was the level's and the night's;
    He's for the morning.
Step to a tune, square chests, erect each head,
    'Ware the beholders!
This is our master, famous, calm, and dead,
    Borne on our shoulders.

Sleep, crop and herd! sleep, darkling thorpe and croft,
    Safe from the weather!   30
He, whom we convoy to his grave aloft,
    Singing together,

He was a man born with thy face and throat,
   Lyric Apollo!
Long he lived nameless; how should Spring take note
   Winter would follow?
Till lo, the little touch, and youth was gone!
   Cramped and diminished,
Moaned he, "New measures, other feet anon!
   My dance is finished"?   40
No, that 's the world's way (keep the mountain-side,
   Make for the city!).
He knew the signal, and stepped on with pride
   Over men's pity;
Left play for work, and grappled with the world
   Bent on escaping.
"What 's in the scroll," quoth he, "thou keepst furled?
   Show me their shaping,
Theirs who most studied man, the bard and sage—
   Give!"—So, he gowned him,   50
Straight got by heart that book to its last page;
   Learned, we found him.
Yea, but we found him bald, too, eyes like lead,
   Accents uncertain.
"Time to taste life," another would have said,
   "Up with the curtain!"
This man said rather, "Actual life comes next?
   Patience a moment!
Grant I have mastered learning's crabbed text,
   Still there 's the comment.   60
Let me know all! Prate not of most or least,
   Painful or easy!
Even to the crumbs I 'd fain eat up the feast,
   Aye, nor feel queasy."
Oh, such a life as he resolved to live,
   When he had learned it,
When he had gathered all books had to give!
   Sooner, he spurned it.

Imagine the whole, then execute the parts,
   Fancy the fabric   70
Quite, ere you build, ere steel strike fire from quartz,
   Ere mortar dab brick!

(Here's the town-gate reached; there's the market-
    place
   Gaping before us.)
Yea, this in him was the peculiar grace
   (Hearten our chorus!)
That before living he'd learn how to live—
   No end to learning.
Earn the means first—God surely will contrive
   Use for our earning.   80
Others mistrust and say, "But time escapes;
   Live now or never!"
He said, "What's time? Leave Now for dogs and apes!
   Man has Forever."
Back to his book then; deeper drooped his head;
   Calculus racked him.
Leaden before, his eyes grew dross of lead;
   Tussis attacked him.
"Now, master, take a little rest!"—not he!
   (Caution redoubled,   90
Step two abreast, the way winds narrowly!)
   Not a whit troubled,
Back to his studies, fresher than at first,
   Fierce as a dragon
He (soul-hydroptic with a sacred thirst)
   Sucked at the flagon.
Oh, if we draw a circle premature,
   Heedless of far gain,
Greedy for quick returns of profit, sure
   Bad is our bargain!   100
Was it not great? did not he throw on God,
   (He loves the burthen)—

God's task to make the heavenly period
   Perfect the earthen?
Did not he magnify the mind, show clear
   Just what it all meant?
He would not discount life, as fools do here,
   Paid by installment.
He ventured neck or nothing—heaven's success
   Found, or earth's failure: 110
"Wilt thou trust death or not?" He answered "Yes!
   Hence with life's pale lure!"
That low man seeks a little thing to do,
   Sees it and does it;
This high man, with a great thing to pursue,
   Dies ere he knows it.
That low man goes on adding one to one,
   His hundred's soon hit;
This high man, aiming at a million,
   Misses an unit.   120
That, has the world here—should he need the next,
   Let the world mind him!
This, throws himself on God, and unperplexed
   Seeking shall find him.
So, with the throttling hands of death at strife,
   Ground he at grammar;
Still, through the rattle, parts of speech were rife.
   While he could stammer,
He settled *Hoti's* business—let it be!—
   Properly based *Oun*—   130
Gave us the doctrine of the enclitic *De*,
   Dead from the waist down.
Well, here's the platform, here's the proper place.
   Hail to your purlieus,
All ye highflyers of the feathered race,
   Swallows and curlews!
Here's the top-peak; the multitude below
   Live, for they can, there:

This man decided not to Live but Know—
    Bury this man there?   140
Here—here's his place, where meteors shoot, clouds form,
    Lightnings are loosened,
Stars come and go! Let joy break with the storm,
    Peace let the dew send!
Lofty designs must close in like effects. Loftily lying,
Leave him—still loftier than the world suspects,
    Living and dying.

1855

ONE WORD MORE

TO E. B. B.

London, September, 1855

There they are, my fifty men and women
Naming me the fifty poems finished!
Take them, Love, the book and me together;
Where the heart lies, let the brain lie also.

Rafael made a century of sonnets,
Made and wrote them in a certain volume
Dinted with the silver-pointed pencil
Else he only used to draw Madonnas.
These, the world might view—but one, the volume.
Who that one, you ask? Your heart instructs you.   10
Did she live and love it all her lifetime?
Did she drop, his lady of the sonnets,
Die, and let it drop beside her pillow
Where it lay in place of Rafael's glory,
Rafael's cheek so duteous and so loving—
Cheek, the world was wont to hail a painter's,
Rafael's cheek, her love had turned a poet's?

You and I would rather read that volume,
(Taken to his beating bosom by it)
Lean and list the bosom-beats of Rafael,   20

Would we not? than wonder at Madonnas—
Her, San Sisto names, and Her, Foligno,
Her, that visits Florence in a vision,
Her, that's left with lilies in the Louvre—
Seen by us and all the world in circle.

You and I will never read that volume.
Guido Reni, like his own eye's apple
Guarded long the treasure-book and loved it.
Guido Reni dying, all Bologna   29
Cried, and the world cried too, "Ours, the treasure!"
Suddenly, as rare things will, it vanished.
Dante once prepared to paint an angel;
Whom to please? You whisper "Beatrice."
While he mused and traced it and retraced it,
(Peradventure with a pen corroded
Still by drops of that hot ink he dipped for,
When, his left hand i' the hair o' the wicked,
Back he held the brow and pricked its stigma,
Bit into the live man's flesh for parchment,
Loosed him, laughed to see the writing rankle,   40
Let the wretch go festering through Florence)—
Dante, who loved well because he hated,
Hated wickedness that hinders loving,
Dante standing, studying his angel—
In there broke the folk of his Inferno.
Says he—"Certain people of importance"
(Such he gave his daily dreadful line to)
"Entered and would seize, forsooth, the poet."
Says the poet—"Then I stopped my painting."

You and I would rather see that angel,   50
Painted by the tenderness of Dante,
Would we not?—than read a fresh Inferno.

You and I will never see that picture.
While he mused on love and Beatrice,

While he softened o'er his outlined angel,
In they broke, those "people of importance."
We and Bice bear the loss forever.

What of Rafael's sonnets, Dante's picture?
This: no artist lives and loves, that longs not
Once, and only once, and for one only   60
(Ah, the prize!), to find his love a language
Fit and fair and simple and sufficient—
Using nature that's an art to others,
Not, this one time, art that's turned his nature.
Aye, of all the artists living, loving,
None but would forego his proper dowry—
Does he paint? He fain would write a poem—
Does he write? He fain would paint a picture,
Put to proof art alien to the artist's,
Once, and only once, and for one only,   70
So to be the man and leave the artist,
Gain the man's joy, miss the artist's sorrow.

Wherefore? Heaven's gift takes earth's abatement!
He who smites the rock and spreads the water,
Bidding drink and live a crowd beneath him,
Even he, the minute makes immortal,
Proves, perchance, but mortal in the minute,
Desecrates, belike, the deed in doing.
While he smites, how can he but remember,
So he smote before, in such a peril,   80
When they stood and mocked—"Shall smiting help us?"
When they drank and sneered—"A stroke is easy!"
When they wiped their mouths and went their journey,
Throwing him for thanks—"But drought was pleasant."
Thus old memories mar the actual triumph;
Thus the doing savours of disrelish;
Thus achievement lacks a gracious somewhat;
O'er-importuned brows becloud the mandate,

Carelessness or consciousness—the gesture.
For he bears an ancient wrong about him,   90
Sees and knows again those phalanxed faces,
Hears, yet one time more, the 'customed prelude—
"How shouldst thou, of all men, smite, and save us?"
Guesses what is like to prove the sequel—
"Egypt's flesh-pots—nay, the drought was better."

Oh, the crowd must have emphatic warrant!
Theirs, the Sinai-forehead's cloven brilliance,
Right-arm's rod-sweep, tongue's imperial fiat.
Never dares the man put off the prophet.
Did he love one face from out the thousands,   100
(Were she Jethro's daughter, white and wifely,
Were she but the Aethiopian bondslave),
He would envy yon dumb patient camel,
Keeping a reserve of scanty water
Meant to save his own life in the desert;
Ready in the desert to deliver
(Kneeling down to let his breast be opened)
Hoard and life together for his mistress.

I shall never, in the years remaining,
Paint you pictures, no, nor carve you statues,   110
Make you music that should all-express me;
So it seems; I stand on my attainment.
This of verse alone, one life allows me;
Verse and nothing else have I to give you.
Other heights in other lives, God willing;
All the gifts from all the heights, your own, Love!

Yet a semblance of resource avails us—
Shade so finely touched, love's sense must seize it.
Take these lines, look lovingly and nearly,
Lines I write the first time and the last time.   120
He who works in fresco steals a hair-brush,
Curbs the liberal hand, subservient proudly,

Cramps his spirit, crowds its all in little,
Makes a strange art of an art familiar,
Fills his lady's missal-marge with flowerets.
He who blows through bronze may breathe through silver,
Fitly serenade a slumbrous princess.
He who writes may write for once as I do.

Love, you saw me gather men and women,
Live or dead or fashioned by my fancy,   130
Enter each and all, and use their service,
Speak from every mouth—the speech, a poem.
Hardly shall I tell my joys and sorrows,
Hopes and fears, belief and disbelieving.
I am mine and yours—the rest be all men's,
Karshish, Cleon, Norbert, and the fifty.
Let me speak this once in my true person,
Not as Lippo, Roland, or Andrea,
Though the fruit of speech be just this sentence:
Pray you, look on these my men and women,   140
Take and keep my fifty poems finished;
Where my heart lies, let my brain lie also!
Poor the speech; be how I speak, for all things.

Not but that you know me! Lo, the moon's self!
Here in London, yonder late in Florence,
Still we find her face, the thrice-transfigured.
Curving on a sky imbrued with color,
Drifted over Fiesole by twilight,
Came she, our new crescent of a hair's-breadth.
Full she flared it, lamping Samminiato,   150
Rounder 'twixt the cypresses and rounder,
Perfect till the nightingales applauded.
Now, a piece of her old self, impoverished,
Hard to greet, she traverses the house-roofs,
Hurries with unhandsome thrift of silver,
Goes dispiritedly, glad to finish.

What, there's nothing in the moon noteworthy?
Nay; for if that moon could love a mortal,
Use, to charm him (so to fit a fancy),
All her magic ('tis the old sweet mythos),   160
She would turn a new side to her mortal,
Side unseen of herdsman, huntsman, steersman—
Blank to Zoroaster on his terrace,
Blind to Galileo on his turret,
Dumb to Homer, dumb to Keats—him, even!
Think, the wonder of the moonstruck mortal—
When she turns round, comes again in heaven,
Opens out anew for worse or better!
Proves she like some portent of an iceberg
Swimming full upon the ship it founders,   170
Hungry with huge teeth of splintered crystals?
Proves she as the paved work of a sapphire
Seen by Moses when he climbed the mountain?
Moses, Aaron, Nadab, and Abihu
Climbed and saw the very God, the Highest,
Stand upon the paved work of a sapphire.
Like the bodied heaven in his clearness
Shone the stone, the sapphire of that paved work,
When they ate and drank and saw God also!

What were seen? None knows, none ever shall know.
Only this is sure—the sight were other,   181
Not the moon's same side, born late in Florence,
Dying now impoverished here in London.
God be thanked, the meanest of his creatures
Boasts two soul-sides, one to face the world with,
One to show a woman when he loves her!

This I say of me, but think of you, Love!
This to you—yourself my moon of poets!
Ah, but that's the world's side, there's the wonder, 189
Thus they see you, praise you, think they know you!
There, in turn I stand with them and praise you—

Out of my own self, I dare to phrase it.
But the best is when I glide from out them,
Cross a step or two of dubious twilight,
Come out on the other side, the novel
Silent silver lights and darks undreamed of,
Where I hush and bless myself with silence.

Oh, their Rafael of the dear Madonnas,
Oh, their Dante of the dread Inferno,
Wrote one song—and in my brain I sing it,
Drew one angel—borne, see, on my bosom!   —R. B.
1855

PROSPICÉ

Fear death?—to feel the fog in my throat,
    The mist in my face,
When the snows begin, and the blasts denote
    I am nearing the place,
The power of the night, the press of the storm,
    The post of the foe;
Where he stands, the Arch Fear in a visible form,
    Yet the strong man must go;
For the journey is done and the summit attained,
    And the barriers fall,   10
Though a battle's to fight ere the guerdon be gained,
    The reward of it all.
I was ever a fighter, so—one fight more,
    The best and the last!
I would hate that death bandaged my eyes, and forbore,
    And bade me creep past.
No! let me taste the whole of it, fare like my peers,
    The heroes of old,
Bear the brunt, in a minute pay glad life's arrears
    Of pain, darkness, and cold.   20
For sudden the worst turns the best to the brave,
    The black minute's at end,

And the element's rage, the fiend-voices that rave,
    Shall dwindle, shall blend,
Shall change, shall become first a peace out of pain,
    Then a light, then thy breast,
O thou soul of my soul! I shall clasp thee again,
And with God be the rest!

                        1864

THE RING AND THE BOOK

(SELECTION FROM BOOK I)

. . . . . .

O lyric Love, half angel and half bird,
And all a wonder and a wild desire—
Boldest of hearts that ever braved the sun,
Took sanctuary within the holier blue,
And sang a kindred soul out to his face—
Yet human at the red-ripe of the heart—
When the first summons from the darkling earth
Reached thee amid thy chambers, blanched their blue,
And bared them of the glory—to drop down,   1391
To toil for man, to suffer or to die—
This is the same voice. Can thy soul know change?
Hail then, and harken from the realms of help!
Never may I commence my song, my due
To God who best taught song by gift of thee,
Except with bent head and beseeching hand—
That still, despite the distance and the dark,
What was, again may be; some interchange
Of grace, some splendor once thy very thought,   1400
Some benediction anciently thy smile:
—Never conclude, but raising hand and head
Thither where eyes, that cannot reach, yet yearn
For all hope, all sustainment, all reward,
Their utmost up and on—so blessing back
In those thy realms of help, that heaven thy home,

Some whiteness which, I judge, thy face makes proud,
Some wanness where, I think, thy foot may fall!

1868

PHEIDIPPIDES
Χαίρετε, νικωμεν*

First I salute this soil of the blessed, river and rock!
Gods of my birthplace, daemons and heroes, honour to all!
Then I name thee, claim thee for our patron, co-equal in
    praise
—Ay, with Zeus the Defender, with Her of the aegis and
    spear!
Also, ye of the bow and the buskin, praised be your peer,
Now, henceforth and forever,—O latest to whom I upraise
Hand and heart and voice! For Athens, leave pasture and
    flock!
Present to help, potent to save, Pan—patron I call!

Archons of Athens, topped by the tettix, see, I return!
See, 'tis myself here standing alive, no specter that speaks!
Crowned with the myrtle, did you command me, Athens
    and you,   11
"Run, Pheidippides, run and race, reach Sparta for aid!
Persia has come, we are here, where is She?" Your com-
    mand I obeyed,
Ran and raced: like stubble, some field which a fire runs
    through,
Was the space between city and city: two days, two nights
    did I burn
Over the hills, under the dales, down pits and up peaks.

Into their midst I broke: breath served but for "Persia
    has come!
Persia bids Athens proffer slaves'-tribute, water and earth;
Razed to the ground is Eretria—but Athens, shall Athens
    sink,

* Rejoice, we conquer.

Drop into dust and die—the flower of Hellas utterly die, 20
Die, with the wide world spitting at Sparta, the stupid,
    the stander-by?
Answer me quick, what help, what hand do you stretch
    o'er destruction's brink?
How,—when? No care for my limbs!—there's lightning
    in all and some—
Fresh and fit your message to bear, once lips give it birth!"

O my Athens—Sparta love thee? Did Sparta respond?
Every face of her leered in a furrow of envy, mistrust,
Malice,—each eye of her gave me its glitter of gratified
    hate!
Gravely they turned to take counsel, to cast for excuses.
    I stood
Quivering,—the limbs of me fretting as fire frets, an inch
    from dry wood:
"Persia has come, Athens asks aid, and still they debate? 30
Thunder, thou Zeus! Athene, are Spartans a quarry beyond
Swing of thy spear? Phoibos and Artemis, clang them
    'Ye must'!"

No bolt launched from Olumpos! Lo, their answer at last!
"Has Persia come,—does Athens ask aid,—may Sparta
    befriend?
Nowise precipitate judgment—too weighty the issue at
    stake!
Count we no time lost time which lags through respect to
    the gods!
Ponder that precept of old, 'No warfare, whatever the odds
In your favor, so long as the moon, half-orbed, is unable to
    take
Full-circle her state in the sky!' Already she rounds to it
    fast:
Athens must wait, patient as we—who judgment sus-
    pend."   40

Athens,—except for that sparkle,—thy name, I had
    mouldered to ash!
That sent a blaze through my blood; off, off and away was
    I back,
—Not one word to waste, one look to lose on the false and
    the vile!
Yet "O gods of my land!" I cried, as each hillock and plain,
Wood and stream, I knew, I named, rushing past them
    again,
"Have ye kept faith, proved mindful of honours we paid
    you erewhile?
Vain was the filleted victim, the fulsome libation! Too rash
Love in its choice, paid you so largely service so slack!

"Oak and olive and bay,—I bid you cease to enwreathe
Brows made bold by your leaf! Fade at the Persian's foot,
You that, our patrons were pledged, should never adorn a
    slave!   51
Rather I hail thee, Parnes,—trust to thy wild waste tract!
Treeless, herbless, lifeless mountain! What matter if
    slacked
My speed may hardly be, for homage to crag and to cave
No deity deigns to drape with verdure? at least I can
    breathe,
Fear in thee no fraud from the blind, no lie from the
    mute!"

Such my cry as, rapid, I ran over Parnes' ridge;
Gully and gap I clambered and cleared till, sudden, a bar
Jutted, a stoppage of stone against me, blocking the way.
Right! for I minded the hollow to traverse, the fissure
    across: 60
"Where I could enter, there I depart by! Night in the
    fosse?
Athens to aid? Though the dive were through Erebos,
    thus I obey--

Out of the day dive, into the day as bravely arise! No
    bridge
Better!"—when—ha! what was it I came on, of wonders
    that are?

There, in the cool of a cleft, sat he—majestical Pan!
Ivy drooped wanton, kissed his head, moss cushioned his
    hoof:
All the great god was good in the eyes grave-kindly—the
    curl
Carved on the bearded cheek, amused at a mortal's awe,
As, under the human trunk, the goat-thighs grand I saw.
"Halt, Pheidippides!"—halt I did, my brain of a whirl:
"Hither to me! Why pale in my presence?" he gracious
    began: 71
"How is it,—Athens, only in Hellas, holds me aloof?

"Athens, she only, rears me no fane, makes me no feast!
Wherefore? Than I what godship to Athens more helpful
    of old?
Ay and still, and forever her friend! Test Pan, trust me!
Go, bid Athens take heart, laugh Persia to scorn, have faith
In the temples and tombs! Go, say to Athens, 'The Goat-
    God saith:
When Persia—so much as strews not the soil—is cast in
    the sea,
Then praise Pan who fought in the ranks with your most
    and least,
Goat-thigh to greaved-thigh, made one cause with the free
    and the bold!'   80

"Say Pan saith: 'Let this, foreshowing the place, be the
    pledge!'"
(Gay, the liberal hand held out this herbage I bear
—Fennel—I grasped it a-tremble with dew—whatever it
    bode)

"While, as for thee" . . . But enough! He was gone.
    If I ran hitherto—
Be sure that the rest of my journey, I ran no longer, but
    flew.
Parnes to Athens—earth no more, the air was my road:
Here I am back. Praise Pan, we stand no more on the
    razor's edge!
Pan for Athens, Pan for me! I too have a guerdon rare!

Then spoke Miltiades. "And thee, best runner of Greece,
Whose limbs did duty indeed,—what gift is promised
    thyself?   90
Tell it us straightway,—Athens the mother demands of her
    son!"
Rosily blushed the youth: he paused: but, lifting at length
His eyes from the ground, it seemed as he gathered the
    rest of his strength
Into the utterance—"Pan spoke thus: 'For what thou hast
    done
Count on a worthy reward! Henceforth be allowed thee
    release
From the racer's toil, no vulgar reward in praise or in pelf!'

"I am bold to believe, Pan means reward the most to my
    mind!
Fight I shall, with our foremost, wherever this fennel may
    grow,—
Pound—Pan helping us—Persia to dust, and, under the
    deep,   99
Whelm her away forever; and then,—no Athens to save,—
Marry a certain maid, I know keeps faith to the brave,—
Hie to my house and home: and, when my children shall
    creep
Close to my knees,—recount how the God was awful yet
    kind,
Promised their sire reward to the full—rewarding him—
    so!"

Unforseeing one! Yes, he fought on the Marathon day:
So, when Persia was dust, all cried "To Akropolis!
Run, Pheidippides, one race more! the meed is thy due!
'Athens is saved, thank Pan,' go shout!" He flung down
    his shield,
Ran like fire once more: and the space 'twixt the Fennel-
    field
And Athens was stubble again, a field which a fire runs
    through,   110
Till in he broke: "Rejoice, we conquer!" Like wine
    through clay,
Joy in his blood bursting his heart, he died—the bliss!

So, to this day, when friend meets friend, the word of salute
Is still "Rejoice!"—his word which brought rejoicing
    indeed.
So is Pheidippides happy forever,—the noble strong man
Who could race like a god, bear the face of a god, whom a
    god loved so well;

He saw the land saved he had helped to save, and was
    suffered to tell
Such tidings, yet never decline, but, gloriously as he began,
So to end gloriously—once to shout, thereafter be mute:
"Athens is saved!"—Pheidippides dies in the shout for his
    meed.

1079

EPILOGUE TO ASOLANDO

At the midnight in the silence of the sleep-time,
    When you set your fancies free,
Will they pass to where—by death, fools think, im-
    prisoned—
Low he lies who once so loved you, whom you loved so,
      —Pity me?

Oh, to love so, be so loved, yet so mistaken!
  What had I on earth to do
With the slothful, with the mawkish, the unmanly?
Like the aimless, helpless, hopeless, did I drivel!
    —Being—who?   10

One who never turned his back but marched breast for-
    ward,
  Never doubted clouds would break,
Never dreamed, though right were worsted, wrong would
    triumph,
Held we fall to rise, are baffled to fight better,
    Sleep to wake.

No, at noonday in the bustle of man's work-time
  Greet the unseen with a cheer!
Bid him forward, breast and back as either should be,
"Strive and thrive!" cry "Speed—fight on, fare ever
    There as here!"

                               1889

WALT WHITMAN (1819–1892)

I HEAR AMERICA SINGING

I hear America singing, the varied carols I hear:
Those of mechanics—each one singing his, as it should be,
    blithe and strong;
The carpenter singing his, as he measures his plank or
    beam;
The mason singing his, as he makes ready for work, or
    leaves off work;
The boatman singing what belongs to him in his boat—the
    deckhand singing on the steamboat deck;
The shoemaker singing as he sits on his bench—the hatter
    singing as he stands;
The wood-cutter's song—the plowboy's, on his way in the
    morning, or at the noon intermission, or at sundown;

The delicious singing of the mother—or of the young wife
 at work—or of the girl sewing or washing—each sing-
 ing what belongs to her, and to none else;
The day what belongs to the day—at night, the party of
 young fellows, robust, friendly,
Singing, with open mouths, their strong melodious songs.

                                              1860

VIGIL STRANGE I KEPT ON THE
FIELD ONE NIGHT

Vigil strange I kept on the field one night.
When you, my son and my comrade, dropped at my side
 that day,
One look I but gave, which your dear eyes returned, with a
 look I shall never·forget;
One touch of your hand to mine, O boy, reached up as
 you lay on the ground;
Then onward I sped in the battle, the even-contested
 battle;
Till late in the night relieved, to the place at last again I
 made my way;
Found you in death so cold, dear comrade—found your
 body, son of responding kisses (never again on earth
 responding);
Bared your face in the starlight—curious the scene—cool
 blew the moderate night-wind.
Long there and then in vigil I stood, dimly around me
 the battlefield spreading;
Vigil wondrous and vigil sweet, there in the fragrant silent
 night;   10
But not a tear fell, not even a long-drawn sigh—long, long
 I gazed;
Then on the earth partially reclining, sat by your side,
 leaning my chin in my hands;

Passing sweet hours, immortal and mystic hours with you,
    dearest comrade—not a tear, not a word;
Vigil of silence, love and death—vigil for you my son and
    my soldier,
As onward silently stars aloft, eastward new ones upward
    stole;
Vigil final for you, brave boy (I could not save you, swift
    was your death,
I faithfully loved you and cared for you living—I think
    we shall surely meet again);
Till at latest lingering of the night, indeed just as the dawn
    appeared,
My comrade I wrapped in his blanket, enveloped well his
    form,
Folded the blanket well, tucking it carefully over head,
    and carefully under feet;   20
And there and then, and bathed by the rising sun, my
    son in his grave, in his rude-dug grave I deposited;
Ending my vigil strange with that—vigil of night and
    battlefield dim;
Vigil for boy of responding kisses (never again on earth
    responding);
Vigil for comrade swiftly slain—vigil I never forget, how
    as day brightened,
I rose from the chill ground, and folded my soldier well
    in his blanket,
And buried him where he fell.

                                        1865

WHEN LILACS LAST IN THE DOORYARD BLOOMED

1

When lilacs last in the dooryard bloomed,
And the great star early drooped in the western sky in
    the night,

I mourned, and yet shall mourn with ever-returning spring.
Ever-returning spring, trinity sure to me you bring,
Lilac blooming perennial and drooping star in the west,
And thought of him I love.

2

O powerful western fallen star!
O shades of night—O moody, tearful night!
O great star disappeared—O the black murk that hides
   the star!
O cruel hands that hold me powerless—O helpless soul of
   me!   10
O harsh surrounding cloud that will not free my soul.

3

In the dooryard fronting an old farmhouse near the white-
   washed palings,
Stands the lilac-bush tall-growing with heart-shaped leaves
   of rich green,
With many a pointed blossom rising delicate, with the
   perfume strong I love,
With every leaf a miracle—and from this bush in the
   dooryard,
With delicate-colored blossoms and heart-shaped leaves of
   rich green,
A sprig with its flower I break.-

4

In the swamp in secluded recesses,
A shy and hidden bird is warbling a song.

Solitary the thrush,   20
The hermit withdrawn to himself, avoiding the settlements,
Sings by himself a song.

Song of the bleeding throat,
Death's outlet song of life (for well, dear brother, I know,
If thou wast not granted to sing thou would'st surely die).

5

Over the breast of the spring, the land, amid cities,
Amid lanes and through old woods, where lately the violets
    peeped from the ground, spotting the gray débris,
Amid the grass in the fields each side of the lanes, passing
    the endless grass,
Passing the yellow-speared wheat, every grain from its
    shroud in the dark-brown fields uprisen,
Passing the apple-tree blows of white and pink in the
    orchards,   30
Carrying a corpse to where it shall rest in the grave,
Night and day journeys a coffin.

6

Coffin that passes through lanes and streets,
Through day and night with the great cloud darkening
    the land,
With the pomp of the inlooped flags with the cities draped
    in black,
With the show of the States themselves as of crape-veiled
    women standing,
With processions long and winding and the flambeaus of
    the night,
With the countless torches lit, with the silent sea of faces
    and the unbared heads,
With the waiting depot, the arriving coffin, and the somber
    faces,
With dirges through the night, with the thousand voices
    rising strong and solemn,   40
With all the mournful voices of the dirges poured around
    the coffin,
The dim-lit churches and the shuddering organs—where
    amid these you journey,
With the tolling, tolling bells' perpetual clang,
Here, coffin that slowly passes,
I give you my sprig of lilac.

7

(Nor for you, for one alone,
Blossoms and branches green to coffins all I bring,
For fresh as the morning, thus would I chant a song for
     you, O sane and sacred death.

All over bouquets of roses,
O death, I cover you over with roses and early lilies,   50
But mostly and now the lilac that blooms the first,
Copious I break, I break the sprigs from the bushes,
With loaded arms I come, pouring for you,
For you and the coffins all of you, O death.)

8

O western orb sailing the heaven,
Now I know what you must have meant as a month since
     I walked,
As I walked in silence the transparent shadowy night,
As I saw you had something to tell as you bent to me night
     after night,
As you drooped from the sky low down as if to my side
     (while the other stars all looked on),
As we wandered together the solemn night (for something
     I know not what kept me from sleep),   60
As the night advanced, and I saw on the rim of the west
     how full you were of woe,
As I stood on the rising ground in the breeze in the cool,
     transparent night,
As I watched where you passed, and was lost in the nether-
     ward black of the night,
As my soul in its trouble dissatisfied sank, as where you
     sad orb,
Concluded, dropped in the night, and was gone.

9

Sing on there in the swamp,
O singer bashful and tender, I hear your notes, I hear your
     call,

I hear, I come presently, I understand you;
But a moment I linger, for the lustrous star has detained
    me,
The star my departing comrade holds and detains me.   70

10

O how shall I warble myself for the dead one there I loved?
And how shall I deck my song for the large sweet soul
    that has gone?
And what shall my perfume be for the grave of him I love?

Sea-winds blown from east and west,
Blown from the Eastern sea and blown from the Western
    sea, till there on the prairies meeting,
These and with these and the breath of my chant,
I'll perfume the grave of him I love.

11

O what shall I hang on the chamber walls?
And what shall the pictures be that I hang on the walls,
To adorn the burial-house of him I love?   80

Pictures of growing spring and farms and homes,
With the fourth-month eve at sundown, and the gray
    smoke lucid and bright,
With floods of the yellow gold of the gorgeous, indolent,
    sinking sun, burning, expanding the air,
With the fresh sweet herbage under foot, and the pale
    green leaves of the trees prolific,
In the distance the flowing glaze, the breast of the river,
    with a wind-dapple here and there,
With ranging hills on the banks, with many a line against
    the sky, and shadows,
And the city at hand with dwellings so dense, and stacks
    of chimneys,
And all the scenes of life and the workshops, and the
    workmen homeward returning.

12

Lo, body and soul—this land,
My own Manhattan with spires, and the sparkling and
    hurrying tides, and the ships,   90
The varied and ample land, the South and the North in
    the light, Ohio's shores and flashing Missouri,
And ever the far-spreading prairies covered with grass and
    corn.

Lo, the most excellent sun so calm and haughty,
The violet and purple morn with just-felt breezes,
The gentle soft-born measureless light,
The miracle spreading bathing all, the fulfilled noon,
The coming eve delicious, the welcome night and the stars,
Over my cities shining all, enveloping man and land.

13

Sing on, sing on you gray-brown bird,
Sing from the swamps, the recesses, pour your chant from
    the bushes,   100
Limitless out of the dusk, out of the cedars and pines.
Sing on dearest brother, warble your reedy song,
Loud human song, with voice of uttermost woe.

O liquid and free and tender!
O wild and loose to my soul—O wondrous singer!
You only I hear—yet the star holds me (but will soon
    depart),
Yet the lilac with mastering odor holds me.

14

Now while I sat in the day and looked forth,
In the close of the day with its light and the fields of spring,
    and the farmers preparing their crops,
In the large unconscious scenery of my land with its lakes
    and forests,   110

In the heavenly aërial beauty (after the perturbed winds
    and the storms),
Under the arching heavens of the afternoon swift passing,
    and the voices of children and women,
The many-moving sea-tides, and I saw the ships how they
    sailed,
And the summer approaching with richness, and the fields
    all busy with labor,
And the infinite separate houses, how they all went on,
    each with its meals and minutia of daily usages,
And the streets how their throbbings throbbed, and the
    cities pent—lo, then and there,
Falling upon them all and among them all, enveloping me
    with the rest,
Appeared the cloud, appeared the long black trail,
And I knew death, its thought, and the sacred knowledge
    of death.

Then with the knowledge of death as walking one side of
    me,
                             120
And the thought of death close-walking the other side of
    me,
And I in the middle as with companions, and as holding
    the hands of companions,
I fled forth to the hiding receiving night that talks not,
Down to the shores of the water, the path by the swamp in
    the dimness,
To the solemn shadowy cedars and ghostly pines so still.

And the singer so shy to the rest received me,
The gray-brown bird I know received us comrades three,
And he sang the carol of death, and a verse for him I
    love.
From deep secluded recesses,
From the fragrant cedars and the ghostly pines so still, 130
Came the carol of the bird.

And the charm of the carol rapt me,
As I held as if by their hands my comrades in the night,
And the voice of my spirit tallied the song of the bird.

Come, lovely and soothing death,
Undulate round the world, serenely arriving, arriving,
In the day, in the night, to all, to each,
Sooner or later delicate death.

Praised be the fathomless universe,
For life and joy, and for objects and knowledge curious,   140
And for love, sweet love—but praise! praise! praise!
For the sure-enwinding arms of cool-enfolding death.

Dark mother always gliding near with soft feet,
Have none chanted for thee a chant of fullest welcome?
Then I chant it for thee, I glorify thee above all,
I bring thee a song that when thou must indeed come, come
*   unfalteringly.*

Approach, strong deliveress,
When it is so, when thou hast taken them, I joyously sing the
*   dead,*
Lost in the loving floating ocean of thee,
Laved in the flood of thy bliss, O death.   150

From me to thee glad serenades,
Dances for thee I propose saluting thee, adornments and
*   feastings for thee,*
And the sights of the open landscape and the high-spread sky
*   are fitting,*
And life and the fields, and the huge and thoughtful night.

The night in silence under many a star,
The ocean shore and the husky whispering wave whose voice
*   I know,*

And the soul turning to thee, O vast and well-veiled death,
And the body gratefully nestling close to thee.

Over the tree-tops I float thee a song,
Over the rising and sinking waves, over the myriad fields and
     the prairies wide,   160
Over the dense-packed cities all and the teeming wharves and
     ways,
I float this carol with joy, with joy to thee O death.

                              15

To the tally of my soul,
Loud and strong kept up the gray-brown bird,
With pure deliberate notes spreading, filling the night.

Loud in the pines and cedars dim,
Clear in the freshness moist and the swamp-perfume,
And I with my comrades there in the night.

While my sight that was bound in my eyes unclosed,
As to long panoramas of visions.   170

And I saw askant the armies,
I saw as in noiseless dreams hundreds of battle-flags,
Borne through the smoke of the battles and pierced with
     missiles I saw them,
And carried hither and yon through the smoke, and torn
     and bloody,
And at last but a few shreds left on the staffs (and all in
     silence),
And the staffs all splintered and broken.

I saw battle-corpses, myriads of them,
And the white skeletons of young men, I saw them,
I saw the débris and débris of all the slain soldiers of the
     war,

But I saw they were not as was thought;   180
They themselves were fully at rest, they suffered not,
The living remained and suffered, the mother suffered,
And the wife and the child and the musing comrade
    suffered,
And the armies that remained suffered.

16

Passing the visions, passing the night,
Passing, unloosing the hold of my comrades' hands,
Passing the song of the hermit bird and the tallying song
    of my soul,
Victorious song, death's outlet song, yet varying ever-
    altering song,
As low and wailing, yet clear the notes, rising and falling,
    flooding the night,
Sadly sinking and fainting, as warning and warning, and
    yet again bursting with joy,   190

Covering the earth and filling the spread of the heaven,
As that powerful psalm in the night I heard from recesses,
Passing, I leave thee, lilac with heart-shaped leaves,
I leave thee there in the dooryard, blooming, returning
    with spring.

I cease from my song for thee,
From my gaze on thee in the west, fronting the west,
    communing with thee,
O comrade lustrous with silver face in the night.

Yet each to keep and all, retrievements out of the night,
The song, the wondrous chant of the gray-brown bird,
And the tallying chant, the echo aroused in my soul,   200
With the lustrous and drooping star with the countenance
    full of woe,
With the holders holding my hand nearing the call of the
    bird,

Comrades mine and I in the midst, and their memory ever
    to keep, for the dead I loved so well,
For the sweetest, wisest soul of all my days and lands—
    and this for his dear sake,
Lilac and star and bird twined with the chant of my soul,
There in the fragrant pines and the cedars dusk and dim.

                                 1865–1866

DAREST THOU NOW, O SOUL

Darest thou now, O soul,
Walk out with me toward the unknown region,
Where neither ground is for the feet nor any path to
    follow?

No map there, nor guide,
Nor voice sounding, nor touch of human hand,
Nor face with blooming flesh, nor lips, nor eyes, are in
    that land.

I know it not, O soul,
Nor dost thou; all is a blank before us;
All waits undreamed of in that region, that inaccessible
    land.

Till when the ties loosen,   10
All but the ties eternal, Time and Space,
Nor darkness, gravitation, sense, nor any bounds bounding
    us.

Then we burst forth, we float,
In Time and Space, O soul, prepared for them,
Equal, equipped at last (O joy! O fruit of all!) them to
    fulfill, O soul.

                                   1871

IN CABINED SHIPS AT SEA

In cabined ships at sea,
The boundless blue on every side expanding,
With whistling winds and music of the waves, the large
    imperious waves,
Or some lone bark buoyed on the dense marine,
Where joyous full of faith, spreading white sails,
She cleaves the ether mid the sparkle and the foam of
    day, or under many a star at night,
By sailors young and old haply will I, a reminiscence of
    the land, be read,
In full rapport at last.

Here are our thoughts, voyagers' thoughts,
Here not the land, firm land, alone appears, may then by
    them be said,   10
The sky o'erarches here, we feel the undulating deck beneath
    our feet,
We feel the long pulsation, ebb and flow of endless motion,
The tones of unseen mystery, the vague and vast suggestions
    of the briny world, the liquid-flowing syllables,
The perfume, the faint creaking of the cordage, the melancholy
    rhythm,
The boundless vista and the horizon far and dim are all here,
And this is ocean's poem.

Then falter not, O book, fulfill your destiny,
You not a reminiscence of the land alone,
You, too, as a lone bark cleaving the ether, purposed I
    know not whither, yet ever full of faith,
Consort to every ship that sails, sail you!   20
Bear forth to them folded, my love (dear mariners, for
    you I fold it here in every leaf);
Speed on, my book! spread your white sails, my little
    bark, athwart the imperious waves,

Chant on, sail on, bear o'er the boundless blue from me
    to every sea,
This song for mariners and all their ships.

1871

MATTHEW ARNOLD (1822–1888)

THE BURIED LIFE

Light flows our war of mocking words, and yet,
Behold, with tears mine eyes are wet!
I feel a nameless sadness o'er me roll.
Yes, yes, we know that we can jest,
We know, we know that we can smile!
But there's a something in this breast,
To which thy light words bring no rest,
And thy gay smiles no anodyne.
Give me thy hand, and hush awhile,
And turn those limpid eyes on mine,   10
And let me read there, love! thy inmost soul.

Alas! is even love too weak
To unlock the heart, and let it speak?
Are even lovers powerless to reveal
To one another what indeed they feel?
I knew the mass of men concealed
Their thoughts, for fear that if revealed
They would by other men be met
With blank indifference, or with blame reproved;
I knew they lived and moved   20
Tricked in disguises, alien to the rest
Of men, and alien to themselves—and yet
The same heart beats in every human breast!

But we, my love!—doth a like spell benumb
Our hearts, our voices?—must we, too, be dumb?

Ah! well for us, if even we,
Even for a moment, can get free
Our heart, and have our lips unchained;
For that which seals them hath been deep-ordained!

Fate, which foresaw   30
How frivolous a baby man would be—
By what distractions he would be possessed,
How he would pour himself in every strife,
And well nigh change his own identity—
That it might keep from his capricious play
His genuine self, and force him to obey
Even in his own despite his being's law,
Bade through the deep recesses of our breast
The unregarded river of our life
Pursue with indiscernible flow its way;   40
And that we should not see
The buried stream, and seem to be
Eddying at large in blind uncertainty,
Though driving on with it eternally.

But often, in the world's most crowded streets,
But often, in the din of strife,
There rises an unspeakable desire
After the knowledge of our buried life;
A thirst to spend our fire and restless force
In tracking out our true, original course;   50
A longing to inquire
Into the mystery of this heart which beats
So wild, so deep in us—to know
Whence our lives come and where they go.
And many a man in his own breast then delves,
But deep enough, alas! none ever mines.
And we have been on many thousand lines,
And we have shown, on each, spirit and power;
But hardly have we, for one little hour,
Been on our own line, have we been ourselves—   60

Hardly had skill to utter one of all
The nameless feelings that course through our breast,
But they course on forever unexpressed,
And long we try in vain to speak and act
Our hidden self, and what we say and do
Is eloquent, is well—but 'tis not true!
And then we will no more be racked
With inward striving, and demand
Of all the thousand nothings of the hour
Their stupefying power;   70
Ah, yes, and they benumb us at our call!
Yet still, from time to time, vague and forlorn,
From the soul's subterranean depth upborne
As from an infinitely distant land,
Come airs, and floating echoes, and convey
A melancholy into all our day.

Only—but this is rare—
When a beloved hand is laid in ours,
When, jaded with the rush and glare
Of the interminable hours,   80
Our eyes can in another's eyes read clear,
When our world-deafened ear
Is by the tones of a loved voice caressed—
A bolt is shot back somewhere in our breast,
And a lost pulse of feeling stirs again.
The eye sinks inward, and the heart lies plain,
And what we mean, we say, and what we would, we know.
A man becomes aware of his life's flow,
And hears its winding murmur; and he sees
The meadows where it glides, the sun, the breeze.   90

And there arrives a lull in the hot race
Wherein he doth forever chase
That flying and elusive shadow, rest.
An air of coolness plays upon his face,

And an unwonted calm pervades his breast.
And then he thinks he knows
The hills where his life rose,
And the sea where it goes.

1852

SELF–DEPENDENCE

Weary of myself, and sick of asking
What I am, and what I ought to be,
At the vessel's prow I stand, which bears me
Forwards, forwards, o'er the starlit sea.

And a look of passionate desire
O'er the sea and to the stars I send:
"Ye who from my childhood up have calm'd me,
Calm me, ah, compose me to the end.

"Ah, once more," I cried, "Ye Stars, ye Waters,
On my heart your mighty charm renew: 10
Still, still, let me, as I gaze upon you,
Feel my soul becoming vast like you."

From the intense, clear, star-sown vault of heaven,
Over the lit sea's unquiet way,
In the rustling night-air came the answer—
"Wouldst thou *be* as these are? *live* as they.

"Unaffrighted by the silence round them,
Undistracted by the sights they see,
These demand not that the things without them
Yield them love, amusement, sympathy.   20

"And with joy the stars perform their shining,
And the sea its long moon-silver'd roll.

For alone they live, nor pine with noting
All the fever of some differing soul.

"Bounded by themselves, and unobservant
In what state God's other works may be,
In their own tasks all their powers pouring,
These attain the mighty life you see."

O air-born Voice! long since, severely clear,
A cry like thine in my own heart I hear.   30
"Resolve to be thyself: and know, that he
Who finds himself, loses his misery."

                                                          1852

REQUIESCAT

Strew on her roses, roses,
    And never a spray of yew!
In quiet she reposes;
    Ah, would that I did too!

Her mirth the world required;
    She bathed it in smiles of glee.
But her heart was tired, tired,
    And now they let her be.

Her life was turning, turning,
    In mazes of heat and sound.   10
But for peace her soul was yearning,
    And now peace laps her round.

Her cabined, ample spirit,
    It fluttered and failed for breath.
To-night it doth inherit
    The vasty hall of death.

                                                          1853

THYRSIS

MONODY, TO COMMEMORATE THE AUTHOR'S FRIEND
ARTHUR HUGH CLOUGH, WHO DIED AT FLORENCE, 1861

> Thus yesterday, to-day, to-morrow come,
> They hustle one another and they pass;
> But all our hustling morrows only make
> The smooth to-day of God.
> *From* LUCRETIUS, *an unpublished Tragedy.*

How changed is here each spot man makes or fills!
　In the two Hinkseys nothing keeps the same;
　　The village-street its haunted mansion lacks,
　And from the sign is gone Sibylla's name,
　　And from the roofs the twisted chimney-stacks;
　　　Are ye too changed, ye hills?
　See, 'tis no foot of unfamiliar men
　　To-night from Oxford up your pathway strays!
　　Here came I often, often, in old days;
　Thyrsis and I; we still had Thyrsis then.   10

Runs it not here, the track by Childsworth Farm,
　Up past the wood, to where the elm-tree crowns
　　The hill behind whose ridge the sunset flames?
　The signal-elm, that looks on Ilsley Downs,
　　The Vale, the three lone weirs, the youthful
　　　　Thames?—
　　　This winter-eve is warm,
　Humid the air; leafless, yet soft as spring,
　　The tender purple spray on copse and briers;
　　And that sweet City with her dreaming spires,
　She needs not June for beauty's heightening,   20

Lovely all times she lies, lovely to-night!
　Only, methinks, some loss of habit's power
　　Befalls me wandering through this upland dim;
　Once pass'd I blindfold here, at any hour,
　　Now seldom come I, since I came with him.
　　　That single elm-tree bright

Against the west—I miss it! is it gone?
  We prized it dearly; while it stood, we said,
  Our friend, the Scholar-Gipsy, was not dead;
While the tree lived, he in these fields lived on.   30

Too rare, too rare, grow now my visits here!
  But once I knew each field, each flower, each stick;
    And with the country-folk acquaintance made
  By barn in threshing-time, by new-built rick.
    Here, too, our shepherd-pipes we first assay'd.
      Ah me! this many a year
  My pipe is lost, my shepherd's-holiday!
    Needs must I lose them, needs with heavy heart
    Into the world and wave of men depart;
  But Thyrsis of his own will went away.   40

It irk'd him to be here, he could not rest.
  He loved each simple joy the country yields,
    He loved his mates; but yet he could not keep,
  For that a shadow lower'd on the fields,
    Here with the shepherds and the silly sheep.
      Some life of men unblest
  He knew, which made him droop, and fill'd his head.
    He went; his piping took a troubled sound
    Of storms that rage outside our happy ground;
  He could not wait their passing, he is dead!   50

So, some tempestuous morn in early June,
  When the year's primal burst of bloom is o'er,
    Before the roses and the longest day—
  When garden-walks, and all the grassy floor,
    With blossoms, red and white, of fallen May,
      And chestnut-flowers are strewn—
  So have I heard the cuckoo's parting cry,
    From the wet field, through the vext garden-trees,
    Come with the volleying rain and tossing breeze:
  The bloom is gone, and with the bloom go I.   60

Too quick despairer, wherefore wilt thou go?
  Soon will the high Midsummer pomps come on,
    Soon will the musk carnations break and swell,
  Soon shall we have gold-dusted snapdragon,
    Sweet-William with its homely cottage-smell,
      And stocks in fragrant blow;
  Roses that down the alleys shine afar,
    And open, jasmine-muffled lattices,
    And groups under the dreaming garden-trees,
  And the full moon, and the white evening-star.   70

He hearkens not! light comer, he is flown!
  What matters it? next year he will return,
    And we shall have him in the sweet spring-days,
  With whitening hedges, and uncrumpling fern,
    And blue-bells trembling by the forest-ways,
      And scent of hay new-mown.
  But Thyrsis never more we swains shall see!
    See him come back, and cut a smoother reed,
    And blow a strain the world at last shall heed—
  For Time, not Corydon, hath conquer'd thee.   80

Alack, for Corydon no rival now!—
  But when Sicilian shepherds lost a mate,
    Some good survivor with his flute would go,
  Piping a ditty sad for Bion's fate,
    And cross the unpermitted ferry's flow,
      And relax Pluto's brow,
  And make leap up with joy the beauteous head
    Of Proserpine, among whose crowned hair
    Are flowers, first open'd on Sicilian air,
  And flute his friend, like Orpheus, from the dead.   90

O easy access to the hearer's grace
  When Dorian shepherds sang to Proserpine!
    For she herself had trod Sicilian fields,

She knew the Dorian water's gush divine,
   She knew each lily white which Enna yields,
      Each rose with blushing face;
She loved the Dorian pipe, the Dorian strain.
   But ah, of our poor Thames she never heard!
   Her foot the Cumnor cowslips never stirr'd!
And we should tease her with our plaint in vain.   100

Well! wind-dispers'd and vain the words will be,
   Yet, Thyrsis, let me give my grief its hour
    In the old haunt, and find our tree-topp'd hill!
Who, if not I, for questing here hath power?
   I know the wood which hides the daffodil,
     I know the Fyfield tree,
I know what white, what purple fritillaries
   The grassy harvest of the river-fields,
   Above by Ensham, down by Sandford, yields,
And what sedg'd brooks are Thames's tributaries;   110

I know these slopes; who knows them if not I?—
   But many a dingle on the loved hill-side,
    With thorns once studded, old, white-blossom'd trees,
   Where thick the cowslips grew, and, far descried,
    High tower'd the spikes of purple orchises,
     Hath since our day put by
The coronals of that forgotten time.
   Down each green bank hath gone the ploughboy's
    team,
   And only in the hidden brookside gleam
Primroses, orphans of the flowery prime.   120

Where is the girl, who, by the boatman's door,
   Above the locks, above the boating throng,
    Unmoor'd our skiff, when, through the Wytham flats,
   Red loosestrife and blond meadow-sweet among,
    And darting swallows, and light water-gnats,
     We track'd the shy Thames shore?

Where are the mowers, who, as the tiny swell
  Of our boat passing heav'd the river-grass,
    Stood with suspended scythe to see us pass?—
They all are gone, and thou art gone as well.   130

Yes, thou art gone! and round me too the night
  In ever-nearing circle weaves her shade.
    I see her veil draw soft across the day,
  I feel her slowly chilling breath invade
    The cheek grown thin, the brown hair sprent with gray;
      I feel her finger light
  Laid pausefully upon life's headlong train;
    The foot less prompt to meet the morning dew,
    The heart less bounding at emotion new,
  And hope, once crush'd, less quick to spring again. 140

And long the way appears, which seem'd so short
  To the unpractic'd eye of sanguine youth;
    And high the mountain-tops, in cloudy air,
  The mountain-tops where is the throne of Truth,
    Tops in life's morning-sun so bright and bare!
      Unbreachable the fort
  Of the long-batter'd world uplifts its wall.
    And strange and vain the earthly turmoil grows,
    And near and real the charm of thy repose,
  And night as welcome as a friend would fall.   150

But hush! the upland hath a sudden loss
  Of quiet;—Look! adown the dusk hillside,
    A troop of Oxford hunters going home,
  As in old days, jovial and talking, ride!
    From hunting with the Berkshire hounds they come—
      Quick, let me fly, and cross
  Into yon further field!—'Tis done; and see,
    Back'd by the sunset, which doth glorify
    The orange and pale violet evening-sky,
  Bare on its lonely ridge, the Tree! the Tree!   160

I take the omen! Eve lets down her veil,
  The white fog creeps from bush to bush about,
    The west unflushes, the high stars grow bright,
  And in the scatter'd farms the lights come out.
    I cannot reach the Signal-Tree to-night,
        Yet, happy omen, hail!
  Hear it from thy broad lucent Arno vale
    (For there thine earth-forgetting eyelids keep
    The morningless and unawakening sleep
  Under the flowery oleanders pale),   170

Hear it, O Thyrsis, still our Tree is there!—
  Ah, vain! These English fields, this upland dim,
    These brambles pale with mist engarlanded,
  That lone, sky-pointing tree, are not for him.
    To a boon southern country he is fled,
        And now in happier air,
  Wandering with the great Mother's train divine
    (And purer or more subtle soul than thee,
    I trow, the mighty Mother doth not see!)
  Within a folding of the Apennine,   180

Thou hearest the immortal strains of old.
  Putting his sickle to the perilous grain
    In the hot cornfield of the Phrygian king,
  For thee the Lityerses song again
    Young Daphnis with his silver voice doth sing;
        Sings his Sicilian fold,
  His sheep, his hapless love, his blinded eyes;
    And how a call celestial round him rang
    And heavenward from the fountain-brink he sprang,
  And all the marvel of the golden skies.   190

There thou art gone, and me thou leavest here
  Sole in these fields; yet will I not despair;
    Despair I will not, while I yet descry

'Neath the soft canopy of English air
　　That lonely Tree against the western sky.
　　　Still, still these slopes, 'tis clear,
　Our Gipsy-Scholar haunts, outliving thee!
　　Fields where soft sheep from cages pull the hay,
　　Woods with anemonies in flower till May,
　Know him a wanderer still; then why not me?　　200

A fugitive and gracious light he seeks,
　　Shy to illumine; and I seek it too.
　　　This does not come with houses or with gold,
　With place, with honour, and a flattering crew;
　　　'Tis not in the world's market bought and sold.
　　　　But the smooth-slipping weeks
　Drop by, and leave its seeker still untired;
　　Out of the heed of mortals he is gone,
　　He wends unfollow'd, he must house alone;
　Yet on he fares, by his own heart inspired.　　210

Thou too, O Thyrsis, on like quest wert bound,
　　Thou wanderedst with me for a little hour;
　　　Men gave thee nothing, but this happy quest,
　If men esteem'd thee feeble, gave thee power,
　　　If men procured thee trouble, gave thee rest.
　　　　And this rude Cumnor ground,
　Its fir-topped Hurst, its farms, its quiet fields,
　　Here cam'st thou in thy jocund youthful time,
　　Here was thine height of strength, thy golden prime;
　And still the haunt beloved a virtue yields.　　220

What though the music of thy rustic flute
　　Kept not for long its happy, country tone,
　　　Lost it too soon, and learnt a stormy note
　Of men contention-tost, of men who groan,
　　　Which task'd thy pipe too sore, and tired thy throat—
　　　　It fail'd, and thou wast mute;

Yet hadst thou alway visions of our light,
   And long with men of care thou couldst not stay,
   And soon thy foot resumed its wandering way,
Left human haunt, and on alone till night.   230

Too rare, too rare, grow now my visits here!
   'Mid city-noise, not, as with thee of yore,
     Thyrsis, in reach of sheep-bells is my home!
   Then through the great town's harsh, heart-wearying roar,
    Let in thy voice a whisper often come,
     To chase fatigue and fear:
Why faintest thou? I wander'd till I died.
   Roam on! the light we sought is shining still.
   Dost thou ask proof? Our Tree yet crowns the hill,
Our Scholar travels yet the loved hillside.

       1866

DOVER BEACH

The sea is calm tonight,
The tide is full, the moon lies fair
Upon the Straits—on the French coast the light
Gleams and is gone; the cliffs of England stand,
Glimmering and vast, out in the tranquil bay.
Come to the window; sweet is the night-air!
Only, from the long line of spray
Where the sea meets the moon-blanched land,
Listen! you hear the grating roar
Of pebbles which the waves draw back, and fling, 10
At their return, up the high strand,
Begin, and cease, and then again begin,
With tremulous cadence slow, and bring
The eternal note of sadness in.

Sophocles long ago
Heard it on the Aegean, and it brought
Into his mind the turbid ebb and flow

Of human misery; we
Find also in the sound a thought,
Hearing it by this distant northern sea.   20

The Sea of Faith
Was once, too, at the full, and round earth's shore
Lay like the folds of a bright girdle furled,
But now I only hear
Its melancholy, long, withdrawing roar,
Retreating, to the breath
Of the night-wind, down the vast edges drear
And naked shingles of the world.

Ah, love, let us be true
To one another! for the world, which seems   30
To lie before us like a land of dreams,
So various, so beautiful, so new,
Hath really neither joy, nor love, nor light,
Nor certitude, nor peace, nor help for pain;
And we are here as on a darkling plain
Swept with confused alarms of struggle and flight,
Where ignorant armies clash by night.

1867

RUGBY CHAPEL

November. 1857

Coldly, sadly descends
The autumn evening. The field,
Strewn with its dank yellow drifts
Of withered leaves, and the elms,
Fade into dimness apace,
Silent—hardly a shout
From a few boys late at their play!
The lights come out in the street,
'In the school-room windows—but cold,
Solemn, unlighted, austere,   10
Through the gathering darkness, arise

The chapel walls, in whose bound
Thou, my father! art laid.

There thou dost lie, in the gloom
Of the autumn evening. But ah,
That word, *gloom*, to my mind
Brings thee back, in the light
Of thy radiant vigour again;
In the gloom of November we passed
Days not dark at thy side;   20
Seasons impaired not the ray
Of thy buoyant cheerfulness clear.
Such thou wast! and I stand
In the autumn evening, and think
Of bygone autumns with thee.

Fifteen years have gone round
Since thou arosest to tread,
In the summer morning, the road
Of death, at a call unforeseen,
Sudden. For fifteen years,   30
We who till then in thy shade
Rested as under the boughs
Of a mighty oak have endured
Sunshine and rain as we might,
Bare, unshaded, alone,
Lacking the shelter of thee.

O strong soul, by what shore
Tarriest thou now? For that force,
Surely, has not been left vain!
Somewhere, surely, afar,   40
In the sounding labour-house vast
Of being, is practiced that strength,
Zealous, beneficent, firm!

Yes, in some far-shining sphere,
Conscious or not of the past,

Still thou performest the word
Of the Spirit in whom thou dost live—
Prompt, unwearied, as here!
Still thou upraisest with zeal
The humble good from the ground,   50
Sternly repressest the bad!
Still, like a trumpet, dost rouse
Those who with half-open eyes
Tread the border-land dim
'Twixt vice and virtue; reviv'st,
Succorest! This was thy work,
This was thy life upon earth.

What is the course of the life
Of mortal men on the earth?
Most men eddy about   60
Here and there—eat and drink,
Chatter and love and hate,
Gather and squander, are raised
Aloft, are hurled in the dust,
Striving blindly, achieving
Nothing; and then they die—
Perish—and no one asks
Who or what they have been,
More than he asks what waves,
In the moonlit solitudes mild   70
Of the midmost ocean, have swelled,
Foamed for a moment, and gone.

And there are some, whom a thirst
Ardent, unquenchable, fires,
Not with the crowd to be spent,
Not without aim to go round
In an eddy of purposeless dust,
Effort unmeaning and vain.
Ah, yes! some of us strive
Not without action to die   80

Fruitless, but something to snatch
From dull oblivion, nor all
Glut the devouring grave!
We, we have chosen our path—
Path to a clear-purposed goal,
Path of advance!—but it leads
A long, steep journey, through sunk
Gorges, o'er mountains in snow.
Cheerful, with friends, we set forth—
Then, on the height, comes the storm.   90
Thunder crashes from rock
To rock, the cataracts reply;
Lightnings dazzle our eyes.
Roaring torrents have breached
The track, the stream-bed descends
In the place where the wayfarer once
Planted his footstep—the spray
Boils o'er its borders! aloft
The unseen snow-beds dislodge
Their hanging ruin! alas,   100
Havoc is made in our train!
Friends, who set forth at our side,
Falter, are lost in the storm.
We, we only are left!
With frowning foreheads, with lips
Sternly compressed, we strain on,
On—and at nightfall at last
Come to the end of our way,
To the lonely inn 'mid the rocks;
Where the gaunt and taciturn host   110
Stands on the threshold, the wind
Shaking his thin white hairs—
Holds his lantern to scan
Our storm-beat figures, and asks:
Whom in our party we bring,
Whom we have left in the snow?

Sadly we answer: We bring
Only ourselves! we lost
Sight of the rest in the storm;
Hardly ourselves we fought through,   120
Stripped, without friends, as we are.
Friends, companions, and train,
The avalanche swept from our side.

But thou would'st not *alone*
Be saved, my father! *alone*
Conquer and come to thy goal,
Leaving the rest in the wild.
We were weary, and we
Fearful, and we in our march
Fain to drop down and to die.   130
Still thou turnedst, and still
Beckonedst the trembler, and still
Gavest the weary thy hand.
If, in the paths of the world,
Stones might have wounded thy feet,
Toil or dejection have tried
Thy spirit, of that we saw
Nothing—to us thou wast still
Cheerful, and helpful, and firm!
Therefore to thee it was given   14c
Many to save with thyself;
And, at the end of thy day,
Oh, faithful shepherd! to come,
Bringing thy sheep in thy hand.

And through thee I believe
In the noble and great who are gone;
Pure souls honored and blest
By former ages, who else—
Such, so soulless, so poor,
Is the race of men whom I see—   150

Seemed but a dream of the heart,
Seemed but a cry of desire.
Yes! I believe that there lived
Others like thee in the past,
Not like the men of the crowd
Who all round me today
Bluster or cringe, and make life
Hideous, and arid, and vile;
But souls tempered with fire,
Fervent, heroic, and good,   160
Helpers and friends of mankind.

Servants of God!—or sons
Shall I not call you? because
Not as servants ye knew
Your Father's innermost mind,
His, who unwillingly sees
One of his little ones lost—
Yours is the praise, if mankind
Hath not as yet in its march
Fainted, and fallen, and died!   170

See!   In the rocks of the world
Marches the host of mankind,
A feeble, wavering line.
Where are they tending?—A God
Marshaled them, gave them their goal.
Ah, but the way is so long!
Years they have been in the wild!
Sore thirst plagues them; the rocks,
Rising all round, overawe;
Factions divide them; their host   180
Threatens to break, to dissolve.
—Ah, keep, keep them combined!
Else, of the myriads who fill
That army, not one shall arrive;

Sole they shall stray; in the rocks
Stagger forever in vain,
Die one by one in the waste.

Then, in such hour of need
Of your fainting, dispirited race,
Ye, like angels, appear, 190
Radiant with ardour divine!
Beacons of hope ye appear!
Languor is not in your heart,
Weakness is not in your word,
Weariness not on your brow.
Ye alight in our van! at your voice,
Panic, despair, flee away.
Ye move through the ranks, recall
The stragglers, refresh the outworn,
Praise, reinspire the brave! 200
Order, courage, return.
Eyes rekindling, and prayers,
Follow your steps as ye go.
Ye fill up the gaps in our files,
Strengthen the wavering line,
Stablish, continue our march,
On, to the bound of the waste,
On, to the City of God.

1867

THE LAST WORD

Creep into thy narrow bed,
Creep, and let no more be said!
Vain thy onset! all stands fast.
Thou thyself must break at last.

Let the long contention cease!
Geese are swans, and swans are geese.
Let them have it how they will!
Thou art tired; best be still.

They out-talked thee, hissed thee, tore thee!
Better men fared thus before thee;   10
Fired their ringing shot and passed,
Hotly charged—and sank at last.

Charge once more, then, and be dumb!
Let the victors, when they come,
When the forts of folly fall,
Find thy body by the wall.

1867

PIS–ALLER

"Man is blind because of sin;
Revelation makes him sure.
Without that, who looks within,
Looks in vain, for all's obscure."

Nay, look closer into man!
Tell me, can you find indeed
Nothing sure, no moral plan
Clear prescribed, without your creed?

"No, I nothing can perceive;
Without that, all's dark for men.   10
That, or nothing, I believe."—
For God's sake, believe it then!

1867

AUSTERITY OF POETRY

That son of Italy who tried to blow,
Ere Dante came, the trump of sacred song,
In his light youth amid a festal throng
Sate with his bride to see a public show.

1. Giacopone di Todi.

Fair was the bride, and on her front did glow
Youth like a star; and what to youth belong,
Gay raiment, sparkling gauds, elation strong.
A prop gave way! crash fell a platform! lo,

Mid struggling sufferers, hurt to death, she lay!
Shuddering they drew her garments off—and found 10
A robe of sackcloth next the smooth, white skin.

Such, poets, is your bride, the Muse! young, gay,
Radiant, adorn'd outside; a hidden ground
Of thought and of austerity within.

1867

PALLADIUM

Set where the upper streams of Simois flow
Was the Palladium, high 'mid rock and wood;
And Hector was in Ilium, far below,
And fought, and saw it not, but there it stood.

It stood; and sun and moonshine rain'd their light
On the pure columns of its glen-built hall.
Backward and forward roll'd the waves of fight
Round Troy; but while this stood, Troy could not fall.

So, in its lovely moonlight, lives the soul.
Mountains surround it, and sweet virgin air;   10
Cold plashing, past it, crystal waters roll;
We visit it by moments, ah! too rare.

Men will renew the battle in the plain
Tomorrow; red with blood will Xanthus be;
Hector and Ajax will be there again;
Helen will come upon the wall to see.

Then we shall rust in shade, or shine in strife,
And fluctuate 'twixt blind hopes and blind despairs,
And fancy that we put forth all our life,
And never know how with the soul it fares.   20

Still doth the soul, from its lone fastness high,
Upon our life a ruling effluence send;
And when it fails, fight as we will, we die,
And while it lasts, we cannot wholly end.

1867

DANTE GABRIEL ROSSETTI
(1828–1882)

THE BLESSED DAMOZEL

The blessed damozel leaned out
    From the golden bar of heaven;
Her eyes were deeper than the depth
    Of waters stilled at even;
She had three lilies in her hand,
    And the stars in her hair were seven.

Her robe, ungirt from clasp to hem,
    No wrought flowers did adorn,
But a white rose of Mary's gift,
    For service meetly worn;   10
Her hair that lay along her back
    Was yellow like ripe corn.

Her seemed she scarce had been a day
    One of God's choristers;
The wonder was not yet quite gone
    From that still look of hers;
Albeit, to them she left, her day
    Had counted as ten years.

(To one, it is ten years of years.
   . . . Yet now, and in this place,   20
Surely she leaned o'er me—her hair
   Fell all about my face . . .
Nothing; the autumn fall of leaves.
   The whole year sets apace.)

It was the rampart of God's house
   That she was standing on;
By God built over the sheer depth
   The which is space begun;
So high, that looking downward thence
   She scarce could see the sun.   30

It lies in heaven, across the flood
   Of ether, as a bridge.
Beneath, the tides of day and night
   With flame and darkness ridge
The void, as low as where this earth
   Spins like a fretful midge.

Around her, lovers, newly met
   'Mid deathless love's acclaims,
Spoke evermore among themselves
   Their heart-remembered names;   40
And the souls mounting up to God
   Went by her like thin flames.

And still she bowed herself and stooped
   Out of the circling charm;
Until her bosom must have made
   The bar she leaned on warm,
And the lilies lay as if asleep
   Along her bended arm.

From the fixed place of heaven she saw
   Time like a pulse shake fierce   50

Through all the worlds. Her gaze still strove
   Within the gulf to pierce
Its path; and now she spoke as when
   The stars sang in their spheres.

The sun was gone now; the curled moon
   Was like a little feather
Fluttering far down the gulf; and now
   She spoke through the still weather.
Her voice was like the voice the stars
   Had when they sang together.   60

(Ah sweet! Even now, in that bird's song,
   Strove not her accents there,
Fain to be harkened? When those bells
   Possessed the mid-day air,
Strove not her steps to reach my side
   Down all the echoing stair?)

"I wish that he were come to me,
   For he will come," she said.
"Have I not prayed in heaven?—on earth,
   Lord, Lord, has he not prayed?   70
Are not two prayers a perfect strength?
   And shall I feel afraid?

"When round his head the aureole clings,
   And he is clothed in white,
I'll take his hand and go with him
   To the deep wells of light;
As unto a stream we will step down,
   And bathe there in God's sight.

"We two will stand beside that shrine,
   Occult, withheld, untrod,   80
Whose lamps are stirred continually
   With prayers sent up to God;

And see our old prayers, granted, melt
　Each like a little cloud.

"We two will lie i' the shadow of
　That living, mystic tree
Within whose secret growth the Dove
　Is sometimes felt to be,
While every leaf that His plumes touch
　Saith His Name audibly.   90

"And I myself will teach to him,
　I myself, lying so,
The songs I sing here; which his voice
　Shall pause in, hushed and slow,
And find some knowledge at each pause,
　Or some new thing to know."

(Alas! We two, we two, thou say'st!
　Yea, one wast thou with me
That once of old. But shall God lift
　To endless unity   100
The soul whose likeness with thy soul
　Was but its love for thee?)

"We two," she said, "will seek the groves
　Where the lady Mary is,
With her five handmaidens, whose names
　Are five sweet symphonies,
Cecily, Gertrude, Magdalen,
　Margaret, and Rosalys.

"Circlewise sit they, with bound locks
　And foreheads garlanded;   110
Into the fine cloth, white like flame,
　Weaving the golden thread,
To fashion the birth-robes for them
　Who are just born, being dead.

"He shall fear, haply, and be dumb;
　　Then will I lay my cheek
To his, and tell about our love,
　　Not once abashed or weak;
And the dear Mother will approve
　　My pride, and let me speak. 120

"Herself shall bring us, hand in hand,
　　To Him round whom all souls
Kneel, the clear-ranged unnumbered heads
　　Bowed with their aureoles;
And angels meeting us shall sing,
　　To their citherns and citoles.

"There will I ask of Christ the Lord
　　Thus much for him and me—
Only to live as once on earth
　　With Love, only to be, 130
As then awhile, forever now
　　Together, I and he."

She gazed and listened and then said,
　　Less sad of speech than mild—
"All this is when he comes." She ceased.
　　The light thrilled toward her, filled
With angels in strong, level flight.
　　Her eyes prayed, and she smiled.

(I saw her smile.) But soon their path
　　Was vague in distant spheres; 140
And then she cast her arms along
　　The golden barriers,
And laid her face between her hands,
　　And wept. (I heard her tears.)

1850

EMILY DICKINSON (1830–1886)

XCIX

There is no frigate like a book
  To take us lands away,
Nor any coursers like a page
  Of prancing poetry.

This traverse may the poorest take
  Without oppress of toll;
How frugal is the chariot
  That bears a human soul!

1894

CLXXIV

As if the sea should part
And show a further sea—
And that a further, and the three
But a presumption be
Of periods of seas
Unvisited of shores—
Themselves the verge of seas to be—
Eternity is these.

1929

CLXXV

Not what we did shall be the test
When act and will are done,
But what our Lord infers we *would*—
Had we diviner been.

1929

ALGERNON CHARLES
SWINBURNE (1837–1909)

ATALANTA IN CALYDON

CHORUS

When the hounds of spring are on winter's traces,
   The mother of months in meadow or plain
Fills the shadows and windy places
   With lisp of leaves and ripple of rain;
And the brown bright nightingale amorous
Is half assuaged for Itylus,
For the Thracian ships and the foreign faces,
   The tongueless vigil, and all the pain.
Come with bows bent and with emptying of quivers,
   Maiden most perfect, lady of light,   10
With a noise of winds and many rivers,
   With a clamour of waters, and with might;
Bind on thy sandals, O thou most fleet,
Over the splendour and speed of thy feet;
For the faint east quickens, the wan west shivers,
   Round the feet of the day and the feet of the night.

Where shall we find her, how shall we sing to her,
   Fold our hands round her knees, and cling?
O that man's heart were as fire and could spring to her,
   Fire, or the strength of the streams that spring!   20
For the stars and the winds are unto her
As raiment, as songs of the harp-player;
For the risen stars and the fallen cling to her,
   And the southwest-wind, and the west-wind sing.

For winter's rains and ruins are over,
   And all the season of snows and sins;
The days dividing lover and lover,
   The light that loses, the night that wins;

And time remembered is grief forgotten,
And frosts are slain and flowers begotten,   30
And in green underwood and cover
  Blossom by blossom the spring begins.

The full streams feed on flower of rushes,
  Ripe grasses trammel a traveling foot,
The faint fresh flame of the young year flushes
  From leaf to flower and flower to fruit;
And fruit and leaf are as gold and fire,
And the oat is heard above the lyre,
And the hoofèd heel of a satyr crushes
  The chestnut-husk at the chestnut-root.   40

And Pan by noon and Bacchus by night,
  Fleeter of foot than the fleet-foot kid,
Follows with dancing and fills with delight
  The Maenad and the Bassarid;
And soft as lips that laugh and hide
The laughing leaves of the trees divide,
And screen from seeing and leave in sight
  The god pursuing, the maiden hid.

The ivy falls with the Bacchanal's hair
  Over her eyebrows hiding her eyes;   50
The wild vine slipping down leaves bare
  Her bright breast shortening into sighs;
The wild vine slips with the weight of its leaves,
But the berried ivy catches and cleaves
To the limbs that glitter, the feet that scare
  The wolf that follows, the fawn that flies.

.   .   .   .

CHORUS

Before the beginning of years
  There came to the making of man
Time, with a gift of tears;
  Grief, with a glass that ran;

Pleasure, with pain for leaven;
  Summer, with flowers that fell;
Remembrance fallen from heaven,
  And madness risen from hell;
Strength without hands to smite;
  Love that endures for a breath;   10
Night, the shadow of light,
  And life, the shadow of death.

And the high gods took in hand
  Fire, and the falling of tears,
And a measure of sliding sand
  From under the feet of the years;
And froth and drift of the sea;
  And dust of the labouring earth;
And bodies of things to be
  In the houses of death and of birth;   20
And wrought with weeping and laughter
  And fashioned with loathing and love,
With life before and after
  And death beneath and above,
For a day and a night and a morrow,
  That his strength might endure for a span
With travail and heavy sorrow,
  The holy spirit of man.

From the winds of the north and the south
  They gathered as unto strife;   30
They breathed upon his mouth,
  They filled his body with life;
Eyesight and speech they wrought
  For the veils of the soul therein,
A time for labour and thought,
  A time to serve and to sin;
They gave him light in his ways,
  And love, and a space for delight,

And beauty and length of days,
   And night, and sleep in the night.   40
His speech is a burning fire;
   With his lips he travaileth;
In his heart is a blind desire,
   In his eyes foreknowledge of death;
He weaves, and is clothed with derision;
   Sows, and he shall not reap;
His life is a watch or a vision
   Between a sleep and a sleep.

                      1865

THE GARDEN OF PROSERPINE

   Here, where the world is quiet,
      Here, where all trouble seems
   Dead winds' and spent waves' riot
      In doubtful dreams of dreams,
   I watch the green field growing
   For reaping folk and sowing,
   For harvest-time and mowing;
      A sleepy world of streams.

   I am tired of tears and laughter,
      And men that laugh and weep;   10
   Of what may come hereafter
      For men that sow to reap.
   I am weary of days and hours,
   Blown buds of barren flowers,
   Desires and dreams and powers,
      And everything but sleep.

   Here life has death for neighbour,
      And far from eye or ear
   Wan waves and wet winds labour,
      Weak ships and spirits steer;   20

They drive adrift, and whither
They wot not who make thither;
But no such winds blow hither,
    And no such things grow here.

No growth of moor or coppice,
    No heather-flower or vine,
But bloomless buds of poppies,
    Green grapes of Proserpine,
Pale beds of blowing rushes,
Where no leaf blooms or blushes   30
Save this whereout she crushes
    For dead men deadly wine.

Pale, without name or number,
    In fruitless fields of corn,
They bow themselves and slumber
    All night till light is born;
And like a soul belated,
In hell and heaven unmated,
By cloud and mist abated
    Comes out of darkness morn.   40

Though one were strong as seven,
    He too with death shall dwell,
Nor wake with wings in heaven,
    Nor weep for pains in hell;
Though one were fair as roses,
His beauty clouds and closes;
And well though love reposes,
    In the end it is not well.

Pale, beyond porch and portal,
    Crowned with calm leaves, she stands   5c
Who gathers all things mortal
    With cold immortal hands·

Her languid lips are sweeter·
Than love's who fears to greet her
To men that mix and meet her
    From many times and lands.

She waits for each and other,
    She waits for all men born;
Forgets the earth her mother,
    The life of fruits and corn;   60
And spring and seed and swallow
Take wing for her and follow
Where summer song rings hollow
    And flowers are put to scorn.

There go the loves that wither,
    The old loves with wearier wings;
And all dead years draw thither,
    And all disastrous things;
Dead dreams of days forsaken,
Blind buds that snows have shaken,   70
Wild leaves that winds have taken,
    Red strays of ruined springs.

We are not sure of sorrow,
    And joy was never sure;
Today will die tomorrow;
    Time stoops to no man's lure;
And love, grown faint and fretful,
With lips but half regretful
Sighs, and with eyes forgetful
    Weeps that no loves endure.   80

From too much love of living,
    From hope and fear set free,
We thank with brief thanksgiving
    Whatever gods may be
That no life lives for ever;
That dead men rise up never;

That even the weariest river
Winds somewhere safe to sea.

Then star nor sun shall waken,
Nor any change of light: 90
Nor sound of waters shaken,
Nor any sound or sight:
Nor wintry leaves nor vernal,
Nor days nor things diurnal:
Only the sleep eternal
In an eternal night.

1866

COR CORDIUM

O Heart of hearts, the chalice of love's fire,
Hid round with flowers and all the bounty of bloom;
O wonderful and perfect heart, for whom
The lyrist liberty made life a lyre;
O heavenly heart, at whose most dear desire
Dead love, living and singing, cleft his tomb,
And with him risen and regent in death's room
All day thy choral pulses rang full choir;
O heart whose beating blood was running song,
O sole thing sweeter than thine own songs were,   10
Help us for thy free love's sake to be free,
True for thy truth's sake, for thy strength's sake strong,
Till very liberty make clean and fair
The nursing earth as the sepulchral sea.

1871

A FORSAKEN GARDEN

In a coign of the cliff between lowland and highland,
    At the sea-down's edge between windward and lee,
Walled round with rocks as an inland island,
    The ghost of a garden fronts the sea.

A girdle of brushwood and thorn encloses
   The steep square slope of the blossomless bed
Where the weeds that grew green from the graves of its
     roses
          Now lie dead.

The fields fall southward, abrupt and broken,
   To the low last edge of the long lone land.   10
If a step should sound or a word be spoken,
   Would a ghost not rise at the strange guest's hand?
So long have the gray bare walks lain guestless,
   Through branches and briars if a man make way,
He shall find no life but the sea-wind's, restless
          Night and day.

The dense hard passage is blind and stifled
   That crawls by a track none turn to climb
To the strait waste place that the years have rifled
   Of all but the thorns that are touched not of time. 20
The thorns he spares when the rose is taken;
   The rocks are left when he wastes the plain;
The wind that wanders, the weeds wind-shaken,
          These remain.

Not a flower to be pressed of the foot that falls not;
   As the heart of a dead man the seed-plots are dry;
From the thicket of thorns whence the nightingale calls not,
   Could she call, there were never a rose to reply.
Over the meadows that blossom and wither,
   Rings but the note of a sea-bird's song.   30
Only the sun and the rain come hither
          All year long.

The sun burns sear, and the rain dishevels
   One gaunt bleak blossom of scentless breath.
Only the wind here hovers and revels
   In a round where life seems barren as death.

Here there was laughing of old, there was weeping,
   Haply, of lovers none ever will know,
Whose eyes went seaward a hundred sleeping
              Years ago.   40

Heart handfast in heart as they stood, "Look thither,"
   Did he whisper? "Look forth from the flowers to the
      sea;
For the foam-flowers endure when the rose-blossoms
      wither,
   And men that love lightly may die—but we?"
And the same wind sang, and the same waves whitened,
   And or ever the garden's last petals were shed,
In the lips that had whispered, the eyes that had lightened,
             Love was dead.

Or they loved their life through, and then went whither?
   And were one to the end—but what end who knows? 50
Love deep as the sea as a rose must wither,
   As the rose-red seaweed that mocks the rose.
Shall the dead take thought for the dead to love them?
   What love was ever as deep as a grave?
They are loveless now as the grass above them
            Or the wave.

All are at one now, roses and lovers,
   Not known of the cliffs and the fields and the sea.
Not a breath of the time that has been hovers
   In the air now soft with a summer to be.   60
Not a breath shall there sweeten the seasons hereafter
   Of the flowers or the lovers that laugh now or weep,
When as they that are free now of weeping and laughter
            We shall sleep.

Here death may deal not again forever;
   Here change may come not till all change end.

From the graves they have made they shall rise up never,
　　Who have left naught living to ravage and rend.
Earth, stones, and thorns of the wild ground growing,
　　While the sun and the rain live, these shall be;　　70
Till a last wind's breath, upon all these blowing,
　　　　　　Roll the sea.

Till the slow sea rise, and the sheer cliff crumble,
　　Till terrace and meadow the deep gulfs drink,
Till the strength of the waves of the high tides humble
　　The fields that lessen, the rocks that shrink,
Here now in his triumph where all things falter,
　　Stretched out on the spoils that his own hand spread,
As a god self-slain on his own strange altar,
　　　　　　Death lies dead.

　　　　　　　　　　　　　　　　1878

THOMAS HARDY (1840–1928)

SHE HEARS THE STORM

There was a time in former years—
　　While my roof-tree was his—
When I should have been distressed by fears
　　At such a night as this.

I should have murmured anxiously,
　　"The pricking rain strikes cold;
His road is bare of hedge or tree,
　　And he is getting old."

But now the fitful chimney-roar,
　　The drone of Thorncombe trees,　　　　　　10
The Froom in flood upon the moor,
　　The mud of Mellstock Leaze,

The candle slanting sooty-wicked,
    The thuds upon the thatch,
The eaves-drops on the window flicked,
    The clacking garden-hatch,

And what they mean to wayfarers,
    I scarcely heed or mind;
He has won that storm-tight roof of hers
    Which Earth grants all her kind.

1909

THE MAN HE KILLED

"Had he and I but met
    By some old ancient inn,
We should have sat us down to wet
    Right many a nipperkin!

"But ranged as infantry,
    And staring face to face,
I shot at him as he at me,
    And killed him in his place.

"I shot him dead because—
    Because he was my foe,
Just so—my foe of course he was;
    That's clear enough; although

"He thought he'd 'list, perhaps,
    Off-hand like—just as I—
Was out of work—had sold his traps—
    No other reason why.

"Yes; quaint and curious war is!
    You shoot a fellow down
You'd treat if met where any bar is,
    Or help to half-a-crown."

1909

IN THE MOONLIGHT

"O lonely workman, standing there
In a dream, why do you stare and stare
At her grave, as no other grave there were?

"If your great gaunt eyes so importune
Her soul by the shine of this corpse-cold moon,
Maybe you 'll raise her phantom soon!"

"Why, fool, it is what I would rather see
Than all the living folk there be;
But alas, there is no such joy for me!"

"Ah—she was one you loved, no doubt,   10
Through good and evil, through rain and drought,
And when she passed, all your sun went out?"

"Nay; she was the woman I did not love,
Whom all the others were ranked above,
Whom during her life I thought nothing of."

1911

ROBERT BRIDGES (1844–1930)

THE GROWTH OF LOVE

IV

The very names of things beloved are dear,
And sounds will gather beauty from their sense,
As many a face through love's long residence
Groweth to fair instead of plain and sere:
But when I say thy name it hath no peer,
And I suppose fortune determined thence
Her dower, that such beauty's excellence
Should have a perfect title for the ear.

Thus may I think the adopting Muses chose
Their sons by name, knowing none would be heard   10
Or writ so oft in all the world as those,—
Dan Chaucer, mighty Shakespeare, then for third
The classic Milton, and to us arose
Shelley with liquid music in the word.

1876

L

The world comes not to an end: her city-hives
Swarm with the tokens of a changeless trade,
With rolling wheel, driver and flagging jade,
Rich men and beggars, children, priests, and wives.
New homes on old are set, as lives on lives;
Invention with invention overlaid:
But still or tool or toy or book or blade
Shaped for the hand, that holds and toils and strives.

The men today toil as their fathers taught,
With little bettered means; for works depend   10
On works and overlap, and thought on thought:
And through all change the smiles of hope amend
The weariest face, the same love changed in nought:
In this thing too the world comes not to an end.

1889

ELEGY

The wood is bare: a river-mist is steeping
    The trees that winter's chill of life bereaves:
Only their stiffened boughs break silence, weeping
        Over their fallen leaves;

That lie upon the dank earth brown and rotten,
    Miry and matted in the soaking wet:
Forgotten with the spring, that is forgotten
        By them that can forget.

Yet it was here we walked when ferns were springing,
    And through the mossy bank shot bud and blade:— 10
Here found in summer, when the birds were singing,
        A green and pleasant shade.

'Twas here we loved in sunnier days and greener;
    And now, in this disconsolate decay,
I come to see her where I most have seen her,
        And touch the happier day.

For on this path, at every turn and corner,
    The fancy of her figure on me falls:
Yet walks she with the slow step of a mourner,
        Nor hears my voice that calls.   20

So through my heart there winds a track of feeling,
    A path of memory, that is all her own:
Whereto her phantom beauty ever stealing
        Haunts the sad spot alone.

About her steps the trunks are bare, the branches
    Drip heavy tears upon her downcast head;
And bleed from unseen wounds that no sun stanches,
        For the year's sun is dead.

And dead leaves wrap the fruits that summer planted:
    And birds that love the South have taken wing.   30
The wanderer, loitering o'er the scene enchanted,
        Weeps, and despairs of spring.

        1873

LONDON SNOW

When men were all asleep the snow came flying,
In large white flakes falling on the city brown,
Stealthily and perpetually settling and loosely lying,
    Hushing the latest traffic of the drowsy town;

Deadening, muffling, stifling its murmurs failing;
Lazily and incessantly floating down and down:
 Silently sifting and veiling road, roof and railing;
Hiding difference, making unevenness even,
Into angles and crevices softly drifting and sailing.
 All night it fell, and when full inches seven   10
It lay in the depth of its uncompacted lightness,
The clouds blew off from a high and frosty heaven;
 And all woke earlier for the unaccustomed brightness
Of the winter dawning, the strange unheavenly glare:
The eye marvelled—marvelled at the dazzling whiteness;
  The ear hearkened to the stillness of the solemn
   air;
No sound of wheel rumbling nor of foot falling,
And the busy morning cries came thin and spare.
 Then boys I heard, as they went to school, calling,
They gathered up the crystal manna to freeze   20
Their tongues with tasting, their hands with snowballing;
 Or rioted in a drift, plunging up to the knees;
Or peering up from under the white-mossed wonder,
"O look at the trees!" they cried, "O look at the trees!"
 With lessened load a few carts creak and blunder,
Following alone the white deserted way,
A country company long dispersed asunder:
 When now already the sun, in pale display
Standing by Paul's high dome, spread forth below
His sparkling beams, and awoke the stir of the day. 30
 For now doors open, and war is waged with the snow;
And trains of somber men, past tale of number,
Tread long brown paths, as toward their toil they go:
 But even for them awhile no cares encumber
Their minds diverted; the daily word is unspoken,
The daily thoughts of labor and sorrow slumber
At the sight of the beauty that greets them, for the charm
  they have broken.

              1880

TWENTIETH CENTURY

ALFRED EDWARD HOUSMAN
(1859–   )

A SHROPSHIRE LAD

II

Loveliest of trees, the cherry now
Is hung with bloom along the bough,
And stands about the woodland ride,
Wearing white for Eastertide.

Now, of my threescore years and ten,
Twenty will not come again,
And take from seventy springs a score,
It only leaves me fifty more.

And since to look at things in bloom
Fifty springs are little room,   10
About the woodlands I will go
To see the cherry hung with snow.

IV

REVEILLE

Wake! The silver dusk returning
    Up the beach of darkness brims,
And the ship of sunrise burning
    Strands upon the eastern rims.

Wake! The vaulted shadow shatters,
    Trampled to the floor it spanned,
And the tent of night in tatters
    Straws the sky-pavilioned land.

459

Up, lad, up! 'Tis late for lying;
  Hear the drums of morning play;   10
Hark, the empty highways crying,
  "Who'll beyond the hills away?"

Towns and countries woo together,
  Forelands beacon, belfries call;
Never lad that trod on leather
  Lived to feast his heart with all.

Up, lad! Thews that lie and cumber
  Sunlit pallets never thrive;
Morns abed and daylight slumber
  Were not meant for man alive.   20

Clay lies still, but blood's a rover;
  Breath's a ware that will not keep.
Up, lad; when the journey's over
  There'll be time enough to sleep.

V

O see how thick the goldcup flowers
  Are lying in field and lane,
With dandelions to tell the hours
  That never are told again.
O may I squire you round the meads
  And pick you posies gay?
—'Twill do no harm to take my arm.
  "You may, young man, you may."

Ah, spring was sent for lass and lad,
  'Tis now the blood runs gold,   10
And man and maid had best be glad
  Before the world is old.
What flowers today may flower tomorrow
  But never as good as new.
—Suppose I wound my arm right round—
  "'Tis true, young man, 'tis true."

Some lads there are, 'tis shame to say,
   That only court to thieve,
And once they bear the bloom away
   'Tis little enough they leave.   20
Then keep your heart for men like me
   And safe from trustless chaps.
My love is true and all for you.
   "Perhaps, young man, perhaps."

Oh, look in my eyes, then, can you doubt?
   —Why, 'tis a mile from town.
How green the grass is all about!
   We might as well sit down.
—Ah, life, what is it but a flower?
   Why must true lovers sigh?   30
Be kind, have pity, my own, my pretty—
   "Good-bye, young man, good-bye."

XIII

When I was one-and-twenty
   I heard a wise man say,
"Give crowns and pounds and guineas
   But not your heart away;
Give pearls away and rubies
   But keep your fancy free."
But I was one-and-twenty—
   No use to talk to me.

When I was one-and-twenty
   I heard him say again,   10
"The heart out of the bosom
   Was never given in vain;
'Tis paid with sighs a plenty
   And sold for endless rue."
And I am two-and-twenty,
   And, oh, 'tis true, 'tis true.

XXXVI

White in the moon the long road lies,
    The moon stands blank above;
White in the moon the long road lies
    That leads me from my love.

Still hangs the hedge without a gust,
    Still, still the shadows stay;
My feet upon the moonlit dust
    Pursue the ceaseless way.

The world is round, so travelers tell,
    And straight though reach the track;   10
Trudge on, trudge on, 'twill all be well,
    The way will guide one back.

But ere the circle homeward hies
    Far, far must it remove;
White in the moon the long road lies
    That leads me from my love.

LIV

With rue my heart is laden
    For golden friends I had,
For many a rose-lipped maiden
    And many a lightfoot lad.

By brooks too broad for leaping
    The lightfoot boys are laid;
The rose-lipped girls are sleeping
    In fields where roses fade.

1896

WILLIAM BUTLER YEATS
(1865–   )

THE LAKE ISLE OF INNISFREE

I will arise and go now, and go to Innisfree,
And a small cabin build there, of clay and wattles made;
Nine bean rows will I have there, a hive for the honey bee,
And live alone in the bee-loud glade.

And I shall have some peace there, for peace comes drop-
    ping slow,
Dropping from the veils of the morning to where the
    cricket sings;
There midnight's all a-glimmer, and noon a purple glow,
And evening's full of the linnet's wings.

I will arise and go now, for always night and day   9
I hear lake water lapping with low sounds by the shore;
While I stand on the roadway, or on the pavements gray,
I hear it in the deep heart's core.

1890

THE ROSE OF THE WORLD

Who dreamed that beauty passes like a dream?
For these red lips, with all their mournful pride,
Mournful that no new wonder may betide,
Troy passed away in one high funeral gleam,
And Usna's children died.

We and the labouring world are passing by;
Amid men's souls, that waver and give place,
Like the pale waters in their wintry race,
Under the passing stars, foam of the sky,
Lives on this lonely face.   10

Bow down, archangels, in your dim abode;
Before you were or any hearts to beat,
Weary and kind one lingered by His seat;
He made the world to be a grassy road
Before her wandering feet.

1892

MICHAEL ROBARTES REMEMBERS
FORGOTTEN BEAUTY

When my arms wrap you round I press
My heart upon the loveliness
That has long faded from the world;
The jeweled crowns that kings have hurled
In shadowy pools, when armies fled;
The love-tales wrought with silken thread
By dreaming ladies upon cloth
That has made fat the murderous moth;
The roses that of old time were
Woven by ladies in their hair;   10
The dew-cold lilies ladies bore
Through many a sacred corridor
Where such gray clouds of incense rose
That only the gods' eyes did not close.
For that pale breast and lingering hand
Come from a more dream-heavy land,
A more dream-heavy hour than this;
And when you sigh from kiss to kiss
I hear white Beauty sighing, too,
For hours when all must fade like dew   20
But flame on flame, deep under deep,
Throne over throne, where in half sleep
Their swords upon their iron knees
Brood her high lonely mysteries.

1896

EDWIN ARLINGTON ROBINSON
(1869–   )

THE GIFT OF GOD

Blessed with a joy that only she
Of all alive shall ever know,
She wears a proud humility
For what it was that willed it so—
That her degree should be so great
Among the favoured of the Lord
That she may scarcely bear the weight
Of her bewildering reward.

As one apart, immune, alone,
Or featured for the shining ones,   10
And like to none that she has known
Of other women's other sons—
The firm fruition of her need,
He shines anointed; and he blurs
Her vision, till it seems indeed
A sacrilege to call him hers.

She fears a little for so much
Of what is best, and hardly dares
To think of him as one to touch
With aches, indignities, and cares;   20
She sees him rather at the goal,
Still shining; and her dream foretells
The proper shining of a soul
Where nothing ordinary dwells.

Perchance a canvass of the town
Would find him far from flags and shouts,
And leave him only the renown
Of many smiles and many doubts;

Perchance the crude and common tongue
Would havoc strangely with his worth;   30
But she, with innocence unwrung,
Would read his name around the earth.

And others, knowing how this youth
Would shine, if love could make him great,
When caught and tortured for the truth
Would only writhe and hesitate;
While she, arranging for his days
What centuries could not fulfill,
Transmutes him with her faith and praise,
And has him shining where she will.   40

She crowns him with her gratefulness,
And says again that life is good;
And should the gift of God be less
In him than in her motherhood,
His fame, though vague, will not be small,
As upward through her dream he fares,
Half clouded with a crimson fall
Of roses thrown on marble stairs.

1914

CASSANDRA

I heard one who said: "Verily,
    What word have I for children here?
Your Dollar is your only Word,
    The wrath of it your only fear.

"You build it altars tall enough
    To make you see, but you are blind;
You cannot leave it long enough
    To look before you or behind.

"When Reason beckons you to pause,
   You laugh and say that you know best;   10
But what it is you know, you keep
   As dark as ingots in a chest.

"You laugh and answer, 'We are young;
   Oh, leave us now, and let us grow,'
Not asking how much more of this
   Will Time endure or Fate bestow.

"Because a few complacent years
   Have made your peril of your pride,
Think you that you are to go on
   Forever pampered and untried?   20

"What lost eclipse of history,
   What bivouac of the marching stars
Has given the sign for you to see
   Millenniums and last great wars?

"What unrecorded overthrow
   Of all the world has ever known,
Or ever been, has made itself
   So plain to you, and you alone?

"Your Dollar, Dove, and Eagle make
   A Trinity that even you   30
Rate higher than you rate yourselves;
   It pays, it flatters, and it's new.

"And though your very flesh and blood
   Be what your Eagle eats and drinks,
You'll praise him for the best of birds,
   Not knowing what the Eagle thinks.

"The power is yours, but not the sight;
   You see not upon what you tread;
You have the ages for your guide,
   But not the wisdom to be led.   40

"Think you to tread forever down
   The merciless old verities?
And are you never to have eyes
   To see the world for what it is?

"Are you to pay for what you have
   With all you are?"—No other word
We caught, but with a laughing crowd
   Moved on. None heeded, and few heard.

1914

FLAMMONDE

The man Flammonde, from God knows where,
With firm address and foreign air,
With news of nations in his talk
And something royal in his walk,
With glint of iron in his eyes,
But never doubt, nor yet surprise,
Appeared, and stayed, and held his head
As one by kings accredited.

Erect, with his alert repose
About him, and about his clothes,   10
He pictured all tradition hears
Of what we owe to fifty years.
His cleansing heritage of taste
Paraded neither want nor waste;
And what he needed for his fee
To live, he borrowed graciously.

He never told us what he was,
Or what mischance, or other cause,
Had banished him from better days
To play the Prince of Castaways.   20
Meanwhile he played surpassing well
A part, for most, unplayable;

In fine, one pauses, half afraid
To say for certain that he played.

For that, one may as well forego
Conviction as to yes or no;
Nor can I say just how intense
Would then have been the difference
To several, who, having striven
In vain to get what he was given, 30
Would see the stranger taken on
By friends not easy to be won.

Moreover, many a malcontent
He soothed and found munificent;
His courtesy beguiled and foiled
Suspicion that his years were soiled;
His mien distinguished any crowd,
His credit strengthened when he bowed;
And women, young and old, were fond
Of looking at the man Flammonde. 40

There was a woman in our town
On whom the fashion was to frown;
But while our talk renewed the tinge
Of a long-faded scarlet fringe,
The man Flammonde saw none of that,
And what he saw we wondered at—
That none of us, in her distress,
Could hide or find our littleness.

There was a boy that all agreed
Had shut within him the rare seed 50
Of learning. We could understand,
But none of us could lift a hand.
The man Flammonde appraised the youth,
And told a few of us the truth;
And thereby, for a little gold,
A flowered future was unrolled.

There were two citizens who fought
For years and years, and over nought;
They made life awkward for their friends,
And shortened their own dividends.   60
The man Flammonde said what was wrong
Should be made right; nor was it long
Before they were again in line,
And had each other in to dine.

And these I mention are but four
Of many out of many more.
So much for them. But what of him—
So firm in every look and limb?
What small satanic sort of kink
Was in his brain? What broken link   70
Withheld him from the destinies
That came so near to being his?

What was he, when we came to sift
His meaning, and to note the drift
Of incommunicable ways,
That make us ponder while we praise?
Why was it that his charm revealed
Somehow the surface of a shield?
What was it that we never caught?
What was he, and what was he not?   80

How much it was of him we met
We cannot ever know; nor yet
Shall all he gave us quite atone
For what was his, and his alone;
Nor need we now, since he knew best,
Nourish an ethical unrest:
Rarely at once will nature give
The power to be Flammonde and live.

We cannot know how much we learn
From those who never will return,   90

Until a flash of unforeseen
Remembrance falls on what has been.
We've each a darkening hill to climb;
And this is why, from time to time
In Tilbury Town, we look beyond
Horizons for the man Flammonde.

1916

AMY LOWELL (1874–1925)

PATTERNS

I walk down the garden paths,
And all the daffodils
Are blowing, and the bright blue squills.
I walk down the patterned garden paths
In my stiff, brocaded gown.

With my powdered hair and jeweled fan,
I, too, am a rare
Pattern. As I wander down
The garden paths.
My dress is richly figured,   10
And the train
Makes a pink and silver stain
On the gravel, and the thrift
Of the borders.
Just a plate of current fashion,
Tripping by in high-heeled, ribboned shoes.
Not a softness anywhere about me,
Only whalebone and brocade.
And I sink on a seat in the shade
Of a lime tree. For my passion   20
Wars against the stiff brocade.
The daffodils and squills
Flutter in the breeze

As they please.
And I weep;
For the lime tree is in blossom
And one small flower has dropped upon my bosom.
And the plashing of waterdrops
In the marble fountain
Comes down the garden paths. 30
The dripping never stops.
Underneath my stiffened gown
Is the softness of a woman bathing in a marble basin,
A basin in the midst of hedges grown
So thick she cannot see her lover hiding,
But she guesses he is near,
And the sliding of the water
Seems the stroking of a dear
Hand upon her.
What is summer in a fine brocaded gown! 40
I should like to see it lying in a heap upon the ground.
All the pink and silver crumpled up on the ground.

I would be the pink and silver as I ran along the paths,
And he would stumble after,
Bewildered by my laughter.
I should see the sun flashing from his sword hilt and the
    buckles on his shoes.
I would choose
To lead him in a maze along the patterned paths,
A bright and laughing maze for my heavy-booted lover,
Till he caught me in the shade, 50
And the buttons of his waistcoat bruised my body as he
    clasped me,
Aching, melting, unafraid.

With the shadows of the leaves and the sundrops,
And the plopping of the waterdrops,
All about us in the open afternoon—
I am very like to swoon

With the weight of this brocade,
For the sun sifts through the shade.

Underneath the fallen blossom
In my bosom,   60
Is a letter I have hid.
It was brought to me this morning by a rider from the
        Duke.
"Madam, we regret to inform you that Lord Hartwell
Died in action Thursday se'nnight."
As I read it in the white, morning sunlight,
The letters squirmed like snakes.
"Any answer, Madam?" said my footman.
"No," I told him.
"See that the messenger takes some refreshment.
No, no answer."   70
And I walked into the garden,
Up and down the patterned paths,
In my stiff, correct brocade.
The blue and yellow flowers stood up proudly in the sun,
Each one.
I stood upright, too,
Held rigid to the pattern
By the stiffness of my gown.
Up and down I walked,
Up and down.   80

In a month he would have been my husband.
In a month, here, underneath this lime,
We would have broke the pattern;
He for me, and I for him,
He as Colonel, I as Lady,
On this shady seat.
He had a whim
That sunlight carried blessing.
And I answered, "It shall be as you have said."
Now he is dead.   90

In summer and in winter I shall walk
Up and down
The patterned garden paths
In my stiff, brocaded gown.
The squills and daffodils
Will give place to pillared roses, and to asters, and to snow.
I shall go
Up and down,
In my gown.
Gorgeously arrayed,   100
Boned and stayed.
And the softness of my body will be guarded from embrace
By each button, hook, and lace.
For the man who should loose me is dead,
Fighting with the Duke in Flanders,
In a pattern called a war.
Christ! What are patterns for?

1915

JOHN MASEFIELD (1875?–   )

SEA–FEVER

I must down to the seas again, to the lonely sea and the
    sky,
And all I ask is a tall ship and a star to steer her by,
And the wheel's kick and the wind's song and the white
    sail's shaking,
And a gray mist on the sea's face and a gray dawn breaking.

I must down to the seas again, for the call of the running
    tide
Is a wild call and a clear call that may not be denied;
And all I ask is a windy day with the white clouds flying,
And the flung spray and the blown spume, and the sea-
    gulls crying.

I must down to the seas again to the vagrant gypsy life,
To the gull's way and the whale's way, where the wind's
    like a whetted knife; 10
And all I ask is a merry yarn from a laughing fellow-rover,
And quiet sleep and a sweet dream when the long trick's
    over.

1902

THE WEST WIND

It's a warm wind, the west wind, full of birds' cries;
I never hear the west wind but tears are in my eyes.
For it comes from the west lands, the old brown hills,
And April's in the west wind, and daffodils.

It's a fine land, the west land, for hearts as tired as mine,
Apple orchards blossom there, and the air's like wine.
There is cool green grass there, where men may lie at rest,
And the thrushes are in song there, fluting from the nest.

"Will you not come home, brother? You have been long
    away.
It's April, and blossom time, and white is the spray; 10
And bright is the sun, brother, and warm is the rain—
Will you not come home, brother, home to us again?

"The young corn is green, brother, where the rabbits run;
It's blue sky, and white clouds, and warm rain and sun.
It's song to a man's soul, brother, fire to a man's brain,
To hear the wild bees and see the merry spring again.

"Larks are singing in the west, brother, above the green
    wheat,
So will you not come home, brother, and rest your tired
    feet?
I've a balm for bruised hearts, brother, sleep for aching
    eyes,"
Says the warm wind, the west wind, full of birds' cries. 20

It's the white road westwards is the road I must tread
To the green grass, the cool grass, and rest for heart and
    head,
To the violets and the brown brooks and the thrushes' song
In the fine land, the west land, the land where I belong.

1902

CARGOES

Quinquireme of Nineveh from distant Ophir,
Rowing home to haven in sunny Palestine,
With a cargo of ivory,
And apes and peacocks,
Sandalwood, cedarwood, and sweet white wine.

Stately Spanish galleon coming from the Isthmus,
Dipping through the Tropics by the palm-green shores,
With a cargo of diamonds,
Emeralds, amethysts,
Topazes, and cinnamon, and gold moidores.   10

Dirty British coaster with a salt-caked smoke stack,
Butting through the Channel in the mad March days,
With a cargo of Tyne coal,
Road-rails, pig-lead,
Firewood, iron-ware, and cheap tin trays.

1903

LONDON TOWN

Oh, London Town's a fine town, and London sights are
    rare,
And London ale is right ale, and brisk's the London air,
And busily goes the world there, but crafty grows the mind,
And London Town of all towns I'm glad to leave behind.

Then hey for croft and hop-yard, and hill, and field, and
    pond,

With Bredon Hill before me and Malvern Hill beyond.
The hawthorn white i' the hedgerow, and all the spring's
    attire
In the comely land of Teme and Lugg, and Clent, and Clee,
    and Wyre.

Oh, London girls are brave girls, in silk and cloth o' gold,
And London shops are rare shops where gallant things are
    sold, 10
And bonnily clinks the gold there, but drowsily blinks the
    eye,
And London Town of all towns I'm glad to hurry by.

Then hey for covert and woodland, and ash and elm and
    oak,
Tewkesbury inns, and Malvern roofs, and Worcester
    chimney smoke,
The apple trees in the orchard, the cattle in the byre,
And all the land from Ludlow town to Bredon church's
    spire.

Oh, London tunes are new tunes, and London books are
    wise,
And London plays are rare plays, and fine to country eyes,
But wretchedly fare the most there and merrily fare the
    few,
And London Town of all towns I'm glad to hurry through.

So hey for the road, the west road, by mill and forge and
    fold, 21
Scent of the fern and song of the lark by brook, and field,
    and wold,
To the comely folk at the hearth-stone and the talk beside
    the fire,
In the hearty land, where I was bred, my land of heart's
    desire.

1903

ON GROWING OLD

Be with me, Beauty, for the fire is dying;
My dog and I are old, too old for roving;
Man, whose young passion sets the spindrift flying,
Is soon too lame to march, too cold for loving.
I take the book and gather to the fire,
Turning old yellow leaves; minute by minute,
The clock ticks to my heart; a withered wire
Moves a thin ghost of music in the spinet.
I cannot sail your seas, I cannot wander
Your cornland, nor your hill-land nor your valleys,   10
Ever again, nor share the battle yonder
Where the young knight the broken squadron rallies.
   Only stay quiet while my mind remembers
   The beauty of fire from the beauty of embers.

Beauty, have pity, for the strong have power,
The rich their wealth, the beautiful their grace,
Summer of man its sunlight and its flower,
Spring time of man all April in a face.
Only, as in the jostling in the Strand,
Where the mob thrusts or loiters or is loud   20
The beggar with the saucer in his hand
Asks only a penny from the passing crowd,
So, from this glittering world with all its fashion,
Its fire and play of men, its stir, its march,
Let me have wisdom, Beauty, wisdom and passion,
Bread to the soul, rain where the summers parch.
   Give me but these, and though the darkness close
   Even the night will blossom as the rose.

          1906

THE ROSE OF THE WORLD

Dark Eleanor and Henry sat at meat
At Woodstock in the royal hunting-seat.

Eleanor said: "The wind blows bitter chill . . .
Will you go out?" King Henry said, "I will."

Eleanor said: "But on so black a night . . .
Will you still go?" He said, "I take delight . . .

In these wild windy nights with branches swaying
And the wolves howling and the nightmare neighing."

She said "May I come, too?" "But no," said he;
"No, for at night, if robbers set on me   10

I can defend myself . . . I could not you
In the pitch darkness without retinue."

Eleanor said, "Why is it that you go
Thus, and alone?" He said: "You cannot know.

Leave the King's secrets: let the fact suffice;
Duty demands it and I pay the price."

While Henry reached his sword-belt from the ledge
She pinned a tassel in his mantle's edge,

A clue of white silk that would glimmer pale
About his ankles as he trod the gale.   20

    .   .   .   .

Henry went swiftly in the roaring night
Eleanor saw her token glimmer white.

She followed down the hill, along the brook,
Just seeing by the clue the way he took.

He reached the forest where the hazels swayed . . .
Her soul was too intent to be afraid.

He pushed within the forest and was gone
But still among the scrub her token shone.

In the blind forest many trackways led
The hazels swayed, the token shewed ahead.   30

And as she followed she untwined a skein
Of silken floss to lead her out again.

The gale roared in the branches: the beasts shook
Not knowing which direction the step took.

Eleanor knew: she followed thro' the night
King Henry's mantle with its patch of white.

A long long way she followed: but at last . . .
A clearing in the forest sweetly-grassed

With apple-trees in blossom that the gale
Tore and flung forth; the token glimmered pale.   40

Beyond the apple-garth a little house
Stood, shuttered close among the tossing boughs.

Light shone from out the bower window-chinks;
Eleanor crept as cat-like as the lynx.

The white patch lingered at the door: she heard
A signal knock: within doors someone stirred.

All stealthily and still as though for sin
The door undid and Henry passed within.

Then the lock turned and Eleanor crept near.
In the gale's roaring she could nothing hear.   50

Yet near the door a fragrance in the air
Told that a red rose had been crumpled there.

Then in the breaking storm a wild moon shewed
The fashion of that secret wood abode.

The windows high: each crevice tightly shut.
Over the lintel-piece a rose was cut . . .

Eleanor crept about as a cat creeps
In evil midnights when the master sleeps.

No dog was there: no sign of life was there,
Save the faint smell of roses in the air;   60

And hours passed and hurrying showers passed.
Eleanor watched what fish would come to cast.

Then suddenly, before the East grew gray.
The bolt withdrew to let the King away . . .

Eleanor had but time to crouch and hush
Close in the green of a sweet-briar bush.

She heard no word, but someone whispered close
In the King's ear, a someone like a rose.

And white arms, with their clinking bangles, drew
The King's head downward in a long adieu.   70

Then the King turned and quietly the door
Closed, and the house was silent as before.

.   .   .   .

Eleanor watched, but, lo, the patch of white
Was gone, that should have led her through the night.

Yet following on his steps she saw his frame
Retread in front of her the way he came.

And suddenly she saw him halting dead:
His scabbard's end had caught her guiding thread.

She heard him snap it, but she inly knew
He had not guessed the thread to be a clue.   80

Afterwards Henry hurried, for the day
Came swiftly, now the storm had blown away.

And lo, the beanfield sweet and blackbirds waking
Leaping from hedge and setting brambles shaking,

And Woodstock dim in trees with nothing stirring
Save the cats homing after nights of erring.

.   .   .   .

Eleanor decked herself in all her pride,
All that had graced her as King Henry's bride.

"Were you out late?" she asked. He answered, "No . . .
It was not midnight when we rose to go.   90

These midnight councils seldom sit for long."
Eleanor hummed a merry scrap of song.

She went into her turret and undid
Her chest with iron bandings on the lid.

She took a drowsy and a biting draught
And mixed them both and as she mixed she laughed

"This is as heavy sleep upon the life . . .
And this is cutting as an Eastern knife,

Together they will still the April grace
Of Mistress White-Arms in the rosy place."   100

She put the potion in a golden flask,
King Henry's gift, and went upon her task.

King Henry asked her, "Whither are you bound?"
"On charity," she said, "my daily round . . .

The Christian charity I must not spare
To those poor women lying suffering there."

He said, "God bless your charity." And she
Replied "Amen," and went forth quietly.

She visited her sick with bread and wine,
Then searched the forest for her silken sign.   110

She found the floss still clinging, leading in.
"The hunt is up," she said, "The hounds begin."

The forest was all thicket, but the lane
To tread was blazoned by the silken skein.

Though it was dark in covert, her delight
In what her spirit purposed gave her light.

Then lo, the clearing, and the little house
So fair among the blossomed apple-boughs

And once again her spirit was aware
Of midmost summers' roses present there.   120

Within the house she heard a woman sing.
Eleanor knocked the signal of the King.

The chain undid, the bolt was drawn, the key
Turned, and the door was opened, it was she . . .

A girl more beautiful than summer's rose
That in the mid June's beauty burns and glows;

A golden lady graced from foot to tress,
With every simpleness and loveliness,

Who, in the second when she saw the Queen,   129
Knew that her Death had come, for what had been.

Eleanor like a striking python seized
That golden child and dragged her as she pleased.

"O darling of the King," she said, "Behold . . .
I, who am Queen, have brought this flask of gold,

Also the common hangman and his crew.
I, being royal, give a choice to you.

Either you drink this poison, and so end . . .
Or I will call the hangmen who attend

And they shall strip you naked and so hoot
And beat you to the Woodstock gallows-foot　　140

Where they shall hang you: choose, then, sweetest heart."
The girl beheld Death present with his dart.

The present Death with which man cannot strive.
Death that makes beauty be no more alive.

And is so strange the hot blood can but shrink.
"Threaten me not," she said, "For I will drink.

I, too, am royal: and no way remains."
She drank the golden flasket to its drains,

And straight the savage poison in her side
Thrust on her heart-strings that she sank and died.　　150

.　.　.　.　.　.　.

Eleanor dragged the body to the bed,
"Lie there and welcome Henry, Golden Head."

Then forth the grim Queen went, and licked her lips
To think of June's bright beauty in eclipse

And Henry going to his love to find
The candle quenched that shone behind the blind.

"He will thrust in, and find her lying cold."
So Henry did and found the flask of gold

And knew the Queen's contrivance in the Death.
That night the Queen cried "Open . . . give me breath

Open the window, for I cannot breathe, 161
The golden roses' tendrils wreathe and wreathe

Over my mouth. O who has crushed a rose
The perfume stifles me: unclose, unclose."

They told her that she dreamed; but she replied—
"The roses choke me: open windows wide.

Someone had crushed a white rose or a red . . .
Can you not smell the perfume that is shed?

It comes so close, I cannot breathe the air."
Thenceforward every day and everywhere 170

The grim Queen cowered from the haunting scent
Of roses crushed, of sweet rose-petals blent

Red, white and golden, coming where she trod.
Henry and Eleanor are now with God,

Whose Face is in all Beauty, as I say.
The pure White Nuns took Rosamund away.

Within their Quire they showed for many years
A little chest or scatolin of hers,

Painted with birds, that Henry once had given.
There the White Sisters prayed her into Heaven 180

That is the rest for lovers: there they wrought
A white-rose tomb for her from loving thought

So that none thought of her, nor ever will
Save as a lovely thing that suffered ill.

There every May the grass above her bosom
Is strown with hawthorn bloom and apple-blossom.

And on the wild-rose spray the blackbirds sing
"O Rose of all the World, O lovely thing."

1931

ROBERT FROST (1875–   )

TO THE THAWING WIND

Come with rain, O loud Southwester!
Bring the singer, bring the nester;
Give the buried flower a dream;
Make the settled snow-bank steam;
Find the brown beneath the white;
But whate'er you do tonight,
Bathe my window, make it flow,
Melt it as the ices go;
Melt the glass and leave the sticks
Like a hermit's crucifix;   10
Burst into my narrow stall;
Swing the picture on the wall;
Run the rattling pages o'er;
Scatter poems on the floor;
Turn the poet out of door.

1913

THE PASTURE

I'm going out to clean the pasture spring;
I'll only stop to rake the leaves away
(And wait to watch the water clear, I may);
I sha'n't be gone long.—You come too.

I'm going out to fetch the little calf
That's standing by the mother. It's so young,
It totters when she licks it with her tongue.
I sha'n't be gone long.—You come too.

1914

MENDING WALL

Something there is that doesn't love a wall,
That sends the frozen ground-swell under it,
And spills the upper boulders in the sun;
And makes gaps even two can pass abreast.
The work of hunters is another thing:
I have come after them and made repair
Where they have left not one stone on stone,
But they would have the rabbit out of hiding,
To please the yelping dogs. The gaps I mean,
No one has seen them made or heard them made,   10
But at spring mending-time we find them there.
I let my neighbor know beyond the hill;
And on a day we meet to walk the line
And set the wall between us once again.
We keep the wall between us as we go.
To each the boulders that have fallen to each.
And some are loaves and some so nearly balls
We have to use a spell to make them balance:
"Stay where you are until our backs are turned!"
We wear our fingers rough with handling them.   20
Oh, just another kind of out-door game,
One on a side. It comes to little more.
There where it is we do not need the wall:
He is all pine and I am apple orchard.
My apple trees will never get across
And eat the cones under his pines, I tell him.
He only says, "Good fences make good neighbors."
Spring is the mischief in me, and I wonder
If I could put a notion in his head:
"Why do they make good neighbors? Isn't it   30
Where there are cows? But here there are no cows.
Before I built a wall I'd ask to know
What I was walling in or walling out,
And to whom I was like to give offense.

Something there is that doesn't love a wall,
That wants it down." I could say "Elves" to him,
But it's not elves exactly, and I'd rather
He said it for himself. I see him there
Bringing a stone grasped firmly by the top
In each hand, like an old-stone savage armed.   40
He moves in darkness as it seems to me,
Not of woods only and the shade of trees.
He will not go behind his father's saying,
And he likes having thought of it so well
He says again, "Good fences make good neighbors."

1914

CARL SANDBURG (1878-   )

CHICAGO

Hog Butcher for the World,
Tool Maker, Stacker of Wheat,
Player with Railroads and the Nation's Freight Handler;
Stormy, husky, brawling,
City of the Big Shoulders:

They tell me you are wicked and I believe them, for I
have seen your painted women under the gas lamps
luring the farm boys.
And they tell me you are crooked, and I answer: Yes, it is
true I have seen the gunman kill and go free to kill
again.
And they tell me you are brutal and my reply is: On the
faces of women and children I have seen the marks of
wanton hunger.
And having answered so, I turn once more to those who
sneer at this my city, and I give them back the sneer
and say to them: 9
Come and show me another city with lifted head singing so
proud to be alive and coarse and strong and cunning.

Flinging magnetic curses amid the toil of piling job on
 job, here is a tall bold slugger set vivid against the
 little soft cities;
Fierce as a dog with tongue lapping for action, cunning
 as a savage pitted against the wilderness,
   Bareheaded,
   Shoveling,
   Wrecking,
   Planning,
   Building, breaking, rebuilding.
Under the smoke, dust all over his mouth, laughing with
 white teeth,
Under the terrible burden of destiny laughing as a young
 man laughs,
Laughing even as an ignorant fighter laughs who has never
 lost a battle,   20
Bragging and laughing that under his wrist is the pulse,
 and under his ribs the heart of the people,
   Laughing!
Laughing the stormy, husky, brawling laughter of Youth,
 half-naked, sweating, proud to be Hog Butcher, Tool
 Maker, Stacker of Wheat, Player with Railroads, and
 Freight Handler to the Nation.

        1914

LOST

  Desolate and lone,
  All night long on the lake
  Where fog trails and mist creeps,
  The whistle of a boat
  Calls and cries unendingly,
  Like some lost child
  In tears and trouble,
  Hunting the harbor's breast
  And the harbor's eyes.

        1914

THE HARBOR

Passing through huddled and ugly walls,
By doorways where women haggard
Looked from their hunger-deep eyes,
Haunted with shadows of hunger-hands,
Out from the huddled and ugly walls,
I came sudden, at the city's edge,
On a blue burst of lake—
Long lake waves breaking under the sun
On a spray-flung curve of shore;
And a fluttering storm of gulls,   10
Masses of great gray wings
And flying white bellies
Veering and wheeling free in the open.

1914

UNDER THE HARVEST MOON

Under the harvest moon,
When the soft silver
Drips shimmering
Over the garden nights,
Death, the gray mocker,
Comes and whispers to you
As a beautiful friend
Who remembers.

Under the summer roses
When the flagrant crimson   10
Lurks in the dusk
Of the wild red leaves,
Love, with little hands,
Comes and touches you
With a thousand memories,
And asks you
Beautiful, unanswerable questions.

1915

NOCTURNE IN A DESERTED BRICKYARD

Stuff of the moon
Runs on the lapping sand
Out to the longest shadows.
Under the curving willows,
And round the creep of the wave line,
Fluxions of yellow and dusk on the waters
Make a wide dreaming pansy of an old pond in the night.

1915

RUPERT BROOKE (1887–1915)

1914

V—THE SOLDIER

If I should die, think only this of me:
  That there's some corner of a foreign field
That is forever England. There shall be
  In that rich earth a richer dust concealed;
A dust whom England bore, shaped, made aware,
  Gave, once, her flowers to love, her ways to roam,
A body of England's, breathing English air,
  Washed by the rivers, blessed by suns of home.
And think, this heart, all evil shed away,
  A pulse in the eternal mind, no less   10
Gives somewhere back the thoughts by England given;
  Her sights and sounds; dreams happy as her day;
And laughter, learned of friends; and gentleness,
  In hearts at peace, under an English heaven.

1915

THE GREAT LOVER

I have been so great a lover: filled my days
So proudly with the splendor of Love's praise,
The pain, the calm, and the astonishment,
Desire illimitable, and still content,

And all dear names men use, to cheat despair,
For the perplexed and viewless streams that bear
Our hearts at random down the dark of life.
Now, ere the unthinking silence on that strife
Steals down, I would cheat drowsy Death so far,
My night shall be remembered for a star   10
That outshone all the suns of all men's days.
Shall I not crown them with immortal praise
Whom I have loved, who have given me, dared with me
High secrets, and in darkness knelt to see
The inenarrable godhead of delight?
Love is a flame:—we have beaconed the world's night.
A city:—and we have built it, these and I.
An emperor:—we have taught the world to die.
So, for their sakes I loved, ere I go hence,
And the high cause of Love's magnificence,   20
And to keep loyalties young, I'll write those names
Golden for ever, eagles, crying flames,
And set them as a banner, that men may know,
To dare the generations, burn, and blow
Out on the wind of Time, shining and streaming. . . .

These I have loved:
          White plates and cups, clean-gleaming,
Ringed with blue lines; and feathery, faëry dust;
Wet roofs, beneath the lamp-light; the strong crust
Of friendly bread; and many-tasting food;   30
Rainbows; and the blue bitter smoke of wood;
And radiant raindrops couching in cool flowers;
And flowers themselves, that sway through sunny hours,
Dreaming of moths that drink them under the moon;
Then, the cool kindliness of sheets, that soon
Smooth away trouble; and the rough male kiss
Of blankets; grainy wood; live hair that is
Shining and free; blue-massing clouds; the keen
Unpassioned beauty of a great machine;

The benison of hot water; furs to touch; 40
The good smell of old clothes; and other such—
The comfortable smell of friendly fingers,
Hair's fragrance, and the musty reek that lingers
About dead leaves and last year's ferns. . . .
       Dear names,
And thousand others throng to me! Royal flames;
Sweet water's dimpling laugh from tap or spring;
Holes in the ground; and voices that do sing:
Voices in laughter, too; and body's pain,
Soon turned to peace; and the deep-panting train; 50
Firm sands; the little dulling edge of foam
That browns and dwindles as the wave goes home;
And washen stones, gay for an hour; the cold
Graveness of iron; moist black earthen mold;
Sleep; and high places; footprints in the dew;
And oaks; and brown horse-chestnuts, glossy-new;
And new-peeled sticks; and shining pools on grass;—
All these have been my loves. And these shall pass,
Whatever passes not, in the great hour,
Nor all my passion, all my prayers, have power 60
To hold them with me through the gate of Death.
They'll play deserter, turn with traitor breath,
Break the high bond we made, and sell Love's trust
And sacramented covenant to the dust.
—Oh, never a doubt but, somewhere, I shall wake,
And give what's left of love again, and make
New friends now·strangers. . . .
      But the best I've known
Stays here, and changes, breaks, grows old, is blown
About the winds of the world, and fades from brains 70
Of living men, and dies.
    Nothing remains.

O dear my loves, O faithless, once again
This one last gift I give: that after men

Shall know, and later lovers, far-removed,
Praise you, "All these were lovely"; say, "He loved."

1915

EDNA ST. VINCENT MILLAY
(1892-   )

GOD'S WORLD

O world, I cannot hold thee close enough!
Thy winds, thy wide gray skies!
Thy mists, that roll and rise!
Thy woods, this autumn day, that ache and sag
And all but cry with colour! That gaunt crag
To crush! To lift the lean of that black bluff!
World, world, I cannot get thee close enough!

Long have I known a glory in it all,
But never knew I this;
Here such a passion is   10
As stretcheth me apart. Lord, I do fear
Thou'st made the world too beautiful this year;
My soul is all but out of me—let fall
No burning leaf; prithee, let no bird call.

1917

WHEN THE YEAR GROWS OLD

I cannot but remember
    When the year grows old—
October—November—
    How she disliked the cold!

She used to watch the swallows
    Go down across the sky,
And turn from the window
    With a little sharp sigh.

And often when the brown leaves
   Were brittle on the ground,   10
And the wind in the chimney
   Made a melancholy sound,

She had a look about her
   That I wish I could forget—
The look of a scared thing
   Sitting in a net!

Oh, beautiful at nightfall
   The soft spitting snow!
And beautiful the bare boughs
   Rubbing to and fro!   20

But the roaring of the fire,
   And the warmth of fur,
And the boiling of the kettle
   Were beautiful to her!

I cannot but remember
   When the year grows old—
October—November—
   How she disliked the cold!

1917

SONNETS

XXII

Euclid alone has looked on Beauty bare.
Let all who prate of Beauty hold their peace,
And lay them prone upon the earth and cease
To ponder on themselves, the while they stare
At nothing, intricately drawn nowhere
In shapes of shifting lineage; let geese
Gabble and hiss, but heroes seek release
From dusty bondage into luminous air.

O blinding hour, O holy, terrible day,
When first the shaft into his vision shone   10
Of light anatomized! Euclid alone
Has looked on Beauty bare. Fortunate they
Who, though once only and then but far away,
Have heard her massive sandal set on stone.

1923

FATAL INTERVIEW

XIV

Since of no creature living the last breath
Is twice required, or twice the ultimate pain,
Seeing how to quit your arms is very death,
'Tis likely that I shall not die again;
And likely 'tis that Time whose gross decree
Sends now the dawn to clamour at our door,
Thus having done his evil worst to me,
Will thrust me by, will harry me no more.
When you are corn and roses and at rest
I shall endure, a dense and sanguine ghost,   10
To haunt the scene where I was happiest,
To bend above the thing I loved the most;
And rise, and wring my hands, and steal away
As I do now, before the advancing day.

XVI

I dreamed I moved among the Elysian fields,
In converse with sweet women long since dead;
And out of blossoms which that meadow yields
I wove a garland for your living head.
Danaë, that was the vessel for a day
Of golden Jove, I saw, and at her side,
Whom Jove the Bull desired and bore away,
Europa stood, and the Swan's featherless bride.

All these were mortal women, yet all these
Above the ground had had a god for guest;   10
Freely I walked beside them and at ease,
Addressing them, by them again addressed,
And marvelled nothing, for remembering you,
Wherefore I was among them well I knew.

1931

INDEX OF AUTHORS, TITLES, AND FIRST LINES